The Middle-Class New Deal

The Middle-Class New Deal

RESTORING UPWARD MOBILITY AND THE AMERICAN DREAM

A. Mechele Dickerson

UNIVERSITY OF CALIFORNIA PRESS

University of California Press
Oakland, California

Library of Congress Cataloging-in-Publication Data

Names: Dickerson, Mechele (Arletrice Mechele), author.
Title: The middle-class New Deal : restoring upward mobility and the American dream / A. Mechele Dickerson.
Description: Oakland, California : University of California Press, [2026] | Includes bibliographical references and index.
Identifiers: LCCN 2025013852 (print) | LCCN 2025013853 (ebook) | ISBN 9780520423381 (cloth) | ISBN 9780520423398 (paperback) | ISBN 9780520423404 (ebook)
Subjects: LCSH: Middle class—United States—History.
Classification: LCC HT690.U6 D53 2026 (print) | LCC HT690.U6 (ebook) | DDC 305.5/50973—dc23/eng/20250616
LC record available at https://lccn.loc.gov/2025013852
LC ebook record available at https://lccn.loc.gov/2025013853

Manufactured in the United States of America

GPSR Authorized Representative: Easy Access System Europe, Mustamäe tee 50, 10621 Tallinn, Estonia, gpsr.requests@easproject.com

34 33 32 31 30 29 28 27 26
10 9 8 7 6 5 4 3

For my parents, Warner and Arcola Dickerson, who believed in the American Dream and made me who I am.

For my sons, John and Joshua, who I hope will have the same opportunities in life that I have had.

Contents

Acknowledgments

The *Middle-Class New Deal* has been a labor of love. First the "love" part, then the labor.

The book is a tribute to my parents, who spent their entire lives doing things to make sure they could become and remain middle class. They worked hard and made choices and sacrifices that made it possible for me and my brother to become financially stable adults. At times, I gave up and wanted to abandon this project. But my love for my parents and my determination to expose the ways political leaders have abandoned lower- and middle-income adults like my parents gave me the strength I needed to keep writing.

The book has been laborious and has consumed most of my life for the last decade. One reason it has taken so long and almost fell apart is that I started writing it before COVID. Given what the country experienced during the pandemic, I essentially had to start over. I eventually had to forge a new publication path and will forever be grateful that it found the perfect publishing home thanks to Maura Roessner. I could not have made it through the somewhat truncated publication schedule without her encouragement. I am also grateful to the careful guidance (and patience) of Sam Warren and the meticulous copyediting this book received from Sharon Langworthy.

An army of former students either worked with me as research assistants or worked on research projects that contributed to the content of this book. Alejandra Chavira, Nour Haikal, Stacie Nguyen, and Nicole Schilling helped me salvage the book after the 2020 COVID disruption. Other students who have helped me over the last several years include Annie Bennett, David Bujarski, Michelle Chin, Natasha Ertzbischoff, Sam Libby (who helped me think through and prepared charts), Hailey Pulman, Chloe Schmergel, and Warner Scott.

I am thankful for the financial support the University of Texas provided for this project and also wish to thank the anonymous peer reviewers for the University of California Press who helped make the book better. I received helpful comments on early versions of the book at faculty workshops at Sandra Day O'Connor College of Law at Arizona State Law School, Indiana University Maurer School of Law, and the University of Texas School of Law and Department of Government. I thank Melissa Jacoby and Angie Littwin for the time and care they took to read the completed manuscript and provide comments and suggestions.

I am honored to have a loyal group of friends, including Mary Rose, Jolyn Piercy, and David Werth, who have supported me as I labored to write (then rewrite) this book. I especially thank my colleague Wendy Wagner for sticking with me on my tortured publication path for over a decade, and I thank my colleagues Tom McGarity, Bobby Chesney, and Susie Morse for encouraging me to stick with this project when I wanted to jump ship. Finally, it gives me great pride that my son, John McCormick, helped proofread the entire manuscript and offered editorial suggestions.

My two twenty-something sons face a different financial future than I did, even though they have lived lives that are different from most of the lower- and middle-income families I discuss in this book. Because of my parents' grit, hard work, and determination to become and remain middle class, I am financially secure. I am not sure what the future holds for my sons, though. It is my hope that this book encourages political leaders and policymakers to accept that now is the time to make sure that upward mobility is possible for young adults in this country and to pass laws and regulations that give young adults reasons to continue to believe in the American Dream.

Prologue

THE STRUGGLING MIDDLE CLASS

America's middle class is in crisis. Political leaders claim to love the middle class but for decades have done little to help stabilize the finances of middle-class households. If political leaders really wanted to help America's middle-class families, they could. How? By using the same broad and bold legislative approaches to *restore* the middle class that they used to *create* the middle class almost a century ago.

After World War II, local, state, and federal policymakers sprang into action and enacted sweeping laws and regulations to slow rising foreclosures, reverse soaring unemployment rates, and help ensure the US economy fully recovered from the Great Depression. These bold and comprehensive actions ensured that lower- and middle-income (LMI) families and returning GIs could find jobs that offered high wages so they could buy homes, pay for college, pay their bills on time, and comfortably retire. In the process, political leaders created the middle class as we knew it. More recently, the US Department of Commerce observed that "if American families are to realize their middle-class dreams, the nation must have a healthy economy, a responsible private sector that offers decent jobs and benefits, and an effective public sector that provides high quality schools for all children."[1]

Political leaders at all levels know America's middle class has been financially vulnerable for decades. Nonetheless, some either pretend that upward mobility remains possible as long as people work hard and play by the rules or argue that people (like immigrants) or things (like diversity, equity, and inclusion [DEI]/affirmative action or offshoring manufacturing plants) should be blamed for why it is so difficult for LMI children to become and remain middle. Even with a strong postpandemic economy, a bullish stock market that soared to historic highs, the lowest unemployment rates in over fifty years, and the strongest manufacturing sector since the 1950s, polling in 2023 and 2024 reveal that LMI workers feel hopeless. Why such pessimism? Because—for decades—they have been struggling (and failing) to afford the traditional markers of the middle class.[2]

Until recently, most people in this country assumed that, with hard work, grit, and determination, they would become and remain middle class. Since the 1980s, however, LMI workers have struggled to find permanent, full-time jobs with decent wages that offer benefits like health insurance and retirement plans. With unstable employment and stagnant income, they cannot save enough to pay for unexpected emergencies, make a down payment on a home, or pay for their children to attend college. They are burying themselves in debt to pay for the markers of the middle class or just make ends meet. They now believe that debt serves as an income replacement and can be their economic safety net. Living on credit has decimated their household savings, and with no retirement savings, some may have to work for the rest of their lives.

To understand why a group of people that political leaders claim to revere feel hopeless and believe their country has abandoned them, we should remind ourselves how and why political leaders created the middle class in the first place. As has always been true, the creation had more to do with the needs of the country than with the needs of the people in this country.

PART 1 Creating the Middle Class

1 The Birth of America's Middle Class

The concept of the American "middle class" is new. This country's first European colonists came here with rigid class-based views, so until the twentieth century the United States largely consisted of people who were either rich or poor. The colonists' class-based views shaped how they formed governments, so colonial governments were controlled by rich (and White) landowners. For most of the seventeenth and eighteenth centuries, elected leaders were (rich) property owners, so nonlandowners, which included virtually all women and non-White Americans, were powerless and financially vulnerable.[1]

Non-White residents of this country, most notably enslaved Black people and Native Americans, were stripped of most rights and endured brutal treatment at the hands of European settlors. Colonists denied them the right to vote. Enslaved Black people could not even control their own bodies. "Removal" policies let the colonists take Native American land and give it to White settlors. Political leaders were not as physically or economically brutal to poor White Americans, but they nonetheless prevented them from voting, owning land, or running for political office. By the time poor and non-White people and people who did not own land could fully participate in American society, economic inequality was embedded in the fiber of this nation.

Political leaders did little to help poor people be anything other than poor. Until, that is, leaders realized that the country would prosper if it had a large and stable middle class. Although, as we will see in later chapters, politicians have never acted with urgency when *non-White* adults were struggling financially, the robust and comprehensive responses political leaders had to the economic crisis families faced after the Depression and World War II proves that our political leaders can quickly help economically struggling families if they think the help is beneficial to the country.

After the Depression and World War II, America's political leaders enacted a series of educational, employment, housing, and finance laws and policies that saved the US economy and helped LMI families and returning World War II servicemen become more financially secure. For example, the GI Bill (Servicemen's Readjustment Act of 1944) and federal banking policies created a low-cost, fixed-rate, thirty-year mortgage that helped families buy homes and go to college. Political leaders and policymakers did not need to force businesses to create "good" jobs for noncollege workers at that time because the United States was a goods-producing economy that offered an ample supply of manufacturing jobs for workers who lacked a bachelor's degree. Jobs for noncollege workers remained plentiful until the 1980s because organized labor was strong enough to force businesses to provide stable jobs, with decent wages and employee benefits, that paid their workers enough to become and remain middle class.

Since the 1980s, political leaders—at all levels—have largely ignored the economic plight of the middle class and also have refused to admit that their inaction and inertia are why LMI families are facing financial fragility and insecurity. Before explaining just how badly political leaders have neglected America's middle class and why they have an obligation to enact laws and policies that help workers become and remain middle class, I first share the story of my Silent Generation parents and why they appear, at least on paper, to be prototypical members of the middle class.

BECOMING MIDDLE CLASS BEFORE THE 1980S

My parents were not born rich and never became rich, though they eventually acquired the markers of the middle class. My father, the youngest of six children and the only son, was born in rural Hayward County, Tennessee. His mother (Mary Fenny) was a maid, and his father (Henry Fenny) worked for a railroad company. My mother, born in rural Coweta County, Georgia, was the fourth of eight children and the oldest daughter in her family. After her mother (Gertrude Leavell) graduated from high school, she briefly taught in a racially segregated (by law) public school in Newnan, Georgia. Her father (Tommie Leavell) worked briefly as a coal miner and later as a laborer in a warehouse.

My parents' path to the middle class differs somewhat from the typical American story of upward mobility because they are not White. They experienced many of the challenges that a "stereotypical" American worker would face but also faced the barriers public and private actors erected that almost guaranteed that the mobility most non-Whites would have is *downward.* My parents understood then, as young workers understand now, that they would never become financially stable and secure unless they went to some type of college after they graduated from high school.[2]

My father left Memphis to attend Tennessee State University (a historically Black university in Nashville, Tennessee) and paid for most of his college expenses with wages from his part-time job. My mother left Georgia to attend the Nashville Business School, a trade (now commonly called "for-profit") school. She, too, worked part time to pay her college expenses. After they dated for about six months, my parents married, and roughly two years later my brother was born. About eight months later, my parents were expecting their second child (me). With a toddler in tow and an infant on the way, they decided to move to Memphis. To save expenses, they chose to live rent free in my Fenny grandparents' three-bedroom/one-bathroom, 1,016-square-foot house.

My parents decided to live under a multigenerational roof that included my parents, my Fenny grandparents, my paternal great-grandmother, my brother, and (eventually) me to save money for a down payment on their own home. Because they understood how their housing choices would affect their children's educational and vocational opportunities, they wanted to buy a house that would increase in value (to increase their household wealth) in a neighborhood with high-performing public schools their children could attend. My parents assumed that it would be easy for them to accomplish this goal because my father had a stable, full-time job (with benefits) as a public-school math teacher.

They were wrong.

Eventually my parents achieved their housing and educational dreams. Along the way, though, they faced a series of structural and institutional barriers because they were "home buying while Black" at a time when neighborhoods were rigidly *and legally* segregated by race. Even though they succeeded in buying their first home, they made a mistake that many Black homebuyers made during this era: they trusted their real estate agent. The agent betrayed my parents' trust by ignoring their clearly stated goal of buying a home in a neighborhood with high-performing public schools. The agent steered them *away* from homes in high-opportunity (White) neighborhoods and *to* low-appreciating homes in all-Black or unstably integrated neighborhoods where homes were not increasing in value and were zoned for low-performing public schools.[3]

Congress had not yet passed the Fair Housing Act of 1968, and there was little that novice Black homebuyers like my parents could do at that time to protect themselves against real estate agent steering. In this pre-internet era, buyers would not know whether a neighborhood was stably integrated racially or economically. Although they were duped into buying a home that was not their ideal choice, the fact that my parents managed to buy a home in the 1960s was atypical and can be viewed as a success. Only 40 percent of Black households owned homes at that time, which was 25 percentage points lower than White homeownership rates. Unfortunately, my parents soon realized the fleeting nature of their homebuying "success" when they tried to sell their house. They discovered that then (as now) homes in all-Black neighborhoods have lower rates of appreciation relative to homes in White neighborhoods.

As we will see as my parents' education, homebuying, savings, and debt stories unfold throughout this book, they ultimately bought and sold three homes because they worked hard, had dogged determination, and received some financial help from family members. But the primary reason they were able to buy homes, help their children attend college, pay their regular and larger expenses without excessive debt, and retire and live comfortably in a senior living community is that they were young adults at a time when workers could find full-time and permanent jobs that paid them enough to become and remain middle class.

Hard work and determination *alone* are no longer enough for LMI Americans to be financially stable and secure. Young adults now struggle to become and remain middle class because of the radical restructuring of labor, housing, educational, and financial services markets since the 1980s. While it has always been hard for Black and Latino Americans to become and remain middle class, even White LMI families now realize that downward mobility is their new reality.[4]

A recurring question regularly complicates discussions about the middle class and often stymies efforts to help middle-class Americans become financially stable. That question? Just who *is* middle class in this country?

DEFINING THE MIDDLE CLASS

A 1970 *Time Magazine* article described the middle class as people who "sing the national anthem at football games—and mean it."[5] Roughly twenty years after that article was published, the Bill Clinton presidential campaigns used the "It's the Economy Stupid" slogan and cast the middle class as people who want a good job, a house, and the ability to help pay their children's college expenses.[6]

Just after the 2007–2009 Great Recession, a US Department of Commerce report described people who are, or aspire to be, middle class as having "certain common aspirations for themselves and their children. They strive for economic stability and therefore desire to own a home and to save for retirement. They want economic opportunities for their children and therefore want to provide them with a college education. Middle class families want to protect their own and their children's health. And they want enough income for each adult to have a car and for a family vacation each year."[7] This report, as well as polls conducted after the Great Recession, suggest that Americans who aspire to be middle class believe that a middle-class lifestyle means attaining a set of "markers."

The markers of the middle class include big ticket items like buying a home and paying for college. Until recently, the markers also included being able to pay for routine but necessary expenses (like medical care, clothing, food, and childcare) as well as being able to afford things beyond the bare minimum necessities, like owning a TV, more than one car in a multiworker household, and a smartphone. Being middle class also meant having enough of a financial cushion to indulge in occasional splurges, like eating in a restaurant, getting your hair cut by a trained stylist, occasionally attending a movie or athletic event, or traveling out of town for weddings or family reunions. Being a middle-class worker also meant that, after a lifetime of hard work, you could stop working and use your retirement savings to pay your living expenses for the rest of your life.[8]

Most discussions of the meaning of being middle class focus on financial stability. But a 2008 Congressional Research Service report aptly observed that there is no "consensus definition of 'middle class,' neither is there an official government definition. What constitutes the middle class is relative, subjective, and not easily defined."[9] Anyone whose beliefs, aspirations, or emotions align with the "middle class" ostensibly can proclaim to be middle class, which caused one political scientist to quip that "in America . . . you are middle class if you say so."[10]

One reason we have no precise definition for a group that all political leaders claim to love is that no organization or federal agency is tasked with collecting financial data by class or providing a definitive definition for the middle class. For example, the US Census Bureau is tasked with reporting the state of household finances for families in this country, but it collects and reports data by grouping households into income quartiles, *not* in economic classes. Likewise, while some state and federal assistance programs use means tests to determine how they will allocate financial assistance to eligible recipients, these programs focus on how much a potential recipient earns, *not* their class status.

Middle Class in America examined the emotional, psychological, and financial dimensions of being middle class and noted that even rich people might self-identify as middle class because they align themselves with the forward-looking views of middle-class families who "know that . . . they must work hard, plan ahead and save for the future. Indeed, being middle class may be as much about setting goals and working to achieve them as it is about their attainment."[11] Moreover, because of the explosion in the number of billionaires in this country, even mere millionaires may not "feel" rich. A 2023 Treasury Department report admits that there is not a technical definition of *middle class*, noting that the term is defined using absolute measures (like occupational status or education level) or relative measures like social self-identification, income, or wealth.[12]

With no official definition for the middle class, people who earn enough to own summer homes or are members of country clubs have felt emboldened to use their political clout to lobby political leaders for laws and policies that make it easier for them to afford an otherwise unaffordable lifestyle. For example, people who call themselves "upper middle class" demand tax relief if they cannot easily buy homes in cities like Austin, Texas, Boston, Massachusetts, or San Jose, California. Likewise, well-heeled parents demand tax relief that would let them save (tax-free) money to pay for their children's educational expenses because they do not feel they should be forced to take out parent loans or borrow against their (often expensive) homes to pay to send their children to private K–12 schools or to college.

A widely publicized 2016 article, "The Secret Shame of Middle-Class Americans," epitomizes the financial struggles of the "upper-middle-class" worker. The author, journalist, and film critic Neal Gabler faced many of the financial challenges that LMI Americans have been facing since the 1980s. Gabler poignantly described the shame he felt because he—like many middle-class Americans—did not have $400 in savings to pay for an emergency, and he struggled to amass household savings because he (like many LMI workers) was paid on a piecemeal basis in a labor market that increasingly employed only part-time or freelance workers. With unstable income and minimal savings, Gabler could not afford to pay his daughters' college and weddings expenses and also could not afford to pay for annual maintenance and upkeep for his home.[13]

Gabler's confessions provided a much-needed national platform to publicize the financially precarious middle class. He was excoriated, however, for claiming to be middle class because of the seismic differences between his lifestyle and the lifestyles of typical LMI families. For example, while Gabler's employment and income as a writer were in fact unstable, his work has appeared in the *New York Times;* he sold one of his screenplays to award-winning film director Martin Scorsese; he has appeared on major TV networks on shows including *The Today Show*, *CBS Morning News*, and *Good Morning America;* and he recently published a biography of Barbra Streisand.

In addition to Gabler's wildly fluctuating and unpredictable income as a contracted worker making it harder for him to accumulate savings, he struggled to amass household savings because his wife chose not to earn wages in the paid labor market—something that is not economically feasible for most families. Another significant difference between Gabler and most LMI workers is that he had access to wealth, which generally is defined as the total value of the assets you own minus any liabilities or outstanding debt. And in Gabler's case, some of that wealth was generational.

Gabler could not afford to pay for his two daughters' college expenses to attend Stanford (and then Harvard Medical School) and Emory (and then the University of Texas). His daughters eventually attended those universities, however, because Gabler's parents could afford to pay their educational expenses. Similarly, while Gabler did not earn enough to pay for his daughters' weddings, he tapped his retirement savings to pay those expenses. Likewise, while he lacked $400 in savings to pay for desperately needed repairs to the roof and porch of his home, that home was in the Hamptons—one of the most expensive communities in the country.

While "upper" middle-class workers like Gabler may genuinely *feel* middle class, they are not the focus of this book. Moreover, the book defines *middle class* using financial metrics and ignores emotional or psychological criteria. People who self-describe themselves as "upper middle class" typically are in the top 20 percent of earners in this country. Moreover, while not true for all members of that class, as this book will show in later chapters, "upper" middle households are more likely to inherit wealth that can help them attain the markers of the middle class. Given that, this book uses the term *lower rich*, not *upper middle class*, for people like Gabler even if they might otherwise "feel" they are middle class.[14]

This book does not attempt to create a definition of who is (or is not) middle class. Instead, it considers the definitions that public and not-for-profit private colleges use when deciding who is eligible for full or partial financial aid under their "middle-class" initiatives. Colleges vary in their financial aid eligibility rules, but based on their 2024–2025 ranges, being middle class for the purposes of this book means people whose 2024 annual household earnings range from approximately $75,000 to $130,000.[15]

ABANDONING THE MIDDLE CLASS

Most state and federal policymakers since the 1980s have expressed abiding concern for the well-being of the middle class and have genuflected toward the middle class "so reflexively that failing to do so in a speech or a statement about the economy seem[ed] almost heretical."[16] Despite these professions of concern, politicians have consistently failed to implement a comprehensive framework of laws and policies to secure the financial stability of the middle class. Indeed, rather than commit themselves to eliminating the factors that make it difficult for LMI Americans to become or remain middle class, political leaders have contented themselves with placing America's middle class under a microscope, then inspecting it with the detached curiosity of an anthropologist examining the fossilized remains of an unknown species.

For decades, Congress has conducted hearings with titles like *Innovative Ideas to Strengthen and Expand the Middle Class*, *The Power of Pensions: Building a Strong Middle Class and Strong Economy*, *Beyond Mother's Day: Helping the Middle Class Balance Work and Family*, *State of the American Dream: Economy Policy and the Future of the Middle Class*, and *The Endangered Middle Class: Is the American Dream Slipping Out of Reach for American Families?* More than a decade ago, during a Senate committee hearing, then Senator Tom Harkin quoted a middle-class Iowa voter who lamented, "My own disposable income has disappeared and I am not alone. Where I once joined friends occasionally for a lunch out, that no longer happens. I don't buy new clothes. I don't travel. My friends and neighbors, formerly middle class all, are in the same boat. We are the new poor."[17] The revelation by this Iowan, while distressing, should not have been "news" to the Senate committee in 2011. Had they been paying more than scant attention, they would have noticed that LMI workers have been struggling to afford the markers of the middle class for more than forty years.

Joe Biden (as senator, presidential candidate, vice president, and president) and former President Clinton both understood the financial struggles middle-class Americans were facing, and both made these struggles centerpieces of their political campaigns. Most political leaders, however, are members of what some refer to as the *comfort class*, a group with generational wealth who control a society they do not understand. Thus, although the 2016 and 2024 presidential campaigns were dominated by the trope of the "angry middle-class voter," and candidates were forced to focus on what it would take for them to be less angry, people who were born into lives of financial stability (like Donald Trump) or who consistently associate with millionaires and billionaires often have no clue just how hard it is for poor and middle-class households to survive and thrive.[18]

Trump also has never seemed to believe he was accountable to LMI workers. Despite this, he won both presidential races by harnessing and unleashing the rage of the angry voters who could not find stable and secure jobs that provided health insurance and retirement benefits. However, the angry voters who supported him, and the only ones who really mattered to him, were White. This is not terribly surprising, as the "middle class" has always been cast as White (male) manufacturing workers who live in the Midwest and who lost their jobs to global outsourcing.[19]

RACE AND THE MIDDLE CLASS

Political pundits ranging from *New York Times* opinion writer Thomas B. Edsall to Jared Bernstein (a member of the Biden administration's Council of Economic Advisers) to organizations like The Brookings Institution struggled to accept before Trump was elected president in 2016 that discussions of the plight of the "middle class" have always ignored race.[20] Although most Latino males voted for Trump in 2024, few politicians or political analysts have seriously examined why most middle-class Black and Latina voters have chosen not to align with the vocal, angry (White) middle-class bloc that passionately supports Trump.

It is possible, of course, that middle-class Black and Latina voters believed traditional political candidates have protected their economic interests and assumed they (and their children) would have a bright economic future as long as they worked hard and played by the rules. The more plausible explanation for why these voters did not seem as enraged as White voters were in the 2016, 2020, and 2024 elections, however, is that they were not swayed by the middle-class crisis. This crisis was not new for them, as non-White workers have *always* struggled to become financially secure and stable.

My parents' experiences show why it has *never* been easy for Black (or Latino) Americans to become and remain middle class even if they work hard and play by the rules. Banking, housing, transportation, and educational laws and policies that state and federal policymakers enacted to create the middle class routinely and intentionally prevented non-White families from seizing the economic opportunities that were created for White families. Ongoing biases and market discrimination continue to make it harder for non-White families to become and remain middle class. Political officials can no longer directly discriminate against non-Whites. But the lingering legacies of the racially tinged actions political leaders took after the Depression and World War II, combined with more recent legislative and judicial rollbacks of affirmative action and diversity initiatives in schools and in the workforce, have all but guaranteed that Black and Latino Americans will continue to struggle to become and remain middle class unless political leaders enact new laws and policies.

My parents had to overcome racist obstacles in housing markets that similarly situated White Americans did not. Still, their path to the middle class was normal for the Silent Generation and baby boomers who worked hard and played by the rules. At that time, financial assistance from relatives or friends and wages from a part-time job were all young adults needed to pay their college expenses. With stable jobs and secure income and benefits, they could buy homes and retire comfortably. It is harder now for LMI young adults of all races to find stable jobs with secure income. Employment instability means they save less, borrow more, and often cannot afford to retire. Sadly, the path to the middle class that was possible before the 1980s is no longer realistic for most young LMI adults. That path is essentially blocked for young adults who are not White and who do not have a bachelor's degree.

THE MIDDLE-CLASS CRISIS

Political leaders who profess support for the middle class but feign ignorance about why it is struggling are being disingenuous. Political leaders know that we have not always had a middle class in this country, and they know that the middle class did not develop spontaneously or organically. They also know what it will take to restore the middle class, because they know that the only reason the United States has a middle class is that their predecessors made bold political decisions almost one hundred years ago. America's middle class is shrinking and struggling *not* because political leaders do not know *how* to act. It is struggling because politicians *refuse* to act.

This book urges federal, state, and local political leaders to respond to the problems facing people who are struggling to become middle class with the same zeal and urgency they had when they created the middle class almost a century ago. Part 1 examines how political leaders created the middle class and explores how the type of K–12 school children attend significantly influences whether they will attend college, *particularly* the elite colleges whose graduates are more likely to find good jobs that pay them enough to afford the markers of the middle class.

Part 2 shows how LMI workers have struggled to find good jobs, buy their own homes, and generally become and remain middle class. Part 3 explains that a combination of too much debt and too little savings has caused LMI families to fall out of the middle class. The book ends by arguing that restoring the middle class will require political leaders to use the comprehensive approach that their predecessors used when they created the middle class almost a century ago.

2 Educating Lower- and Middle-Income Children

A bachelor's degree largely determines whether a worker will have a permanent, full-time job that pays them enough to be financially stable and pay for the markers of the middle class. Sadly, LMI children may never become or remain middle class unless they can successfully navigate a complex K–12 educational labyrinth. That is, whether children will grow up, attend, and graduate from college is largely determined by the type of K–12 school they attend. But whether a child will attend a K–12 school that prepares them to attend and graduate from college is largely determined by where their parents can afford to live.

NAVIGATING K–12 EDUCATION BEFORE THE 1980S

After my father received his bachelor's degree from Tennessee State, my parents moved to Memphis and were determined to buy a home in a neighborhood that was zoned for high-performing public schools. When they bought their first home, public schools in this country could no longer be legally segregated by race because of the 1954 Supreme Court decision in *Brown v. Board of Education*. Despite this, Memphis public schools, like most public school systems in southern states, were still segregated by race and often by income in the 1960s. The principal reason local K–12 schools were racially and economically segregated then, and remain segregated now, is that where a child lives determines where they will go to school.

Eventually my parents bought a home in a predominantly White neighborhood, and my brother and I graduated from a high-performing, racially integrated high school. But the first home my parents bought was in a mixed-race neighborhood that was rapidly becoming all Black and lower income. The homes in that neighborhood were zoned to attend K–12 schools that, unbeknownst to my parents, had already declined in quality. While my parents did not know the neighborhood was transitioning, the real estate agent who steered them to that neighborhood certainly did.

Once they had bought a home zoned for low-performing elementary schools, my parents had only limited options: send us to the zoned school, enroll us in a high-performing private school, or try to transfer us to another elementary school in Memphis. They quickly rejected option 1 (the zoned school), as they understood schools that primarily educated poor and non-White children were poorly maintained, had fewer educational resources, and did not offer the type of extracurricular activities found in schools that educated middle- or higher-income White students.

My parents briefly flirted with option 2 (private school), primarily because the elite (and expensive) private schools in Memphis were desperately trying to increase the diversity of their student bodies. To make these schools more affordable, admissions counselors were offering middle-class Black parents financial assistance. My parents believed in the sincerity of the admission officers' overtures and seriously considered this option because they knew that if we attended one of those schools they would achieve the educational goals they had set for us. Option 2 was a professionally awkward one for my parents, however, because my father was a public-school teacher, and my mother had already applied to Memphis State University (now the University of Memphis) to earn a bachelor's degree and become a public-school teacher. This option also presented social challenges for them.

My parents were worried that sending their children to an all-White private school in Memphis, in the racially tense climate that existed after

Dr. Martin Luther King Jr. was assassinated in that city, might detrimentally harm us socially and emotionally. Ultimately they rejected option 2 for both social and financial reasons. Even with financial assistance, paying private school tuition would have derailed their goal of saving enough money to buy a high-appreciating home in a neighborhood zoned for high-performing public schools. They chose their only remaining option, number 3, and used the intradistrict transfer process to send us to a public elementary school (Idlewild) that was racially and economically integrated. The main reason this option was available, though, was where Idlewild was located.

Due to my mother's class schedule at Memphis State and my father's public-school teaching schedule, coordinating daily school drop-offs and pickups posed significant challenges. Then (and now) the standard school day schedule for children did not align with the standard workday schedule for their parents. Sending us to Idlewild helped align my mother's college class schedule and our elementary school schedules because the school was within walking distance of a public library. So, after school ended, my brother and I walked to the library, read books there, and remained in a safe environment until my mother finished her college classes and came there to take us home.

My brother and I were one of a handful of middle-income Black students at Idlewild. The teaching and administrative staff lacked racial diversity, and the student body was composed of approximately 75 percent White students and 25 percent Black students, virtually all of whom resided in subsidized public housing. My parents were generally pleased with the education we received at Idlewild, but they ultimately transferred us to Memphis State University's selective and high-performing elementary laboratory school, Campus School. Campus School achieved all their educational goals for us, as the student body was more diverse (racially and economically), it employed Black teachers, and our school day was perfectly aligned with my mother's class schedule.

After resolving the issue of where we would attend elementary school, my parents were quickly confronted with their next educational challenge: finding a junior high school for my brother. Given the school day and workday scheduling conflicts, this time my parents reluctantly decided to enroll my brother in the neighborhood school because I was still at

Campus School, and they could not manage the logistics of having two children attend different out-of-zone schools. The year he attended the zoned junior high school was an unmitigated disaster academically, emotionally, and socially. Fortunately a timely inheritance my mother received from the sale of the Leavell farm, along with my parents' savings and my father's stable income, allowed them to buy a home in an all-White, middle-class neighborhood at the end of my brother's calamitous first year of junior high.

Throughout our time at Wooddale Junior and Senior High, my brother and I were the only Black students whose parents owned a home in the neighborhoods zoned for those schools. Although my parents would have preferred to enroll us in middle and high schools that had the same economic and racial diversity as Campus School, their housing choices worked the way they had hoped. Both my brother and I graduated from high school and went on to attend and complete college, and all four of my parents' grandchildren graduated from high school and are attending college or are college graduates.[1]

So much has changed since then.

LMI children, particularly if they are non-White, are increasingly likely to attend separate and unequal K–12 schools. Many of these schools fail to equip them with the educational or vocational skills needed to compete for higher-wage, full-time, permanent jobs that pay them enough to afford the markers of the middle class. While state political leaders cannot legally create racially segregated K–12 public school systems, state laws enable school segregation by condoning school assignments by street address. In addition to using school attendance boundary laws to warehouse LMI families in low-performing and less-resourced public schools, political leaders facilitate K–12 school segregation by allowing parents (who are likely to be rich, lower rich, or White) to orchestrate school "successions." Parents who successfully implement school successions legally withdraw their children—and their associated property tax dollars—from racially and economically integrated districts and then form wealthier, predominantly White districts that will educate their children.

Perhaps the biggest reason that LMI students are less competitive in the college admissions process is that their parents cannot afford to give them a "shadow education" of private tutors and summer school enrichment activities. This shadow education increases the likelihood that a student will perform well in high school, then attend and graduate from college, particularly elite public and private colleges. College is the gateway to the middle class for *all* workers, but the type of postsecondary institution students attend often dictates whether they will have jobs that pay them enough to afford the markers of the middle class.

SEPARATE (AND UNEQUAL) K–12 SCHOOL FUNDING

As the US Supreme Court observed in its 1954 ruling in *Brown v. Board of Education*, "it is doubtful that any child may reasonably be expected to succeed in life if he is denied the opportunity of an education."[2] Recognizing the role that education plays in helping children become upwardly mobile, the *Brown* Court barred states from operating dual racially segregated school systems. While *Brown* admonished states to provide an education that was "available to all on equal terms," the Court ruled that wealth is not a suspect class and that public school systems are not constitutionally required to offer poor (or non-White) students the same quality of education that rich and lower-rich students receive.[3]

Although some public school systems tried to circumvent the Court's ruling in *Brown*,[4] high school (or GED) graduation rates for Black and Latino children have increased over the last fifty years. High school graduation rates for Black students increased tenfold from 1940 to 2020 though their graduation rates remain somewhat lower (and dropout rates slightly higher) than rates for White students. Racial achievement gaps in K–12 education have significantly narrowed since *Brown*, but the educational disparities between rich and lower-rich students and LMI (or non-White) students remain, largely due to how state and local leaders fund public schools and establish school attendance boundaries.[5]

Public school districts in this country are mostly funded through state and local governments.[6] States and localities use various funding formulas, though most formulas allocate funds to school districts based on the amount of property tax revenue the state collects from businesses and homes within those districts. These funding formulas all but guarantee that the public schools rich and lower-rich students attend will be better funded because their parents are more likely to live in neighborhoods with homes and businesses that have high property values. In addition, even within a school district, local leaders can decide whether to evenly allocate funds between high- and low-wealth schools in that district.

Some states have tried to narrow funding disparities by creating allocation formulas that give low-wealth districts a disproportionately large share of state funds or by directly transferring funds from high- to lower-wealth districts. These Robin Hood–style practices are well-intentioned and commendable, but they rarely fully close budgetary gaps. Moreover, they often spark resentment from rich or lower-rich parents, who bemoan that *their* money is being siphoned away to support children in low-wealth districts rather than funding programs and activities that benefit *their* children.[7]

The main reason parents in high-wealth districts believe that *their* money should be used only to pay for *their* children's education is that public K–12 school assignments are almost always determined by the student's home address. Local leaders who create school attendance zones using street addresses inextricably link housing choices to educational options for children. Although state and local officials cannot constitutionally operate dual, racially segregated school districts, creating or condoning school attendance zone policies that rely on where a student's parents can afford to live virtually guarantees that the racial and economic composition of students in individual school buildings will be as segregated as the neighborhoods themselves.[8] Indeed, recent research indicates that nearly two-thirds of the racial and economic segregation found in K–12 schools is the result of school district boundary lines.[9]

Schools that educate rich and lower-rich students are also better funded because of private, parent-controlled booster clubs that function as school financing supplements. While there have always been public school fundraisers, most efforts until recently were modest and mostly involved charging membership dues for a parent-teacher association or conducting small-scale carnivals or fairs. Since the 1980s, however, both the number and scope of fundraising organizations and the amount of revenue private fundraising generates for some schools have increased exponentially. For example, between 1995 and 2010, the number of parent-teacher associations, athletic booster clubs, alumni organizations, and other auxiliary school organizations expanded from 3,500 to 11,500, and the amount these groups raised quadrupled, increasing from $197 million to approximately $880 million.[10]

Parents or alumni are the ones who typically operate these organizations and arrange the fundraisers. Parents/alumni generally are allowed to stipulate how the monies raised can be used and, in almost all cases, those funds can be used only at their child's school. Funds often are designated for things like buying additional (or more expensive) musical instruments, hiring more coaches, or hiring teachers who can offer advanced (or additional) language or specialized technology classes. Private funding thus exacerbates funding disparities and educational opportunities between high- and low-wealth schools, as we saw vividly during the COVID pandemic.

When schools shut down in the spring of 2020, students at well-resourced schools had an easier transition to online classes because many already owned personal laptops or iPads or attended schools that provided them with technology they could take home. After the initial shutdown, schools serving rich or lower-rich students reopened sooner than those attended by LMI students, in part because rich or lower-rich parents could afford to purchase and donate masks and ventilation equipment that schools needed to safely reopen. Additionally, as I discuss shortly, these schools were safer and posed fewer health risks to students and school personnel because they were generally in better condition and already had more effective ventilation systems.

Despite the disparities that parent-controlled fundraising creates, local school boards and state leaders have little incentive to discourage parents from donating money to public schools although a few cities and districts require high-wealth schools to share a portion of their private funds with schools that educate poor students. Because neither property-based funding allocations nor existing Supreme Court rulings mandate that the education LMI children receive must be comparable to the public school education that rich or lower-rich students receive, state and local officials are not legally required to pass laws or policies that could reduce the growing funding or educational disparities between high- and low-wealth schools.

K–12 SEGREGATION, REDUX

As was true when my parents attended racially segregated high schools in the 1950s, many of the schools that LMI, Black, and Latino students attend are drastically different from *and decidedly unequal* to the schools that White students attend. Despite *Brown*, many K–12 public schools are segregated by race and income in part because US neighborhoods are largely segregated by race and income. While parents in some districts can enroll their children in any school in the district where they reside, because local school officials create school assignments using street addresses, most students can only attend their assigned school.

A 2022 report prepared by the Government Accountability Office (GAO) found that more than a third of students attend schools where 75 percent or more of students were of the same race or ethnicity. The average White student attends a school that is predominantly White, and White students are more likely to attend low-poverty schools in rural and suburban communities. In contrast, Black and Latino children are significantly more likely to attend schools with poor children, and in large urban cities and they are disproportionately less likely to attend schools with White students.[11] Although most states promise children a free and "appropriate" K–12 education, many poor and non-White students receive an education that fails to prepare them for college or to secure full-time, permanent jobs that pay them enough to afford the markers of the middle class.

Litigation filed in 2016 involving Detroit parents, who alleged that the State of Michigan violated their children's constitutional right to a minimally adequate education, illustrates just how inadequate an "appropriate" free education can be. Specifically, the children involved in this litigation attended low-resourced, low-performing public schools in Detroit. State and local officials all knew that some of the students' standardized tests scores were the lowest for students *in all large cities in the United States*, not just in Detroit or Michigan. State and local officials likewise knew the schools lacked books, were infested with vermin, and had leaking roofs and outdated heating and cooling systems. Ironically, one reason schools in Detroit had deteriorated is that the Supreme Court's 1974 ruling in *Milliken v. Bradley* struck down a Detroit metropolitan plan that was designed to decrease the number of racially and economically segregated school buildings in the city of Detroit.[12]

The federal judge who reviewed the parents' claims acknowledged that "literacy—and the opportunity to obtain it—is of incalculable importance" and agreed that the public education the students received was "nothing short of devastating."[13] Despite these findings, the court refused to find that the students had a fundamental right to be literate when (or if) they graduated from high school. Later, an appellate court acknowledged the "unique role" public education serves and concluded that a public education is a source of opportunity that is separate from the income or wealth of a child's parents.[14] This appellate panel further concluded that students have a fundamental right to a "basic minimum education—meaning one that plausibly provides access to literacy" given that the burdens poor children face impose "a heightened social burden to provide at least a minimal education."[15]

Unfortunately, a later appellate panel reversed the initial panel's finding that students have a constitutional right to be literate. The Michigan governor eventually settled the case and agreed to give the Detroit Public Schools Community District $2.7 million and promised to seek an additional $94.5 million from the state legislature. This amount, though, was far less than the estimated $1 billion needed to repair the physical deficiencies in the schools, which consigned these students to attending underfunded and high-poverty school that did not have the resources to ensure that the students would be prepared to graduate from high school.[16]

Even if the students in the Detroit litigation earn a high school diploma, they will not be competitive in the college admissions process if they are functionally illiterate, Likewise, giving children an education that is "nothing short of devastating" makes it less likely they will be hired for jobs that pay them enough to afford the markers of the middle class.[17] This case, combined with the earlier Supreme Court opinion, shows why litigation alone will not ensure that LMI and non-White children will receive a better educational experience. Whether concerned about the separation of powers or fearing political repercussions, judges generally are unwilling to tell governors or public school officials what it means to provide an "adequate" education, and the Supreme Court's refusal to rule that states cannot segregate public schools by income means that K–12 schools likely will remain segregated by income, and by race.

Parents who are rich and lower rich can ensure that their children attend schools that do not have vermin, have books, and provide an education that ensures the children are literate. Unlike poor parents, they can avoid living in neighborhoods whose homes are zoned for low-performing schools. Rich and lower rich parents typically have better information about school quality and, unlike most LMI parents, they can avoid buying homes in neighborhoods that are zoned for low-performing schools. Moreover, rich and lower-rich parents who conclude that the quality of the education their zoned school provides can enroll their children in private schools or move to a different neighborhood in the same or a different city that has better quality schools. One reason they can more easily transfer their children to higher-performing schools within either the same or neighboring districts is that they are more likely to have the money or occupational flexibility to handle the logistics of getting their children to and from school each day.[18]

Money—alone—does not determine the type of K–12 education a student will receive, and neither race nor socioeconomic status dictates how well an individual student will perform academically. Nonetheless, the amount of poverty in a neighborhood and its zoned schools is now a proxy for the neighborhood's (and thus the school's) quality. And as discussed next, the students who attend well-resourced schools fare better scholastically than students who attend low-wealth schools.

THE ADVANTAGES OF BETTER AND MORE RESOURCES

Students who attend well-resourced schools tend to achieve higher educational outcomes because these schools are typically newer, better maintained, and equipped with up-to-date technology, and they offer more advanced college preparatory courses. Students in well-resourced public high schools also have more elaborate sports complexes and access to a wider range of athletic and nonathletic extracurricular offerings, like robotics clubs, tennis, or water polo teams. One reason students who attend well-resourced schools have a sizeable educational advantage over students who attend less-resourced schools is that school officials in low-wealth schools must triage how to use their budgeted funds.[19]

School administrators in low-resourced schools can rarely afford to fund a golf team, buy multiple tubas for high school bands, or afford the supplies needed for robotics classes from their budgets, and they rarely receive much funding from parent fundraisers. Instead, these administrators often are forced to use funds for nonessential activities to pay for basic academic services and tutoring (or remediation) in core subjects like English and math. Indeed, some administrations now turn to crowdsourcing to cover the costs of nonacademic services because they know they are unlikely to secure substantial funding from private sources. Given these infrastructure, curricular, and extracurricular disparities, students who attend high-wealth schools are more competitive in both the college admissions process and labor markets.[20]

Another reason students who attend high-wealth schools perform better academically is that they typically have more qualified and experienced teachers and counselors. Because high-wealth schools experience lower teacher turnover rates than low-wealth schools, their students generally are taught by more experienced and specialized educators. While the COVID pandemic created a nationwide teacher shortage, turnover rates for teachers, counselors, coaches, and administrators in low-wealth districts and schools (particularly non-White ones) have always exceeded turnover rates in high-wealth districts/schools.[21] Turnover rates in those schools are also disproportionately high because high-wealth districts/schools lure away their experienced teachers with offers of higher pay and the promise of working in newer, better maintained, and better resourced schools.[22]

Another reason rich and lower-rich students are more competitive when they apply to college is that their schools have more (and more specialized) guidance counselors. Schools in high-wealth districts often employ specialized professionals like "college and career counselors" or "dual credit counselors." These specialized counselors focus on (1) guiding students into high school courses that provide college credit and (2) positioning them academically to be admitted to college once they graduate from high school. While students at high-wealth schools also receive help from their parents (or from private counselors), college and career counselors in public schools provide invaluable assistance by helping students (1) pick "safety" and "dream" schools, (2) keep track of college application deadlines, and (3) apply for scholarships or grant aid.

In stark contrast to the college and career counseling students receive in high-wealth schools, some low-wealth schools do not even *have* permanent guidance counselors on-site, and even if they do, the counseling staff is almost always smaller than the number of counselors at high-wealth schools. Similarly, although counselors at low-wealth schools also give students advice during the college application process, these schools cannot afford to provide specialized college counselors. Because of this, existing staff must do more than help juniors and seniors apply to college. Students at these schools are less likely to apply to selective colleges even when they are qualified, and they are left to navigate the college application process alone or with whatever help they might receive from their parents or family friends.[23]

EXCLUDING LMI CHILDREN FROM CERTAIN SCHOOLS

Brown prevents states from creating racially separate districts/schools, but some rich and lower-rich parents nonetheless engage in extreme efforts to prevent poor children from going to school with their children. Unlike the informational gaps my parents faced when they unknowingly purchased a home in a neighborhood with low-performing schools, parents today often research school ratings online before deciding where to buy or rent a home. Moreover, real estate agents and online sources like Homes.com and Redfin mention the ratings of the zoned schools when describing homes for sale or rent. Similarly, online real estate search engines frequently reference or link to the test scores and ratings of zoned schools, often using color-coded indicators that are eerily reminiscent of the now-outlawed practice of residential redlining.[24]

The widespread online access to school quality metrics—such as test scores—along with publicly available data on the racial and economic composition of students in individual schools legally exacerbates existing neighborhood and school building segregation. While real estate agents cannot legally tell parents not to buy in a home in a neighborhood whose schools are majority non-White or LMI, parents can obtain that information online as they decide where to live. This information can also help parents decide when it is time for them to sell their home because the neighborhood has started to shift demographically. When predominantly non-White neighborhoods start to gentrify and White parents move into those neighborhoods, some will not enroll their children in zoned lower-performing K–12 schools and will instead send their children to private schools. Some who opt to enroll their children in neighborhood schools often find ways to exclude non-White and LMI children from those schools.

As an example, a 2020 *New York Times* article reviewed the *Nice White Parents* podcast and described "the 60-year relationship between White parents and the public school down the block." Recognizing that White parents are "arguably the most powerful force in our schools," both the article and the podcasters recounted how self-described progressive parents often collude to exclude poor and non-White children from their children's schools or demand changes in the zoned schools that might harm the children who were attending those schools before they moved to the neighborhood. Both the *Times* article and podcast episodes acknowledge that state and local officials often are unwilling to guarantee that all children will receive an equal education because some higher-income and college-educated White parents do not *want* schools to be equal.

Rich and lower-rich parents exert tremendous power over local school decisions. For instance, when local school officials propose redrawing attendance zones or relaxing intradistrict transfer policies in ways that might allow more LMI or non-White children to attend their children's school, rich and lower-rich parents often mobilize and arrive at school board meetings in large numbers (often accompanied by a lawyer) to ensure that the boundaries for their children's schools are not redrawn. Rich and lower-rich parents do more, though, than just avoid buying homes in racially and economically mixed neighborhoods or use their political leverage to keep poor and non-White children out of *their* children's schools. In a disturbing throwback to the pre–*Brown v. Board of Education* era, these parents are also creating separate public school districts to keep schools racially and economically segregated.

Over the last few decades, parents have lawfully used school (or city) "secessions" to splinter existing school districts and create new, smaller, richer, and less diverse school districts. Parent-driven school secessions have created more than 120 communities or schools, centered mostly in southern states. A 2022 GAO study of school secessions concluded that the demographics of secessionist districts almost always differ from the demographics of the abandoned district, because secessionist districts almost always have more White students and measurably fewer poor children (defined as students who are eligible for free or reduced meals) than the original district.[25]

For example, the GAO study discusses a 2018 school secession involving mostly higher-income and White parents in communities near my hometown of Memphis. These parents were determined to make sure that *their* children would not be forced to remain in a school district that was predominantly non-White and mostly poor, so a year after Memphis City Schools merged with the Whiter and richer Shelby County School District, parents in richer neighborhoods sought to secede from the combined school district. The secession worked in six municipalities (Arlington, Bartlett, Collierville, Germantown, Lakeland, and Millington), and parents were allowed to form new school districts that were richer and Whiter than the consolidated countywide district. Similar results occurred in East Baton Rouge Parish, when parents were allowed to create a Whiter and richer city (St. George) that resulted in a significant decrease in the percentage of White students in the abandoned school district.[26]

State laws generally do not require secessionist parents to consider the fiscal (or socioeconomic) impact the secession will have on the original district. Because the rich and lower-rich parents who create these new districts are not state actors, they cannot be sued under applicable antidiscrimination law. Some states have codified the process parents must use to create a separate school district, and others require parent-driven secession requests to be approved by a state agency. Unfortunately, there is little most parents in the abandoned districts can do to prevent secessionist parents from fleeing the school district and taking their children, property, and political clout.

Parents like those in Shelby Country or East Baton Rouge Parish inflict financial harm on the children in the old district when they create a secessionist district. As noted earlier in this chapter, state and local funding formulas rely heavily on property values when distributing money to public school districts. When parents flee a school district (or city), they take the value of real property from the original district and transfer it to the newer (and Whiter) district. Removing property from the original district makes it even harder for schools to provide an adequate education for the students left behind. When parents create secessionist districts, they also take their political clout and their departure stigmatizes the original district because the reputation of a school's quality is often measured by the number of upper-income and White students in the school or district.

Secessionist parents consistently espouse race- and class-neutral factors or "local control" rhetoric to justify their decision to remove their children from diverse schools or school districts. They typically protest that their decision to create another district has nothing to do with their desire to avoid having their children attend school with LMI or non-White children and that they simply want to ensure that their children receive the type of education the parents believe they deserve. The best way to ensure their children get that education is by creating smaller, more efficient, and less bureaucratic districts that are more responsive to *their* children's needs and the needs of *their* subcommunity.[27]

Secessionist parents are never required to consider how their decision to flee poorer and less White districts affects the overwhelmingly non-White and poor students left behind. State political leaders who let parents orchestrate school secessions give those parents a permission structure to ignore the harm their acts inflict on schools and students in the abandoned districts. Political leaders also let those parents maintain the appearance of neutrality rather than forcing them to admit that their primary motive is to ensure their children do not have to attend schools with too many non-White and low-income students.[28] Moreover, when secessionist parents remove their children, their political clout, and valuable property from existing districts, they often go to great lengths to make sure that the children in the abandoned district cannot follow their children to the secessionist district.

Most parents in the abandoned district cannot afford to buy or rent homes in the successionist district, where real estate prices almost always are higher than the prices in the abandoned district, and school officials in the new district will almost certainly use street addresses to determine school attendance zones and often will not permit out-of-district transfers to the schools in the new district. As a result, parents who create secessionist districts can achieve something legally (segregated schools) that school officials cannot legally do on their own.

Rich and lower-rich parents may avoid schools that have too many poor and non-White students but they happily tolerate having their children attend schools with poor and non-White children if the school is highly ranked and may provide educational options the parents conclude may be beneficial for their children. A recent example involves The Booker T. Washington High School for the Performing and Visual Arts, a school that lists as alumni Norah Jones and Erykah Badu. This prestigious public school is located in an urban neighborhood in the Dallas Independent School District (DISD), and it regularly sends its students to Julliard. Once rich and lower-rich parents concluded that the extracurricular offerings at this inner-city performing arts school would enhance their children's college applications, they found ways to finagle their children's admission to this predominantly non-White and LMI high-performing *public* school by renting or buying homes in the DISD attendance boundaries.

While they may have rented or owned property in the DISD attendance boundaries, these parents were not willing to actually *live* in any of the neighborhoods zoned to attend the school. Instead, they continued to live in suburban neighborhoods outside of the Dallas district. After blisteringly bad publicity, DISD local school officials started to investigate where students who attended the school actually lived. They soon learned (or were forced to admit) that many of the White students who attended this inner-city high school had attended middle schools in higher-income suburban school districts. Local officials further discovered that some parents convinced (or coerced) friends or coworkers who lived in DISD to put their (the suburban parents') names on utility bills to create the illusion that their child lived in the DISD attendance zone.[29]

THE SHADOW EDUCATION

Rich and lower-rich parents do more than just move to neighborhoods with high-performing schools or manipulate or maneuver around school attendance zone policies. To ensure their children will be more competitive in the college admissions process and in employment markets, rich and lower-rich parents now spend an inordinate amount of time (and money) "parenting" their children.[30] The best predictor of a child's academic and occupational success or achievement is no longer race or even whether the student is smart. Instead, whether a child's parent can afford to provide an elaborate and expensive "shadow education" is now one of the best predictors of whether a student will succeed in high school and college and also determines whether they will have upward or downward mobility.[31]

In addition to organizing fundraising drives *for* their children's public schools, rich and lower-rich parents are increasingly present *in* their children's schools during regular business hours, which allows teachers to dedicate more time to instruction. Rich and lower-rich parents spend more time providing free administrative assistance for teachers or participating in classroom activities during the school day, in part because one of the parents (typically the father) often earns enough for the other parent to leave the workforce or work part time. These parents (typically mothers) also help teachers by agreeing to serve as chaperones for field trips or out-of-school activities like field days.

Rich and lower-rich parents are also more likely to have the occupational flexibility to arrive at work late, leave work early, or take an extended break in the middle of a workday. In contrast, LMI schools are less likely to have a cadre of *voluntarily unemployed* parents or parents whose jobs give them the occupational flexibility to be regularly present inside their children's schools. Parents who are actively present in their children's schools gain valuable face time with teachers and administrators, which helps them build social capital they can leverage to support their children's education.[32]

In addition to being physically present in their children's schools or classrooms, since the 1980s rich and lower-rich parents have invested in their children's future success by giving them an expensive and time-consuming "shadow education" outside of regular school hours. As documented in books like *The Meritocracy Trap: How America's Foundational Myth Feeds Inequality*, rich and lower-rich families have raised the stakes of "parenting" and invest a dizzying amount of time and money providing tutoring and other educational opportunities for their children during both the summer and the school year. Data show that the time parents spent providing a shadow education for their children started increasing in the 1970s, and by the mid-2000s, higher-income parents were dedicating nearly three times as much time to their children's activities as other families.[33]

Rich and lower-rich parents also spend a staggering amount of time coordinating elite extracurricular events and activities, particularly involving sports, to ensure that their children will be admitted to colleges that will give them the best chance to be upwardly mobile. Poor, Black, and Latino children often cannot participate in the expensive extracurricular activities, particularly "pay to play" activities, that rich, lower-rich, and White children can. Their participation rates are lower because their parents often face financial and logistical barriers, such as (1) the "pay-to-play" costs involved with travel for soccer, volleyball, AAU basketball, or Olympic sports like swimming and diving; (2) difficulty transporting their children to practices and games; and (3) the inability to meet required parental time commitments. Additionally, because public K–12 schools now regularly charge athletic participation fees, these costs can prevent low-income students from joining school teams, which further limits them from including these extracurricular activities on college applications.[34]

In addition to ensuring that their children participate in activities that enhance their chances of admission to competitive colleges, the knowledge rich and lower-rich parents have—*particularly* if they are college graduates—gives their children significant advantages in the competitive college admissions process. Parents who are college graduates or who can afford to hire college admissions counselors know how to use time management to play and win the college admissions game. For example, parents make sure their children balance advanced classes (that help in the college admissions process) with less-demanding ones to make it easier for them to perform well in the more challenging classes. Likewise, parents who have submitted applications for college when they were in high school can advise their children when to scale back extracurricular activities or take a break from a part-time job to prioritize studying for final exams, high-stakes state tests, or national standardized tests.

Perhaps the most significant advantage rich and lower-rich students receive from their shadow education is the ability to minimize the "summer slide." Almost *all* students forget some of the things they learned during the school year when they are on summer break, but the slide is less severe for children who receive tutoring or participate in camps or other academic enrichment activities during the summer. The most recent example of the devastating effects of educational slides occurred during COVID shutdowns, as shown in National Assessment of Educational Progress data that detail that reading, history, and math test scores dropped to their lowest levels in decades after the pandemic. The COVID slide was particularly calamitous for poor and non-White students and for students who lived in communities with the highest COVID death rates (which were disproportionately lower income and LMI).

The academic slide for LMI and non-White children was more severe during the pandemic because they lost more classroom time than rich, lower-rich, and White children. LMI children attended schools that were closed for longer periods, which meant that these students were more likely to be offered remote-only education. In turn, this forced LMI parents to choose between staying home to supervise their children's remote learning or returning to work to earn income for their families. LMI and non-White parents were less likely to have the occupational flexibility to work remotely and supervise or help their children in virtual classes during the COVID school shutdowns, which is why some poor children vanished altogether from formal education during the pandemic.[35]

After schools reopened, research revealed that some schools would need to teach 150 percent of a typical year's academic materials *for three consecutive years* to close the pandemic learning loss gap, and the pandemic disruptions may have caused students overall to lose the equivalent of two decades of educational advancement in reading and math.[36] Though rich and lower-rich children also suffered learning losses, their shadow education of private tutors combined with neighborhood in-person "learning pods" (often taught by teachers in their school districts) helped lessen those losses. Hiring private tutors or even splitting the cost to hire someone to teach in a pandemic learning pod simply was not a financially feasible option for LMI parents.[37]

Summer slides have never been as severe for rich and lower-rich children as for LMI children because of their shadow education of tutors and academic camps. Rich and lower-rich parents can more readily give their children a robust shadow education because they can afford to outsource some of their "parenting" to strangers. For example, parents who cannot (or prefer not to) take their children to before- or after-school tutoring or extracurricular activities can outsource these tasks to babysitters/nannies, private academic tutors, or athletic trainers. Although most school districts offer remedial summer classes or educational activities for students who fail classes, few offer the type of educational opportunities rich and lower-rich parents give their children. Rich and lower-rich children typically do not attend remedial classes in the summer and instead are more likely to take classes or attend camps that focus on subjects like robotics or coding. Or they attend programs on the campuses of elite colleges or at places like Interlochen Center for the Arts.[38]

Even if their children's schools do not have guidance counselors who focus on the college admissions process, rich and lower-rich parents can afford to hire private college admissions consultants, who do things like tell rich and lower-rich parents to take their children on college visits during spring or summer breaks to signal "interest" in those colleges. While some admissions offices deny that they use "engagement metrics" as an admissions factor, some continue to use campus visits to measure a student's demonstrated interest in the college. Using this signal in the admission process places LMI students who cannot afford to visit campuses at a competitive disadvantage relative to their richer peers. Similarly, parents who understand the college admissions "game" and the importance of standardized tests in the college admissions and financial aid process also send their children to summer abroad programs or enroll them in expensive SAT/ACT prep camps.[39]

This shadow education that rich and lower-rich students receive helps them retain information but also prepares them to be more competitive when they submit college applications. LMI students are also at a disadvantage in the admissions process relative to rich and lower-rich children because the latter are more likely to submit applications for early action or early decision, often with the assistance of private college counselors. Rich and lower-rich children apply for early decision at roughly twice the rate of students with similar academic credentials whose families earn less than $50,000. Because data show that early action/decision applicants have higher college admissions rates than students who apply in regular action, students who can complete and submit their applications before the regular deadline are more likely to be accepted to their preferred college.[40]

Recent media exposés show other ways a shadow education can help boost admissions prospects for rich and lower-rich high school students.

A recent *ProPublica* article reveals a gimmick some parents now use to make their children appear more qualified to be admitted to college. The gimmick? Using "publication" counselors and research services to help students write and publish "research papers" in peer-reviewed journals. While students write articles (or at least participate in the writing process) that ultimately are published in a journal, many of the peer-reviewed journals are operated by the research services that are employing the publication counselors who are helping supervise the students' writing.[41]

Another, even more blatant and unethical, ruse that rich and lower-rich parents have used to make their children more competitive was revealed in the highly publicized "Operation Varsity Blues" college admissions bribery scandal. The parents who participated in Varsity Blues paid a company to perform a range of tasks, many illegal, to help their children gain admission to their preferred colleges. For example, parents paid the company to hire people to take their students' standardized tests and paid for sham psychological "diagnoses" that would give their children additional time on standardized tests.

Perhaps the most shocking and brazen aspect of Varsity Blues was that parents (or the company) paid college coaches to convince college admissions officers that applicants who were *not* athletes should nonetheless be admitted using the less rigorous admissions standard that colleges often apply to student-athletes. Though these children have had a lifetime of educational advantages (including tutoring, summer enhancement activities, and college counselors at their high schools), rich and lower-rich parents were willing to risk being sent to prison or fined to guarantee their children would be the victors in the competitive college admissions game.[42]

Operation Varsity Blues no doubt represents an extreme version of parenting, and one assumes (or at least hopes) that not *all* rich and lower-rich parents are willing to risk jail time to make their children more competitive in the college admissions process. Even if the scandal is an aberration, it is the natural extension of the intensive and expensive helicopter/snowplow/curling parenting that has blossomed since the 1980s. Ultra-parenting has exacerbated the K–12 educational gaps that school funding formulas, school secessions, and the shadow education created. Though galling and appalling, intensive parenting unfortunately works.[43]

CREATING SAFE AND HEALTHY LEARNING ENVIRONMENTS FOR LMI STUDENTS: A TARGETED APPROACH

Chapter 8 presents a comprehensive "Middle-Class New Deal" that incorporates proposals to link K–12 education, postsecondary training, housing, and employment options for LMI workers. Although it is impossible to rebuild the middle class unless political leaders implement bold and innovative changes, they should also implement smaller, targeted measures to ensure that LMI children receive a K–12 education that equips them to become and remain middle class. The proposals contained in the Biden administration's Department of Education *ED COVID-19 Handbook: Roadmap to Reopening Safely and Meeting all Students' Needs* exemplify such an approach.[44] The glaring educational disparities revealed during and after the COVID pandemic prompted the Biden administration to respond to lost instructional time, including proposals to help create safe and healthy learning environments and to increase access to technology for poor K–12 students. Of course, the pandemic did not create the educational disparities that have existed in this country for almost fifty years, but the roadmap nonetheless presents a useful framework policymakers could use to respond to some of the educational disparities discussed in this chapter.

Increasing funding for K–12 schools that educate LMI children will not be enough by itself to help them become and remain middle class, but additional funding can close some critical gaps. For example, additional funds can make it less likely that LMI students will be educated in unhealthy, vermin-infested buildings with leaking roofs and outdated heating and cooling systems. Money can also help improve the infrastructure of buildings that educate LMI children, which could encourage experienced teachers and guidance counselors to come and remain in those schools rather than flee to high-wealth school districts.

The main educational goal for the Trump administration, governors, mayors, and school superintendents during the pandemic was to reopen public schools as quickly as possible and have children return to in-person classrooms, which succeeded in the high-wealth schools, schools in rural areas, and schools in Republican-controlled states that reopened in fall

2020. Schools in urban LMI neighborhoods reopened later than those schools, often because the school buildings lacked windows that opened, modern ventilation systems, hallways that were large enough for social distancing, or an adequate supply of personal protective equipment (like masks) and portable ventilation systems.

Building deficiencies, like vermin and leaky roofs, are open and obvious disparities, but a less visible disparity that became open and obvious during the pandemic was the lack of reliable and affordable high-speed internet. Indeed, until the pandemic shutdown, few people understood that LMI schools are often located in neighborhoods (including some in large cities and in rural areas) that have deficient broadband. The pandemic exposed these disparities and revealed the digital divide that made online learning a near impossibility for some LMI students and has always made it harder for LMI children to complete schoolwork or participate in online college preparatory activities at home.

The lack of stable internet access did more than just widen educational achievement gaps and make it harder for students to learn during the pandemic. The digital divide also made it harder for some workers, including teachers, to do their jobs. That is, teachers who lived in neighborhoods that lacked stable broadband struggled to teach online classes or homeschool their own children during the shutdowns, and even workers who were given the option to work remotely often could not do so because of unstable internet access.

Because local school officials stubbornly adhere to the practice of assigning children to K–12 schools based on their parents' street address, they must ensure that the buildings in the neighborhoods that educate LMI children have amenities that are comparable to the ones found in neighborhoods that educate rich and lower-rich children. At a bare minimum, political leaders must make sure those buildings have reliable high-speed internet access. Likely because broadband easily fits in the "infrastructure" box, the Biden American Jobs Plan proclaimed that "broadband internet is the new electricity," declaring it "necessary for Americans to do their jobs, participate equally in school learning, health care, and to stay connected."[45]

While the Emergency Broadband Benefit Program (part of the American Rescue Plan Act of 2021) allocated funding to subsidize broadband for some low-income households, like many pandemic programs, the funding was temporary. To ensure that students and workers who live in broadband deserts have high-quality, reliable, and affordable access to the internet and to help close educational disparities between LMI children and their wealthier peers, federal leaders should treat the internet like a utility and allocate direct funding for high-speed fiber construction projects in underserved neighborhoods. The federal government should also work with private-sector partners to ensure that high-speed internet service is more accessible in Wi-Fi hot spots near rural and urban schools, community centers, and churches. Without stable broadband in their neighborhoods, even LMI students who attend resource-rich schools will struggle to complete school assignments, take online classes, or participate in academic enrichment activities offered on platforms like Khan Academy in their homes.[46]

CONCLUSION

Brown v. Board of Education prevents states from legally segregating public schools by race. Nonetheless, children who attend high-poverty schools in this country receive an education that is decidedly unequal to the education students in high-wealth schools receive. The pandemic shutdowns put those inequalities in plain view for all of us to see. Despite this, political leaders will not admit that the way this country educates LMI children makes them less competitive in the college admissions game and also makes it less likely they will find jobs that pay them enough to afford the markers of the middle class. As the next chapter shows, a bachelor's degree is the gateway to the middle class. Being a college graduate may not ensure that a worker will become and remain middle class, but adult workers who lack that degree should assume that their only mobility will be downward.

3 Educating Lower- and Middle Income Adults

A 2022 report prepared by The Pell Institute, a research organization for the Council for Opportunity in Education, discusses President Franklin Delano Roosevelt's proposed "Second Bill of Rights." While Roosevelt never succeeded in having the Second Bill of Rights enacted into law, it would have guaranteed a right to a college education at a time when roughly 26 percent of White and 8 percent of Black people over the age of twenty-five had a high school diploma, but only 5 percent of White and 1 percent of Black adults had a bachelor's degree. Although college attainment rates have significantly increased since the 1940s, as we saw in the last chapter, the Supreme Court has refused to declare that Americans have a constitutional right to receive anything beyond even a minimally adequate high school education.[1]

One way Congress helped LMI students earn a college degree was by enacting the Servicemen's Readjustment Act of 1944 (commonly known as the GI Bill). The GI Bill gave returning veterans benefits they could use to pay for college or other postsecondary training and to help pay their families' living expenses while they were in school. At that time, workers could secure stable and reliable jobs without a college degree because of the abundance of high-wage manufacturing jobs. Nonetheless, Congress passed this legislation to help veterans achieve upward mobility and to mitigate the risk that returning veterans would overwhelm labor markets and destabilize an economy that had barely recovered from the Great Depression. The GI Bill boosted enrollments at public colleges and generally democratized higher education because, until then, most people who went to college attended private institutions.[2]

By enacting the GI Bill, federal legislators ensured that going to college was no longer accessible only for wealthy students whose parents could afford to send them to private colleges. This legislative act also signaled that Congress recognized the critical link between a college degree, higher earnings, upward mobility, and economic stability. The bill significantly increased college enrollment rates, helped increase lifetime earnings for the veterans who used the benefits, and also helped them buy homes (which increased their household wealth). As students were not required to repay GI benefits, veterans never needed to bury themselves in debt to get a college degree or postsecondary training.

Although the legislation had positive results for the mostly male veterans who used their benefits to attend college (or buy homes), for several reasons, it overwhelmingly benefited White male veterans. One reason is that many public flagship universities, and virtually all those in southern states, used racist admissions policies that would not admit Black students. As a result, Black veterans could only use their GI benefits at chronically and intentionally underfunded historically Black colleges and universities (HBCUs) and trade schools. Another reason the educational options available to Black veterans were not comparable to those available to White GIs is that educational policies at that time prevented most public HBCUs from offering graduate degrees or programs in fields like engineering.[3]

As discussed in chapter 1, my parents understood that they would need more than just a high school diploma to become middle class. Both received additional education after they graduated from high school. My father was not a veteran, so he was not eligible for GI benefits. Fortunately, both graduated from their postsecondary educational programs and, unlike many LMI college students today, they graduated largely without debt. As chapter 6 shows, that is in stark contrast to the reality facing many young adults (and their parents) today.

After my mother graduated from a legally segregated all-Black high school (Warner High School) in Newnan, Georgia, she moved to Nashville to attend a secretarial trade school (the Nashville Business School). No one encouraged her to further her education, and she understood that with four younger siblings still living at home with her parents, the only way she could pay for her education was to follow the path most young Black women took in the 1950s: get a job and work her way through college. So my mother worked as a nanny for a White family in Newnan for a year and a half after she graduated from high school.

My mother aggressively saved her wages and the monetary gifts the family gave her. She had enough savings to pay her travel expenses to Nashville, but not enough to pay her college expenses. So when she arrived in Nashville, she found a part-time clerical job. Her transition to the workforce was effortless. Thanks to the Nashville Business School's commitment to guaranteed job placement once students completed their skills training, my mother secured a permanent, full-time secretarial position once she finished her studies. She had that job when she married my father and kept it until she became pregnant with my brother.

Like my mother, my father also graduated from a legally segregated all-Black high school (Booker T. Washington High School). He left Memphis after he graduated and attended Tennessee State University (TSU), an HBCU in Nashville. Unlike my mother, my father's family and high school teachers encouraged him to attend college, and my Fenny grandfather's job with a railway company paid him enough to cover my father's freshman year college expenses. When my grandfather suffered a debilitating work injury after my father's first year of college, my father was forced to leave school for a semester and work full time to earn money.

To pay his remaining college costs at Tennessee State, my father found part-time jobs at a chicken processing plant and in a boiler room at Fisk University (another HBCU). My father's earnings from part-time jobs, my mother's full-time earnings from her secretarial job, and monetary gifts that my father occasionally received from one of his sisters (Beatrice) was enough to pay his bachelor's degree expenses and their living expenses once they married.[4] Savings, wages, and relatively low tuition and fees in the 1950s meant my parents never had to bury themselves in debt to pay their college expenses.[5]

Although few non-White or female veterans could use GI benefits to go to college, and their college attendance and graduation rates vastly lagged behind rates for White and male high school graduates, young adults of all races and genders now have higher college attendance and graduation rates. By 2020, 41 percent of White adults, 28 percent of Black adults and 21 percent of Latino adults had a bachelor's degree. Unfortunately, overall college enrollment rates peaked at roughly 70 percent in 2009 after the Great Recession, dipped during the COVID pandemic, and rates for eighteen-year-olds dipped again in 2024, continuing a decade-long trend caused by lower overall US birth rates.[6]

As the next section explains, while more students were graduating from college and the bachelor's degree became the gateway to the middle class, for several reasons college costs were rising faster than inflation. The main reason is that state legislatures decreased public funding for state colleges and universities. In response, cash-strapped colleges and universities increased tuition but simultaneously reduced need-based financial aid policies and are now as likely to award "merit" scholarships to students with no demonstrated financial need as to award aid to financially needy students. As chapter 6 discusses in more detail, many LMI students and their parents are now drowning in debt to pay for this marker of the middle class.

COLLEGE COSTS

Higher education at public colleges has shifted from being mainly supported by public funding to being predominantly financed by parents and students. The total cost (including tuition, room and board, and fees) to attend college has soared at all colleges—especially for-profits—since the 1980s. Costs have increased in part because colleges are in a fierce battle to attract a dwindling number of potential applicants, given declining US birth rates. Though colleges can be blamed for administrative bloat and for building state-of-the-art dorms, recreational centers, football stadiums, and dining halls, since the 2007–2009 Great Recession, they have had to compete for a smaller pool of college-age students.

Lower birth rates forced colleges to implement "enrollment management programs" and to expand student support services to entice students with the promise of having a memorable social experience, access to luxurious dorms and facilities, and on-time graduation. Though those investments might improve student satisfaction and increase enrollment, the costs are typically passed on to students through increased tuition and fees. Moreover, these services are primarily designed to attract students whose parents can afford to pay most (if not all) of their children's college costs. The main reason costs have soared at public colleges and universities, however, is not high-end facilities but that state officials have systematically reduced their support and funding for higher education.

Until the 1980s, public colleges received approximately 75 percent of their funding from state appropriations and the remainder from students and their parents in the form of tuition and fees. Although total state funding for public colleges and universities has increased since the 1990s, it has not kept pace with the rising costs of attending college. Furthermore, the proportion of funding that public colleges and universities receive from state and local sources has not increased. For example, in 1975 state and local funding accounted for nearly 60 percent of the total funding for public colleges and universities. By 2000, however, this share had dropped by almost 15 percentage points, with roughly half of state colleges relying primarily on tuition and fees, rather than on government appropriations, for their funding.[7]

An unfortunate financial convergence makes it particularly difficult for LMI students to afford college. That is, state financial support for public institutions declined at roughly the same time that LMI parents were facing stagnating income. Moreover, student funding declines also coincided with an increase in college enrollments for Black, Latino, and LMI students. Although perhaps this is mere happenstance, public divestment from higher education has been particularly notable in states controlled by politically conservative legislatures. Indeed, many Republican federal and state political leaders now openly question the value and purpose of higher education.[8] Faced with budget cuts and the understanding that students and their parents can take out student loans to pay for college, public colleges and universities have responded by increasing tuition and fees. Some states responded by imposing tuition freezes to prevent colleges from increasing in-state undergraduate tuition and fees, but faced with tuition freezes, colleges have chosen to enroll more nonresident or international students or to expand graduate and nondegree programs.[9]

Though tuition freezes help LMI families, most political leaders have done little else to make college more affordable for LMI students. One reason political leaders, particularly older ones, may struggle to understand why it is so difficult for LMI families to afford college is that they attended college during a time when it was easier for parents to pay for their children to go to college and for students to "work their way through" college.[10] A recent Dēmos report highlighted the sharp rise in college costs and compared the tuition that members of Congress paid during their college years to current tuition at their alma maters. The report showed that college costs have far outpaced wages and inflation, but also signaled why political leaders have utterly failed to respond to the crisis LMI young adults face if they want to go to college.

The report noted that students who attended Yale University roughly a decade after the 2007–2009 Recession paid 261 percent more than congressional members who graduated from Yale in 1965. Similarly, Harvard graduates in Congress paid 260 percent less to receive their degrees in the late 1960s than Harvard students paid in the mid-2010s. The most striking increases, however, were for public colleges. That is, tuition at the University of Alabama increased by 594 percent from 1957 to 2016 and by 387 percent from 1976 to 2016. During that approximate time period, tuition at the University of Texas increased by more than 800 percent (for 1985 graduates) and almost 450 percent (for 1990 graduates).[11]

Since 1980, college costs have increased at rates that are up to three times faster than increases in household income, inflation, and the price of other consumer goods and services. Average costs to attend four-year public institutions were roughly 150 percent higher just before the pandemic (in 2019–2020) than they were in 1974–1975, and the Biden administration observed in 2022 that "the total cost of both four-year public and four-year private college has nearly tripled" since 1980.[12] Decreased state education appropriations combined with tuition increases have caused LMI students and their families to bury themselves in student loan debt to pay for college, and this caused the Biden administration to enact student loan forgiveness policies. Unfortunately, Republican political leaders and some Trump-appointed federal judges have halted many of these policies, and the current Trump administration has refused to cancel educational debt even for borrowers who may be unable to repay their loans.

Rich or wealthy families can often afford to pay for their children's college costs using savings or current income. In contrast, most LMI students use a combination of scholarships, grants, and their parents' income or savings to pay for college. The *mix* of parental contributions, scholarships and grants, wages, savings, and student loans that a student uses to pay for college varies—often dramatically—depending on their parents' income and the level of educational attainment. For example, until the 1980s, LMI students often paid for their college expenses with small gifts from friends or family or by working their way through college. As my father did in the 1950s, many paid for college using money from part-time jobs during the school year or full-time jobs in the summer and most students who attend community college and virtually all students who attend for-profits work (often full time) while they go to school.

The difference between the 1950s and today is how much students will need to work. Students who attend traditional four-year colleges typically do not work full time and, in fact, college advisers discourage students from working more than fifteen hours a week. Research shows that students who work more than fifteen hours each week get worse grades, are less likely to graduate on time, and often miss out on building the social capital formed through informal networking with classmates in extracurricular activities or in casual encounters.[13] Even if working too many hours did not have these negative educational consequences, it is no longer logistically possible for students to "work their way" through college, given that college costs have increased faster than wages for most workers.[14]

Because they view college as a worthwhile investment and the gateway to the middle class, LMI students (particularly non-White and first generation) often borrow excessively, and this borrowing exacerbates income and racial inequality gaps.[15] As chapter 6 addresses in more detail, most borrowers do not have excessive student loan balances, and most borrowers repay their loans on time. Nonetheless, cumulative outstanding student loan debt was roughly $1.6 trillion at the start of the pandemic, and some commentators (and politicians) have criticized students and their parents for drowning themselves in debt. As discussed in more detail at the end of this chapter, LMI students are correct to view a bachelor's degree as an investment in their future, given that average earnings for college graduates exceed earnings for high school graduates by as much as $1 million over a lifetime.[16]

Poor students can use Pell Grants to pay for college, though this is no longer enough to prevent them (and their parents) from drowning themselves in debt. When Congress created the Pell Grant program, it covered roughly three-quarters of the total cost to attend a four-year public college. In 2024, Congress increased the amount students can receive in Pell Grants, though the annual maximum covers *less than half* the costs in 2022 to attend a two-year community college, just over one-quarter of the cost to attend a four-year in-state public college, and less than 10 percent of the total cost to attend Ivy League and other elite schools.[17] In 2025 the Trump administration proposed draconian budget cuts to programs administered by the Department of Education, including the Pell Grant program and the program that funds work-study (a program that helps students earn money to pay for their college expenses).

Until recently, rich or lower-rich parents assumed their children would not qualify for *any* assistance, as financial aid traditionally was based on financial need. Because of federal tax credits enacted during the Clinton administration, that is no longer true. With the exception of the University of North Carolina's Morehead-Cain scholarship, virtually no public universities before the 1990s offered all-expense, non-need scholarships. "Merit-based" programs—like Georgia's Helping Outstanding Pupils Educationally (HOPE) scholarship—that give students with no demonstrated financial need financial assistance have proliferated since then, and state political and higher education leaders have reduced the proportion of *need*-based financial aid relative to "merit" grants. Most states now offer college financial aid that is not based on need, the share of students receiving non-need grants since the 1990s has roughly doubled at both public and private colleges, and the average amount of "merit" awards often surpasses that of need-based aid in some areas.[18]

Colleges that award financial assistance to students who have no demonstrated financial need typically consider the applicants' grade point averages or standardized test scores. But the term *merit* is broadly defined, as highlighted in a 2011 report by the US Department of Education that revealed that almost 20 percent of freshmen at four-year colleges with SAT scores below 700 (out of 1,600) were awarded "merit" aid and that 20 percent of those with GPAs lower than 2.0 (out of 4.0) also received "merit" scholarships. Admissions or financial aid offices at colleges often determine what constitutes "merit," and state and university leaders are willing to accept the vagaries associated with "merit" scholarships because of the type of students universities typically attract with these awards.[19]

College admissions offices often engage in what can best be described as financial aid arbitrage to decide which students will receive financial assistance denominated as a merit-based award, and some now use algorithms to award discounts based more on what parents will pay than on the applicant's qualifications. The students most likely to get non-need-based awards are rich and lower-rich students. Given the K–12 educational disparities that already exist between LMI students and their rich and lower-rich peers who attended well-resourced high schools and received a shadow education of private tutors and expensive test prep courses, these ostensibly income-neutral "merit" awards further disadvantage smart but less wealthy students.[20] As legal scholar Daniel Markovits has noted, "meritocracy has become the single greatest obstacle to equal opportunity in America today" because, whether or not the student has truly earned the "merit" scholarship, non-need merit grants almost always shift financial aid funds from LMI students to rich or lower-rich students.[21]

State spending on non-need financial assistance has increased faster than spending on need-based financial aid. Starting in 1995 and through the beginning of the 2007–2009 Recession, the proportion of rich students who received non-need merit grants *increased*, while the proportion of low-income students who received need-based grants *decreased*. State elected officials and college administrators often brush off criticisms of merit scholarships by arguing that these programs keep the best and brightest high-scoring (and higher-income) students in state. College administrators likewise contend that these non-need financial awards help them target wealthy, high-scoring, out-of-state undergraduates who might be willing to enroll at their colleges. Particularly if legislatures have mandated tuition freezes for in-state undergraduates, universities have an incentive to view out-of-state students as revenue generators. Public colleges charge out-of-state students higher tuition but award a "merit" scholarship that results in them paying significantly less than the advertised tuition for out-of-state students. In essence, states use wealthy parents of out-of-state students to help to close the budget gaps that state officials created when they cut state funding for public colleges and universities.[22]

While state political leaders may approve of non-need financial aid, it is not clear that these "merit" grants actually encourage rich and lower-rich students to remain in state for college. That is, while merit aid makes it somewhat less likely that high-scoring students will leave their states to attend a *public* college in another state, research does not show that these grants convince high-income students (or their parents) to remain in state (and pay lower tuition) if they are admitted to attend an elite *private* college.[23] Moreover, while financial aid (whether merit or need based) often determines whether a poor student will attend college, the same is not true for non-need-based grants that rich and lower-rich students receive. Empirical data do not support the proposition that higher-income students who receive non-need financial assistance would forego college without these grants. Instead, what is clear is that these non-need grants shift funds from poor students (who likely will *not* attend college without financial aid) to rich or lower-rich students (who likely *will* attend even if they receive no financial aid).[24]

In addition to making it harder for LMI students to afford to pay for college, many private colleges also make it harder for them to be admitted. This is consistent with sentiments James Carville (one of former President Clinton's longtime campaign managers) expressed in his 2012 book *It's the Middle Class, Stupid!*, which recent media reports and guidance counselors essentially confirm: it actually may be better to be rich than to be smart if you want to go to college. Specifically, while college admissions policies historically prioritized admitting qualified students regardless of their financial need, financial aid directors now admit that their admission process is no longer "need-blind," and they confess that they routinely consider a student's need for financial aid when making admissions decisions. They also admit that they use "gapping" (offering low-income students less financial aid than they need to cover expenses) to discourage them from enrolling.[25] While admissions officers may view this practice as ethical,[26] nearly twenty elite colleges were sued for conspiring to limit financial aid for financially needy students, though many have recently settled.[27]

Of course, not all educational leaders have prioritized winning the favor and financial support of rich and lower-rich families over ensuring that LMI students and their families can afford to pay college costs. Indeed, most private and public colleges with large endowments have enacted programs that grant free (or nearly free) tuition to students from families earning $65,000 or less. Some of these programs also provide grants that cover the full cost of attendance. While eligibility requirements vary and are often restricted to in-state residents at public colleges, most programs also award financial assistance to middle-income students to help defray tuition costs.[28]

IS COLLEGE WORTH IT?

Despite the costs, most parents understand the value of a college degree. Still, there is an odd but dramatic mismatch between the value some parents/students place on a bachelor's degree and the criteria many employers use when they make hiring decisions. Polls conducted during the 2016, 2020, and 2024 election cycles indicated that many parents and students no longer believe a college degree is "worth it" given the number of college graduates who have jobs that do not explicitly require a college degree. Lower-income families are less likely (84%) to agree that college is an investment in their children's future than middle (89%) or high (96%) income families. These parents are also less likely (65%) to believe that college is part of the American dream than middle (75%) and higher (79%) income families.[29]

Although it is understandable that LMI parents and students may want to avoid drowning themselves in student loans to get a degree that may not be worth the return on their investment, as discussed in more detail in the next chapter, many employers will not hire noncollege workers even if the job historically would have been performed by someone who did not have a college degree. So, even if some families may no longer believe that college is "worth it," the bachelor's degree nonetheless remains the gateway to the middle class because of the value employers place on the degree.

Until the 2007–2009 Recession, almost 80 percent of high school students believed they would attend and complete college, more than

90 percent of parents with children in grades 6–12 expected their children to attend college, and 65 percent of parents who assumed their children would attend college expected them to earn at least a bachelor's degree. Expectations and assumptions about whether a child will attend and graduate from college vary, sometimes drastically, based on parental income and educational level, just as actual graduation rates vary based on income and race.[30]

A 2008 report found that students with noncollege parents (first-generation, or first-gen, students) are significantly less likely (barely half) to expect they will earn a bachelor's degree, compared to 70 percent of students with parents who are college graduates (continuing generation, or continuing-gen, students). Similarly, more than two-thirds of the highest income students believed they would become college graduates, but only 45 percent of middle-income children and barely one-third of the country's poorest children shared that belief. In addition to variations among students in their expectations and assumptions, rich and lower-rich parents and parents with college degrees are also more likely to expect their children to earn *at least* a bachelor's degree.[31]

One reason rich and lower-rich students expect they will graduate from college and earn a professional or doctoral degree is that rich, lower-rich, and college-educated parents believe they have a *duty* to help pay their children's college expenses. It is no great surprise that parents who willingly pay for private tutors and other expensive facets of a shadow education to give their children a competitive advantage in the college admissions process also are willing to pay their children's college costs. Consequently, this parental willingness to pay contributes to higher college enrollment and graduation rates for rich and lower-rich students.[32]

Low-income parents are less likely to believe they are primarily or solely responsible for paying their children's college expenses. Those beliefs are understandable given soaring college costs, reductions in need-based financial aid awards, and stagnant income since the 1980s for all but the highest earners in the country. Even if LMI parents cannot afford to pay all their children's college costs, LMI students who receive even modest financial support (as my father received from my Aunt Bea and the teachers at his all-Black high school) are more likely to attend (and graduate from) college than LMI students whose families do not support them. Similarly, the college attendance rates for lower-income students who receive encouragement or emotional support from their families are comparable to overall attendance rates.[33]

Another reason that lower-income students may not receive financial support from their parents and, indeed, may *assume* their parents will not pay for their college expenses is the prevalence of student-to-parent financial transfers in lower-income households. Though transferring money (which sometimes includes part of their student loan proceeds) to parents increases the risk that a student will not graduate from college, poor students routinely give their parents or other older relatives money because they believe that, as adults, they have an obligation to support family members even if they are college students.[34]

ENROLLMENT AND GRADUATION DISPARITIES

Despite racial and income college enrollment and attendance disparities, since the mid-1970s rates have increased for young adults from all racial groups at both two- and four-year colleges, though attendance rates for rich and lower-rich students have remained roughly a third higher than rates for poor students. While college attendance rates dropped for all income groups and across all races when most classes went fully online during the pandemic, students from most income and racial groups returned to college campuses by 2024.[35]

One reason college enrollment rates increased for non-White (and female) students in the 1970s is that colleges adopted affirmative-action and need-blind admissions policies. College attendance and graduation rates may regress, of course, given the Supreme Court's recent ruling that bans the use of race-conscious college admissions decisions and the Trump administration's 2025 executive order that authorizes the US attorney general to scrutinize how universities are complying with the Court's ruling.[36] Female enrollment, attendance, and graduation rates now exceed comparable male rates, particularly for White students (whose enrollment rates have been declining principally because of their lower birth rates). While people born since the 1980s are the most educated and credentialed generation, soaring costs combined with stagnant family income discourage many capable and competent LMI students from even applying to college.[37]

Racial and income disparities in college *enrollment* rates contribute to college *graduation* gaps. One factor that consistently determines whether students will attend and graduate from college is whether they are continuing-gen or first-gen students. Continuing-gen students are disproportionately rich, lower rich, and White and have higher college enrollment and graduation rates compared to first-gen young adults, who are disproportionately LMI, Black, and Latino. Although attendance rates for white students have seen steep drops in recent years, the shadow education (discussed in the last chapter) that rich and lower-rich students, particularly if they are continuing-gen, receive helps explain their higher college enrollment and graduation rates.[38]

Research shows that poor children with high test scores in kindergarten are less likely to keep those high scores through high school and only have a three in ten chance of earning a college degree. In contrast, children from families in the top income quartile with *low* test scores in kindergarten have a seven in ten chance of graduating from college. Moreover, regardless of test scores, higher-income students are more likely to apply to the most competitive colleges, enroll in any college, and attain a bachelor's degree than poor students with comparable test scores. Indeed, higher-income students *with bad grades* are more likely to receive a college degree than lower-income students with better grades.[39]

High school graduation and college enrollment rates have increased for all groups since the end of World War II, when political leaders made it easier for veterans to attend college and pay their expenses with GI benefits. Roughly two-thirds of high school graduates enroll in college, but continuing-gen, White, rich and lower-rich students continue to have higher graduation rates overall than non-White and LMI students.[40]

POSTSECONDARY SEGREGATED SILOS

Just as the stereotypical image of a "middle-class American" is a White male who lives in the Midwest and is employed (or formerly employed) by a manufacturing company, there is a stereotypical image of a college student: a person who attends a four-year institution. This image is deceptive, though, as nearly half of *all* college-enrolled students have attended a community college at one point. Community colleges have existed since the mid-nineteenth century and initially were designed to provide additional academic assistance for high school graduates who were not quite ready to attend a four-year college. Though the mission of community colleges has shifted somewhat, they continue to provide a valuable service to students who (1) need to go to school close to their parents' homes, (2) do not need or want to earn a bachelor's degree and prefer to receive specialized workforce skills training, or (3) seek to lower their overall college costs by attending a less expensive community college for two years before transferring to a more expensive four-year college.

Black, Latino, LMI, and first-gen college students (*particularly* males) are disproportionately educated at community colleges, although enrollments for higher-income students increased when overall college costs started to soar, particularly after the 2007–2009 Great Recession. Of all community college students, higher-income students are most likely to start in community college, then transfer their credits to a four-year college.[41] Graduation rates for Black and Latino students who attend selective colleges are comparable to graduation rates for White students who attend those colleges, but students who attend less selective colleges (like community colleges) often have lower graduation rates. It is possible that Black, Latino, LMI, and first-gen students have lower college graduation rates because they are not prepared for the rigor of college classes or just are not as smart as White, rich, lower-rich, and continuing-gen students. The more likely reason graduation rates are lower for students who attend community college and for-profits is that many students are trying to "work their way through college" and also because less selective colleges generally offer fewer academic support services than most selective colleges.

Notwithstanding the racist implications of the common trope that affirmative action allows unqualified Black and Brown students to go to college, research shows that Black and Latino students with above average SAT scores who enroll at a *selective* public college have an 81 percent chance of graduating but only a 46 percent chance of graduating at an open access college.[42] But just as LMI and non-White high school students are more likely to attend segregated high schools, they are also more likely to attend economically segregated and less selective postsecondary institutions even if they are qualified to attend selective private and public colleges.

Like community colleges, HBCUs and Hispanic-serving institutions (HSIs) provide valuable benefits for students who may desire to avoid attending a four-year predominantly White institution (PWI). HBCUs were created to serve the educational needs of Black Americans who wanted to attend college but would not be admitted to PWIs because of their discriminatory admissions policies. HBCUs serve a relatively small percentage of the overall college population and have always prioritized giving their students a higher level of academic support and nonacademic services. Black students who graduate from HBCUs are more likely to experience upward mobility than their peers at predominantly White institutions, and 17 percent of Black students who receive bachelor's degrees and almost 25 percent of Black students who receive science, technology, engineering, and mathematics (STEM) degrees graduate from HBCUs.[43] Although HBCU enrollments are mostly non-White, a growing number of HBCU students are not Black.

The postsecondary institutions that are most racially and economically segregated for reasons unrelated to racist college admissions policies are for-profit institutions. Very few rich or lower-rich students attend for-profits. Compared to public two- or four-year colleges or private nonprofit four-year universities, for-profits disproportionately enroll lower income, first-gen, and non-White students.[44] Historically, for-profits filled an educational niche by offering short-term vocational training for students (like my mother) who did not want to (or could not afford to) enroll in a four-year college. The landscape and mission of for-profits radically shifted in the 1980s, however, when locally owned and operated trade schools (like the Nashville Business School) that offered in-person classes for students were crowded out by large, publicly traded national institutions (like the University of Phoenix or the now defunct ITT Tech) that offered mostly online distance education.[45]

Once private equity or venture capital firms started investing in for-profits, these schools started to shift their educational model from one that focused on offering short-term vocational training to one that focused on competing with public and private nonprofit four-year institutions for students and federal financial aid.[46] For-profits have always been more expensive than community colleges and routinely charge more than many public or private nonprofit four-year colleges. The return on investment for students who attend a for-profit is often minimal, as these programs (particularly online graduate programs) provide woefully deficient job training. Moreover, many offer unaccredited vocational programs that do not prepare students for the occupational licenses they will need for jobs that will pay them enough to repay the debt and generally afford the markers of the middle class.[47]

While most college students in this country attend community colleges or four-year public or not-for-private institutions, enrollments at for-profits have increased at staggering rates, and the number of for-profit institutions grew from approximately 880 in 2005 to more than 1,400 by 2013.[48] Enrollment growth for for-profits slowed in the 2010s when state and federal investigations revealed that many spent significantly more of their operating budgets on recruiting and marketing than they did on instruction/teaching or on academic services such as student outreach and advising. Indeed, while public and not-for-profit private universities spend most of their funds on activities that are designed to enhance student success, investigations revealed that some for-profits (1) intentionally misrepresented the total costs students would pay to attend those institutions, (2) gave recruiters incentives to encourage potential students to falsify financial aid forms, and (3) concealed or outright falsified data about their (dismally low) job-placement rates and overall graduation rates relative to public and nonprofit private colleges.[49]

As shown in figure 1, graduation rates for students (in total and by sex) who attend for-profits are significantly lower than for other college students. Graduation rates are lower in part because many schools are online only, which owners prefer because the online education model increases the institutions' profitability even though remote classes lead to worse educational outcomes for students. The Obama administration's "gainful employment" rule made it harder for nonprofits to receive federally guaranteed student loans, which caused entities like ITT Tech and Corinthian Colleges to shut down. The Trump administration has unfortunately repealed most of the regulations that were designed to protect students

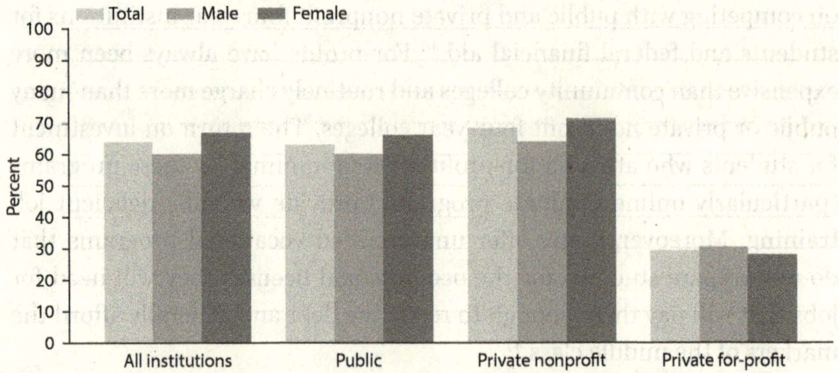

Figure 1. Four-year college graduation rates (within six years of enrollment) at different types of educational institutions.

SOURCE: US Department of Education, National Center for Education Statistics, "Integrated Postsecondary Education Data System (IPEDS), Table 32472, Average Undergraduate Tuition and Required Fees, by Control and Level of Institution, Academic Year," 2025, https://nces.ed.gov/ipeds/search/viewtable?tableId=32472.

from for-profits that did not provide meaningful job prospects and caused students to bury themselves in student loan debt.[50]

LMI and non-White students are more likely to attend community colleges and for-profits, while rich, lower-rich, and White students are more likely to receive degrees from the places whose students have the highest graduation rates and who develop the social ties that help them become economic elites: highly selective and elite colleges and universities.[51] Fewer than 20 percent of undergraduates are enrolled at these colleges, but educational and political leaders are well aware that certain colleges disproportionately educate rich and lower-rich students. As noted earlier, plaintiffs recently sued nearly twenty elite colleges based on allegations that they conspired to limit financial aid for financially needy students, and a civil rights group recently filed a complaint against Harvard University with the US Department of Education Office for Civil Rights. The lawsuit reveals that rich, lower-rich, and White students disproportionately comprise the student bodies at selective colleges and public universities; that many elite schools grant preferences to continuing-gen students; and that first-gen students whose test scores and class ranks are comparable to higher-income students are less likely to attend those colleges. The complaint maintains that Harvard's consideration of legacy preferences violates federal law.[52]

My mother worked her way through the Nashville Business School, had no student loan debt, and received the skills she needed to find a job as a secretary as soon as she finished her training. Unfortunately, today's LMI young adults are likely to find that attending a for-profit will not help them become or remain middle class. Though college enrollment rates for non-Whites are increasing because of their higher birth rates, they are significantly less likely to attend this country's most selective colleges than White students.[53] Although non-White students generally should avoid high-cost for-profits, the best (and perhaps *only*) way for LMI students to become and remain middle class is to earn a bachelor's degree. Without that degree, they may never find jobs that pay them enough to afford the markers of the middle class.

A TARGETED APPROACH TO INCREASE SKILLS TRAINING AND LIFELONG LEARNING

The "college for all" mindset has dominated K–12 educational discussions and policies since the 1980s. Educational leaders, particularly at the national level, seem to have concluded that the sole mission for US high schools is to prepare students to enroll in a four-year college. Rather than develop an educational model that helps LMI high school students achieve financial success in the workplace when they graduate from high school, K–12 educational policies remain myopically focused on ensuring that they excel on standardized tests and achieve high SAT scores so they can go to college.

One reason the "college for all" mantra is so pervasive and corrosive is the unfavorable comparison between income (and wealth) forecasts for college graduates relative to income (and wealth) for noncollege workers. The bachelor's degree is now the clear gateway for LMI workers to the middle class, and the earnings premium college graduates receive results in their earning significantly more over their lifetimes than noncollege graduates.[54] In addition to being beneficial to the individual worker, a bachelor's degree also has intergenerational effects, as continuing-gen college graduates earn more (and have greater wealth) than first-gen college graduates. Because workers who are college graduates (particularly from selective colleges) are more likely to be White, rich, or lower rich, the college attainment disparity has exacerbated racial income and wealth gaps.[55]

US Census Bureau data show that the percentage of people who have a bachelor's degree has never exceeded 40 percent, and it is unlikely that this country likely will *ever* achieve a 100 percent college graduation rate. Not all workers will be *or need* to be college graduates, but employers value workers with postsecondary skills training. Given this, LMI workers need access to low-cost skills training to help them qualify for jobs that pay them enough to afford the markers of the middle class. Because of the transformational changes in labor markets, workers understand the importance of skills training, value "upskilling" opportunities at their jobs, and report that they would prefer to work for employers who have well-defined paths for their career advancement.[56]

State and local political and educational leaders must find ways to offer more free or low-cost job skills training in public high schools. As explored in more detail in the next chapter, changes in US labor markets since the 1980s, combined with more recent AI developments, dictate that political leaders find ways to ensure workers can continually train and retrain to be qualified for jobs that pay them enough to afford the markers of the middle class. Despite the value of a college degree, at a bare minimum, state leaders and local school officials must reject once and for all the "college for all" mantra and accept that not every high school graduate needs to be a college graduate.

As their predecessors did in the past, today's leaders should also reinvest in vocational education programming. Voc-ed was created after World War II to provide reasonably priced skills training for workers. States initially invested in these programs to respond to demands by employers and social reformers that public education be better aligned with business needs. Before the 1980s, most high school graduates completed at least one voc-ed course, but interest in voc-ed credits waned once the "college for all" mantra captured the minds and souls of educational and political leaders. States started cutting funding for high school skills training offerings, and voc-ed ultimately was rebranded as career and technical education (CTE).[57]

High school students and their parents generally shun CTE courses. Some parents reject skills training courses for their children because they perceive that the programs created a class-based, two-tiered system. This perception is not completely untrue, as the students who typically are steered to skills training courses are non-White, LMI, and those with noncollege parents. One reason those students have always participated in voc-ed programming is that guidance counselors have steered them away from advanced placement or other college preparatory classes. This steering, unfortunately, is one reason these courses (and CTE apprenticeships) are stigmatized *particularly* in the minds of rich and lower-rich parents, who concluded that those classes would not help their children perform well on standardized tests or high-stakes, state-mandated tests and might make them less competitive in the college admissions process.[58]

While recent data indicate that school systems had difficulty filling or were unable to fill open CTE positions, there are ways to encourage more students to take skills training classes in high school that do not involve funding. At a bare minimum, educational leaders must find ways to alleviate fears that participating in CTE programming will create rigid workforce or college paths. To give students stronger incentives to take CTE classes, state educational leaders should ensure that students have the option of either (1) using the course credits to earn workforce credentials in high school (and bypass college) or (2) receiving college credits for the skills training they gained through a skills-based course or apprenticeship. Indeed, the primary nonfunding task that local school officials must tackle is to destigmatize high school workforce training classes. This actually may be easier now than it was even a decade ago, now that so many students and parents from all income groups are questioning whether "college is worth it."

Local and state educational leaders should seize this "is college worth it" moment to explain to students and their parents that adult workers must embrace a lifetime of skills training because technological advancements, particularly artificial intelligence, will likely continue to eliminate jobs or restructure workforces. Relatedly, colleges should award more degrees for technical areas, as the University of Northern Iowa recently did when it offered degrees in applied engineering and materials science. Likewise, given the looming enrollment cliff and declining college attendance rates for White rural high school students, colleges should give students partial college credit for training they received in technical fields, as the University of Tennessee-Martin recently did for students who completed a farming operations program at a local technical school.[59]

The shadow education that rich and lower-rich children have received almost since birth prepares them to go to college, but it is simply absurd to force children to choose a career once they enter high school, when they are young teenagers. To encourage students to take CTE classes or participate in skills-based apprenticeships in high school, schools should clearly explain that *not all students* will graduate from college, but that *all* high school graduates will need skills to be hired in jobs that pay them enough to pay for the markers of the middle class.[60] To give students stronger incentives to take CTE classes, state educational leaders should ensure that students have the option of either (1) using the course credits to earn workforce credentials in high school (and bypass college) or (2) receiving college credits for the skills training they gained through a skills-based course or apprenticeship.

Part of the programming in high school CTE courses should focus on financial literacy. While some states offer these classes, as discussed in more detail in chapter 7, few states mandate that students take these classes before they graduate from high school. Encouraging more high school students to take financial literacy courses would help prevent them from drowning themselves in debt to attend a high-cost for-profit institution that may not even give them marketable skills.

CONCLUSION

The final chapter of the book envisions and proposes a bold "New Deal Education Plan" to help LMI students receive the postsecondary training skills needed to find jobs that pay them enough to afford the markers of the middle class. In the interim, though, educational leaders must consider less grandiose and more targeted programs to help non-college LMI workers obtain the skills training they need to compete in the evolving US labor markets, which the next chapter explores.

PART 2 Trying to Remain Middle Class

4 Finding a (Good) Job

The Nobel laureate and former chair of the Council of Economic Advisers Joseph E. Stiglitz proclaimed in his 2013 book, *The Price of Inequality: How Today's Divided Society Endangers Our* Future, that the United States is "no longer the land of opportunity portrayed by Horatio Alger stories of 'rags to riches.'" He argued that if an economic system "leads to so many people without jobs, or with jobs that do not pay a livable wage," the system "has not worked in the way it should." At that point, he maintains, the government must step in.[1]

After the Depression and World War II, the government stepped in to make sure LMI workers could find jobs that helped them join the middle class. Unfortunately, as has become abundantly clear since the 1980s, it is nearly impossible for LMI workers to find full-time and permanent jobs that pay them enough to become and remain middle class. Wages for the lowest paid workers increased after the COVID pandemic, after being stagnant since the 1980s, but LMI workers *still* struggle to acquire the markers of the middle class. Unlike the political leaders who intervened to create the middle class, today's leaders have done little to help LMI workers find good jobs with good benefits.

LMI workers are struggling for the same reasons LMI children struggle in schools: political inaction and neglect. Chapter 2 revealed that some K–12 systems no longer provide an education that prepares LMI students to become and remain middle class. Likewise, chapter 3 stressed that although a bachelor's degree has become the gateway to the middle class, political leaders have done little to make college more affordable or to provide low-cost skills training options for LMI workers who do not want (or need) to go to college. Political leaders are fully aware that businesses have manipulated labor laws in ways that harm LMI adults who work hard and play by the rules. However, rather than intervene as their predecessors did after the New Deal, they stand by and watch workers piece together a patchwork of unstable part-time jobs, temporary gigs, and side hustles.

Before describing why so many LMI workers are warehoused in the low-wage, temporary, and part-time sector with jobs that do not pay them enough money to pay for college for their children (or themselves), buy homes, avoid crushing debt, or build even modest household savings, I first describe what the typical work trajectory looked like when people like my parents entered the workforce as young adults before the 1980s.

FINDING WORK BEFORE THE 1980S

Once my mother completed her course work at the Nashville Business School, a full-time job awaited her—just as the school had promised. She stopped working full time when she became pregnant with my brother, and when my parents lost her income, they patched together money my father earned from his part-time job at a chicken processing plant and money he earned in a side hustle to pay their bills.[2] The only bills they could not pay during his final semester of college were a few months of rent and my mother's obstetrician fees. Fortunately the landlord and doctor agreed that he could pay off those debts over time (which he did) after he started his new job in Memphis.

My father's first full-time job was at George Washington Carver high school, an all-Black public school in Memphis. The job was permanent, was unionized, and had guaranteed annual raises. The security of a permanent full-time job gave my parents the luxury of deciding that my mother would stay home and take care of me and my brother until I began elementary school. Once we were both in elementary school, my mother returned to college to earn her bachelor's degree. Her first full-time job was, by choice, a temporary one as a substitute teacher in the Memphis City Schools system. Soon she was hired full time as a middle-school teacher for Memphis City Schools.

My mother was a public schoolteacher for her entire working career. My father, also a lifelong educator, had jobs that included serving as an assistant commissioner of education for Tennessee and as a school superintendent. All their jobs offered health insurance, a retirement plan, and other benefits like sick and personal leave days. Secure income meant my parents could assume they would be able to pay their living expenses but also build savings they could use to buy homes, pay college expenses (for my mother, my brother, and me), avoid ruinous debt, and eventually retire and use their pension income to pay their living expenses.

Their employment stability may seem fantastical to today's young workers. But their work experiences were not aberrational for adult workers from 1947 through 1974, a period often called the "Great Compression." The typical middle-class workers at the beginning of the Great Compression were white- or pink-collar male workers like office clerks, teachers, or salesmen, à la Willy Loman in *Death of a Salesman*. By the end of the Great Compression, the face of the stereotypical middle-class worker had become a (male) manufacturing worker in a unionized workforce in the rust/steel belt Midwest states in America.[3]

During the Great Compression the United States had a strong and stable middle class, and until the 1980s the wages and benefits workers received from their stable, full-time jobs gave them a fair share of the nation's economic prosperity. My parents and other workers during that timeframe had job security and stability largely because the country was a goods-producing economy that had a strong manufacturing sector. While the wage and nonwage compensations were generous, the main reason workers in my parents' generation felt secure financially is that they knew they were protected by strong labor unions.

VANISHING JOBS AND THE ANTI-UNION POLITICAL AGENDA

Manufacturing jobs peaked in the mid-1940s, dropped after the end of World War II, but then increased fairly consistently until the 1980s. Jobs in rust/steel belt Midwest states started to vanish in the 1980s, and full-time and permanent "good" jobs have declined substantially since then.[4] As shown in figure 2, the manufacturing sector was particularly harmed during the 2007–2009 Great Recession. At the same time political leaders were ritualistically promising to "bring back" good American jobs they were refusing to enact laws to prevent business leaders from shuttering plants and eliminating or offshoring jobs.

Businesses eventually reshored some manufacturing in the 2000s, so political leaders ostensibly could proclaim that they had brought back good American jobs. The main reason businesses reshored jobs was that wages for most US workers had been stagnant ever since the "good" jobs left the country, and they realized that transportation costs made it cheaper to produce goods in the United States now that wage gaps between US and global (notably Chinese) workers had narrowed. When adjusted for inflation, the "good" onshored jobs paid considerably less than the jobs that were outsourced decades earlier.[5]

Another reason "good" manufacturing jobs vanished is the technological advances and the emergence and ultimate dominance of the e-commerce industry. E-commerce decimated brick-and mortar workplaces that historically offered jobs that paid noncollege LMI workers enough to afford the markers of the middle class. Jobs that workers performed physically in buildings before the 1980s are now routinely performed by machines, bots, or robots. Laptops, digital cameras, smartphones, ATMs, self-scanners, digital ordering screens, and drones eliminated pink-and-white and pink-collar jobs like bank tellers, travel agents, photographers, and secretaries. More recently, technology eliminated lower-income starter jobs like store cashiers, baggers, and fast-food servers. Moreover, many of the routine and repetitive tasks workers historically performed in higher-wage manufacturing and mining jobs were mechanized and assigned to robots once businesses realized that robots could perform those tasks cheaply, more efficiently, and with virtually no workplace safety risks.

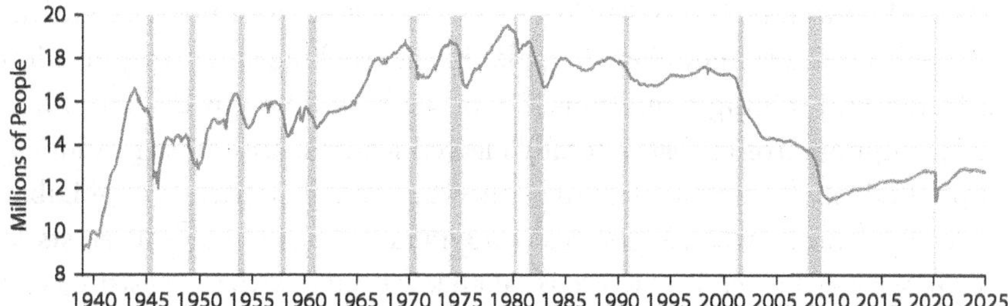

Figure 2. All employees in manufacturing, 1940–2025. Shaded areas indicate US recessions.

SOURCE: Federal Reserve Bank of St. Louis, All Employees, Manufacturing (MANEP), accessed June 25, 2025, https://fred.stlouisfed.org/series/MANEMP.

Most of the jobs that were eliminated by technology had historically been performed by LMI workers, while technological innovations generally have been a boon for college workers with specialized or technical STEM degrees. Now, of course, artificial intelligence threatens their jobs as well.[6] Why has it been so easy for businesses to eliminate or offshore jobs, offer lower wages and benefits when they reshore jobs, or replace humans with robots? Because organized labor is no longer strong enough to stop them.

Until the 1980s, public employers and most large manufacturing companies had unionized workforces. Because of that, employers were required to engage in collective bargaining with labor unions to determine the wages, benefits, and workplace conditions of their workers. Union members overall have better workforce benefits, including retirement plans, medical benefits, life insurance, sick leave, and childcare benefits, than nonunion workers. But unionization has helped all workers because unions fought for a federal minimum wage, unemployment insurance, occupational safety laws, and antidiscrimination civil rights statutes. Union-negotiated collective bargaining agreements (CBA) helped secure health insurance and guaranteed retirement benefits for union members, and CBAs ultimately created standardized wages and benefits for workers across unions and, eventually, helped standardize working conditions in nonunion workplaces.[7]

Nearly one-third of American workers were members of unions during the Great Compression. Unionized workforces were concentrated in the

Rust Belt and industrial East Coast cities and were most prevalent in automobile and steel manufacturing plants, the trucking and transportation industry, and mining operations. Union leaders were powerful and had broad support from most federally elected leaders, and most presidents appointed labor union leaders to be secretary of the Department of Labor until the 1980s.[8] Because political leaders now prioritize the interests of business over the needs of workers, at all levels (and with the assistance of state and federal judges) they have allowed employers to erode workers' rights.

The anti-union blueprint was created well before the 1980s, though, and was largely driven by political leaders in conservative southern states. Indeed, even when labor unions enjoyed the solid support of federal leaders and governors in Midwest and East Coast Rust Belt states, southern political leaders openly expressed hostility to unions. These politicians routinely cast union leaders as communists and used blatantly racist tropes to convince White workers to reject union organizing. To ensure unions would not become powerful in their states, anti-union legislators enacted deceptively titled "right-to-work" (RTW) laws.[9]

RTW laws undermine unions by letting businesses employ workers who refuse to pay union dues or their fair share of the costs of union bargaining *even though* they work in a workplace whose workers are represented by a union. Non-dues-paying workers reap the same employment benefits and protections as dues-paying unionized workers because of federal laws that mandate that unions bargain on behalf of *all* workers in unionized workforces even if they refuse to pay membership dues. The lethal combination of RTW laws, federal labor regulations, and expansive Supreme Court interpretations of those laws gutted union bargaining power and, in the process, made it more likely that workers would have unstable and lower-wage jobs that offered few nonwage benefits.[10]

Many businesses neglect the needs of their LMI workers and focus almost exclusively on maximizing corporate profits and increasing share prices. With tacit and often explicit support from politicians, public-sector employers have balanced their budgets, and private-sector employers have increased corporate profits, at the expense of workers.[11] Once employers decided union wages were excessively high and union-provided benefits (like medical care, long-term disability, and life insurance) were too generous, they realized that the most effective way to reduce their labor costs would be to dismantle or weaken the organizations that protected workers (i.e., unions).

Destabilizing anti-union campaigns in the private sector have included acts to decertify bargaining units, replace union organizers with lower-paid nonunion workers, and illegally discipline or fire workers who participated in union-organizing efforts, as well as threats to file for bankruptcy to force union concessions. Once businesses and political leaders diluted unions and silenced workers' voices, employers realized that there was little workers could do to stop them from eliminating jobs, reducing wage and nonwage compensation, or converting permanent and full-time jobs to temporary or part-time jobs.

Although public unions have fared somewhat better than private unions, then President Ronald Reagan—who was twice president of the Screen Actors Guild—launched arguably the earliest and most brazen political attack on organized labor. After members of the Professional Air Traffic Controllers Organization went on strike without obtaining the required governmental consent, Reagan fired all twelve thousand members. Since then, federal and state political leaders have followed Reagan's playbook. They have slashed the number of local, state, and federal jobs; demonized public workers (particularly at the federal level); and generally made it harder for public employees to bargain individually or collectively. Indeed, one of President Trump's executive orders on the first day he returned to the White House in 2025 took aim at public employees. The order reclassified many federal workers as at-will employees, imposed a hiring freeze, and revoked telework policies. He then authorized former "DOGE" head Elon Musk to make draconian cuts to the federal workforce.[12]

Unionization rates for local, state, and federal government workers (and for US Postal Service workers) remain roughly five times higher than rates for private-sector workers, though those numbers are now declining. Public unions have been relentlessly attacked by conservative (mostly Republican) political leaders, although a few unions—most notably the politically powerful Fraternal Order of Police, which garners almost uniform support from political leaders—continue to have strong bargaining strength. Still, by the early 1980s union membership in the United States had declined from its mid-1950s peak of approximately 33 percent of the workforce.[13]

Although existing labor laws prevent employers from unilaterally dismantling unions, public and private employers suffer few negative consequences if they engage in anti-union campaigns. In fact, the refusal of political leaders to increase sanctions even when businesses repeatedly and willfully violate labor laws during organizing campaigns has emboldened business leaders to be even more aggressive in their anti-union campaigns. In addition to allowing businesses to quash union activity in traditional unionized workforces (particularly the manufacturing sector), lax enforcement of labor laws has ensured that unions will not gain strength in nonmanufacturing sectors like the entertainment or service industries.

Emboldened businesses that are not forced to treat their employees fairly routinely present workers with little more than take-it-or-leave-it job options that force them to either quit or accept jobs that provide lower wages, fewer hours, and minimal nonwage benefits. And although it is less obvious, weaker unions have also allowed businesses to thrust forced arbitration clauses (which prevent them from suing employers in court) and noncompete clauses (which decrease mobility) on even lower-wage LMI workers.[14]

Union organizing had somewhat picked up strength before the COVID pandemic, and the unionized public-sector workforce had grown during the 2007–2009 Great Recession, before contracting during the 2020 COVID recession. Despite historically low overall postpandemic unemployment rates, the public workforce (particularly for K–12 public schoolteachers) has not returned to its pre-COVID strength,[15] and the pay gap between public- and private-sector workers continues to expand. The public workforce was further reduced by the Trump administration's decision (particularly through Elon Musk's DOGE actions) to slash the federal workforce.

While overall union membership remains at roughly 10 percent of the workforce, polls show the public's approval rates for unions are at all-time highs.[16] Indeed, union organizing intensified during the pandemic when workers witnessed the power of collective bargaining in real time. For example, labor unions intervened when Congress debated the $2.2 trillion

Coronavirus Aid, Relief, and Economic Security Act. Specifically, the Association of Flight Attendants-CWA—whose members remembered being duped into agreeing to wage concessions after the September 11, 2001 (9/11) terrorist attacks—successfully lobbied federal leaders to ensure that the pandemic relief airlines received was conditioned on the airlines' agreement to use the funds to save jobs and protect workers rather than engage in stock buybacks, as they had done after 9/11.[17]

Likewise, during the early months of the COVID shutdown, workers—particularly in the health-care industry—saw the benefits of collective bargaining once they realized unionized workers had more job stability, better work protections, lower COVID-19 infection rates, and greater access to personal protective equipment (PPE) than nonunionized workers. In addition, full-time, permanent, temporary, and gig workers in both public and private workforces demanded, and often received, wage increases, paid leave, and additional health and welfare benefits to compensate them for the risks they faced during the pandemic, and many nonunion workers also went on strike or staged small-scale "sickouts" or work slowdowns to publicize what they viewed as unsafe work conditions.[18]

THE ECONOMIC CONSEQUENCES OF HAVING STRONG LABOR VOICES

Unions help LMI workers find jobs that pay them enough to become and remain middle class. Overall wages for unionized households are higher than wages for nonunion households, and wages for union workers typically are higher than wages for nonunion workers *even if* the union worker has a lower educational level than the nonunion worker. Indeed, the mere presence of strong unionized workplaces forces nonunionized workplaces to increase wages and improve working conditions to retain employees and discourage them from engaging in organizing activities at their workplace.[19]

Employers erroneously blame high labor costs for private budget deficits, lower stock prices, and sluggish corporate earnings. Before the 1980s, hourly pay increased in tandem with labor productivity—generally defined as workers' total output divided by total hours worked—and earnings for noncollege and college workers (whether unionized or not) essentially kept pace with inflation. Since then, labor *productivity* has not declined and has, in fact, significantly exceeded labor *compensation*. For example, roughly ten years after the 2007–2009 Great Recession, labor *productivity* was 3.8 times as high as labor productivity in 1950, while labor *compensation* was only 2.7 times higher.[20]

Today's workers are paid less *not* because they are working less or because their wages are harming the employer's bottom line. They are paid less because private businesses understood that political leaders would do little to prevent them from engaging in anti-union campaigns that helped them maximize corporate profits. Rather than share corporate profits with the workers who helped generate those profits, corporate leaders instead gave those profits to themselves (as executive compensation) or to their shareholders (as dividends). Because of weakened unions, inflation-adjusted wages for LMI workers have been stagnant, while income growth for rich and lower-rich workers (who are disproportionately White college graduates) has soared.[21]

As shown in figure 3, college graduates earn more (and have lower unemployment rates) than noncollege workers. While earnings for college graduates are above median wages, earnings for workers who do not have a bachelor's degree are less than average weekly earnings.

Post-COVID labor conditions forced employers to increase pay for lower-wage workers but by 2021 the *bottom 90 percent* of workers earned less than 60 percent of total wages, while the *top 5 percent* earned almost 30 percent.[22] The decrease in union membership and the shrinking union wage premium has widened income gaps between college and noncollege workers and between the top 1 percent of earners and all other earners. Wage gaps are particularly stark between the (mostly) noncollege line workers and the (mostly) college-educated managers, between Black and White men, and between noncollege workers and college graduates who graduated from elite private and public colleges or who have advanced degrees.[23]

Despite the overall benefits of unionization, Black unionized workers received fewer benefits from being union members than their White union peers, in part because they have always been *under*represented in the higher-wage supervisory or managerial unionized jobs. Until Congress

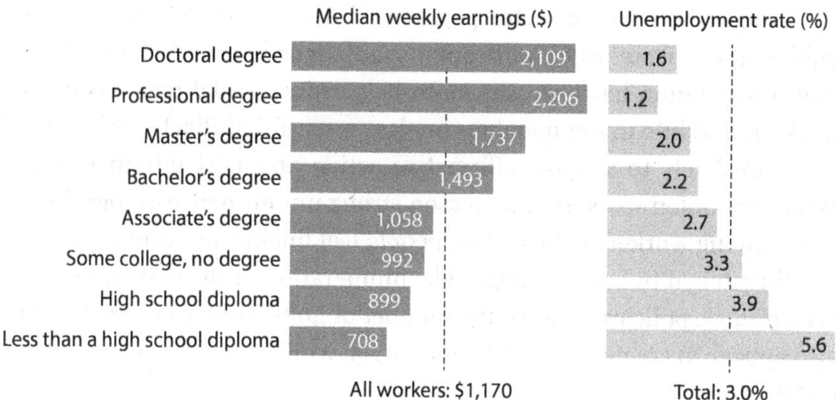

Figure 3. Earnings of adult workers by level of educational attainment.

SOURCE: US Department of Labor, Bureau of Labor Statistics, "Education Pays: Unemployment Rates and Earnings by Educational Attainment," 2024, https://www.bls.gov/emp/chart-unemployment-earnings-education.htm.

and state legislatures passed (and judges enforced) antidiscrimination laws in the 1960s, unions and employers openly discriminated against Black workers. The public sector enforced antidiscrimination laws earlier than the private sector did, and for that reason public sector employment was an easier pathway for Black workers to find jobs that paid them enough to become and remain middle class. Black workers have disproportionately high employment rates in the heavily unionized public workforce, including in K–12 public schools, though, starting in the 1970s, overall membership numbers for Black workers in private unions started to increase, particularly in the heavily unionized blue-collar manufacturing sector. The union wage premium (the difference in earnings between union and *non*union workers) for Black workers has always been larger than the gap for union/nonunion White workers.[24]

Black men have the highest overall union membership rates, and for that reason anti-union campaigns *especially* harm Black workers. When political leaders relentlessly demonize public-sector employees, slash public-sector jobs, or eliminate benefits, these actions disproportionately harm non-White workers, *especially* Black middle-class workers, who are less likely than their White counterparts to find private-sector jobs if they lose their public-sector positions.[25] Another more subtle reason public- and private-sector anti-union campaigns harm Black workers is that unionization has been shown to help reduce racial tensions in the workforce. White union members are less resentful of Black workers and are more likely to support affirmative action and DEI initiatives than White nonunion workers. One reason strong unions may ease racial tensions among workers is that when people feel financially secure, they are less threatened by social changes like immigration or diversity initiatives *even if* those policies increase the number of non-White workers. Unions also appear to create a sense of community, which may also help ease racial tensions.[26]

Most workers in this country are not union members, and unionization still has not returned to pre-1980 numbers. Nonetheless, there is no dispute that unions helped LMI workers become financially stable and find jobs that helped them pay for the markers of the middle class. Indeed, if there was *any* dispute about the importance of union members, it was dispelled when President Biden became the first US president to *ever* march with a union when he joined the UAW picket line in 2023.

LOW WAGES AND THE PART-TIME AND GIG ECONOMY

In addition to their anti-union campaigns, businesses have made it harder for LMI workers to afford the markers of the middle class by dramatically restructuring the US workforce. During much of the Great Compression, the largest employers were high-wage unionized manufacturing companies like General Motors, Exxon, DuPont, AT&T, and U.S. Steel. These employers typically offered permanent and full-time jobs that provided retirement plans, health insurance, and other employee benefits. Since the 1980s, these jobs have *decreased* at roughly the same percentage as temporary, low-wage jobs have *increased*. Now, LMI workers are forced to patch together income through a piecemeal of low-wage and often part-time and temporary jobs.

Since the 1980s, businesses have systematically eliminated secure, permanent, and full-time "good" jobs and replaced them with unstable, temporary, contracted, or part-time jobs. Indeed, by the start of the

2007–2009 Great Recession, America's largest private-sector employers were low-wage retailers like Walmart, McDonald's, and Yum! Brands (which operates KFC, Pizza Hut, and Taco Bell). Not surprisingly, the decline in the number of "good" manufacturing jobs in the 1980s coincided with the emergence of the trope of the "angry" White (male), noncollege, middle-class worker in the Midwest.

Middle-class workers have reason to be angry, as they have been the primary victims of an increasingly polarized labor market that has eliminated their jobs and rewarded larger shares of the economy to college-educated workers who work in finance or other hypertechnical sectors. Sixty percent of the jobs lost during the 2007–2009 Recession were "good" jobs, and significantly fewer (roughly 20%) of the lost jobs were low-wage jobs. In contrast, unstable, low-wage jobs that typically are filled by noncollege workers were more than half of the jobs created during or after this recession, while only 22 percent of the jobs created during that period were higher-wage jobs that would be filled by noncollege workers.[27] The increase in *both* high- and low-wage jobs since the 1980s has made it significantly less likely that LMI workers will be able to find a middle-wage job that pays them enough to pay for the markers of the middle class.

Most workers continue to have only one full-time job, and some workers choose to juggle short-term temporary jobs because they prefer a more flexible work arrangement or have personal obligations (including caring for minor children) that make full-time and permanent jobs less attractive. Some workers juggle multiple part-time or temporary, full-time jobs because they need more money to make ends meet, and most LMI workers prefer to have just one permanent full-time job.[28] Domestic outsourcing has made it less likely, however, that LMI workers will have full-time and permanent jobs that pay them enough to afford the markers of the middle class.

Unlike global outsourcing (which sends full-time US jobs overseas), domestic outsourcing converts full-time and permanent jobs into part-time or temporary jobs. In the first step of domestic outsourcing, businesses eliminate jobs or departments that are not central to the company's main revenue-generating functions, such as accounting, security, or custodial services. In the second step, the company restores those jobs but hires workers (often their recently fired workers) through staffing agencies or hires full-time independent contractors.[29] Typically, wages for jobs that vanish in step 1 of domestic outsourcing are lower when they return as either full- or part-time positions in step 2, and the converted jobs typically do not offer nonwage benefits like health insurance, retirement savings, and paid sick or parental leave.

Perhaps the most pernicious way businesses revolutionized workforces was by creating the "gig" labor market. The gig economy, which did not exist prior to the 1990s, offers workers short-term jobs or tasks like delivering or buying prepared meals or groceries or providing ride sharing. While the gig economy provides part-time and temporary jobs that can help workers supplement their income if they face an unexpected expense or are temporarily unemployed, gig jobs provide absolutely no job security for workers.[30] Gig and contracted workers receive virtually none of the labor law protections full-time statutory employees receive, and even workers who are rehired by their former employers through a contracting agency typically do not receive the same wages, benefits, or work protections they had when they were direct employees of the business.

Even before the pandemic, wage and nonwage compensation had dropped so low for some temporary workers and contractors that they were forced to rely on government benefits, including food stamps and Medicaid, to survive.[31] Although the earliest instances of domestic outsourcing involved jobs with mechanized or routinized tasks, even workers whose jobs *cannot* be mechanized (like professors) are being pushed into temporary or contingent work arrangements. For example, increasingly large shares of faculty at US educational institutions are employed as part-time, full-time adjunct, or non-tenure-track workers.[32]

Tight labor markets improved the situation for LMI workers after the COVID pandemic. Labor economists David Autor, Arindrajit Dube, and Annie McGrew found that postpandemic worker shortages helped some young noncollege workers move from lower-wage to higher-wage jobs, particularly once the 2021 Infrastructure Investment and Jobs Act increased the number of jobs that did not require a college degree. Still, the US Department of Labor projects that the top twenty job-creating industries will mostly be lower wage, including home health care, food preparation, lawn servicing, cleaning, and janitorial services, which do not pay workers enough to afford the markers of the middle class.[33]

INSTABILITY AND UNEMPLOYMENT

Legislators harmed workers and helped businesses implement their anti-union agenda by allowing businesses to place contracted workers at worksites alongside statutory workers. Because only statutory employees have the right to join a union, diluting the number of full-time statutory workers makes it more likely that the workforce will remain nonunionized. State and federal lawmakers and agencies also helped exacerbate job insecurity for part-time, contracted, and temporary workers by refusing to extend labor laws to protect workers from unpredictable work schedules.

Temporary workers in contingent workforces have little control over the hours they work each day, which days they will work, or whether they will even be able to keep their jobs. As David Weil documents in *The Fissured Workplace*, temporary and contracted workers live with constant uncertainty and job insecurity. With little predictability about when they will be called to work, it is difficult for them to have a second (or third) job to earn more money. Unstable work schedules also make it harder for workers to enroll in postsecondary training classes that could lead to permanent full-time (or higher-paying) jobs. Work instability and uncertainty likewise make it harder for workers to structure their personal lives, including scheduling medical appointments, arranging for childcare, figuring out how to get their children to and from school, or attending their children's school activities. Given the uncertainty and instability associated with part-time and temporary jobs, it is little wonder that high school students now view job security and the ability to work full time as equally important as what they earn.[34]

One reason noncollege workers have higher unemployment rates than college graduates is that they are less likely to have full-time permanent jobs and more likely to be employed in temporary and contracted jobs.[35] College graduates have lower unemployment rates than noncollege workers, and there has always been an unemployment gap between college and noncollege workers, as shown in figure 4. The gap increased dramatically after the 2007–2009 Recession before reaching historic highs at the start of the 2020 COVID pandemic.[36]

In addition, while unemployment rates dropped to historic lows in 2023, unemployment rates for Black, Latino, and noncollege workers

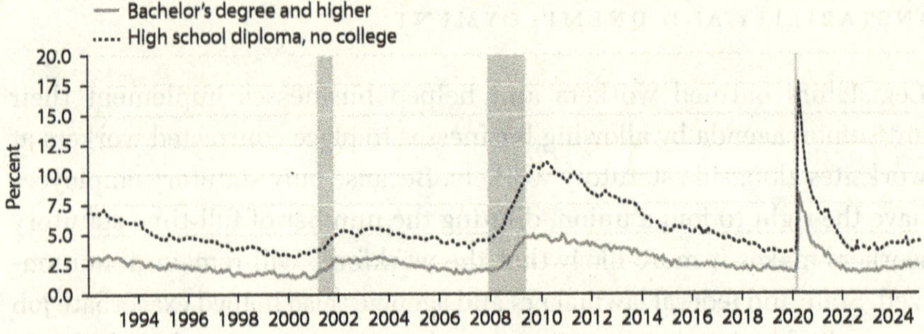

Figure 4. Unemployment rates of adult workers (age 25 and over) by educational level, 1992–2025. Shaded areas indicate US recessions.

SOURCE: Federal Reserve Bank of St. Louis, Unemployment Rate—Bachelor's Degree and Higher, 25 Yrs. & Over and High School Graduates, No College, 25 Yrs. & Over, accessed June, 25, 2025, https://fred.stlouisfed.org/series/LNS14027662.

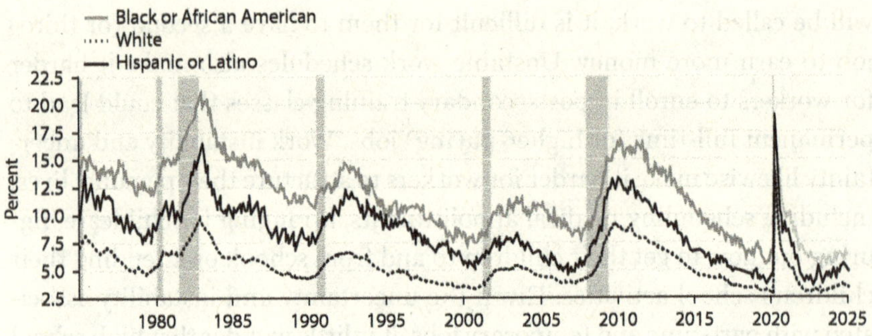

Figure 5. Unemployment rates by race, 1975–2025. Shaded areas indicate US recessions.

SOURCE: US Bureau of Labor Statistics, retrieved from Federal Reserve Bank of St. Louis, "FRED," accessed June 25, 2025, https://fred.stlouisfed.org/series/LNS14000006#.

have always been higher than White and college graduate unemployment rates, as shown in figure 5. One reason noncollege graduates have higher unemployment rates is that they are disproportionately non-White.[37]

In addition to their higher unemployment rates, temporary and contracted workers have no explicit or implicit assurances that they will keep their jobs. This is true even when the contracted workers have full-time jobs with an agency, and they satisfactorily perform their tasks for the business that assigns them work through the agency. Job security for contracted workers is contingent on whether the business elects to continue its contract with their actual employer (the hiring agency). Contracted workers are always at risk of losing their jobs if the business that uses the hiring agency (their employer) informs the agency that it no longer wants the worker at its workplace. Moreover, contracted workers struggle to establish meaningful connections to other workers, as they typically are excluded from things like holiday parties or team meetings and often are excluded from company-sponsored job fairs or the ability to access internal postings for better/permanent jobs.[38]

Gig workers have perhaps the least job security of all workers in the contingent labor force. Businesses routinely insist that gig workers are self-employed independent contractors, *not* statutory employees. Though some gig workers may perform tasks that are similar to those of statutory employees, they have absolutely no job security and few work protections. For example, they do not have the right to mandatory work breaks or to receive a minimum wage or overtime pay, and the businesses that assign them tasks are not required to provide workforce benefits (like paid sick days, family leave, health insurance, or retirement plans) or make social security contributions on their behalf. Although businesses like Lyft and DoorDash exert almost total control over how workers perform their tasks, because gig workers are not direct/statutory employees, they also cannot file for workers' compensation or unemployment benefits.[39]

VANISHING SKILLS TRAINING

As discussed in the last chapter, political and educational leaders historically supported low-cost workforce training for high school students who wanted to learn vocational skills. And throughout the Great Compression trade schools (like the Nashville Business School my mother attended) and community colleges provided relatively low-cost skills training for LMI young adults. Young workers who were union members also could get workplace skills training through an apprenticeship that paid them lower wages in exchange for free on-the-job training. Likewise, manufacturing sector employers historically provided skills training through on-the-job training for new hires.

That has all changed.

Public funding and support for voc-ed and CTE programs have declined, and fewer students are taking skills training classes at their high schools. Shrinking unions and a smaller manufacturing sector mean there are fewer opportunities for young workers to be apprentices or receive on-the-job training at work.[40] While apprenticeships—particularly union-provided ones in the manufacturing sector—gave young workers valuable training skills that helped them get a higher-paying job, it was easier for White males to find an apprenticeship than it was for women or non-White males.

Because unions historically lacked both racial and gender equality, union-sponsored apprenticeships disproportionately benefited White and male workers. Unions can no longer legally engage in gender or racial discrimination, but women and non-White apprentices are still less likely to benefit from apprenticeship programs (whether union sponsored or not) than White males. For example, in 2017 women made up just over 7 percent of all apprentices—a roughly 1 percent increase from 2008—and average hourly wages for women were less than 50 percent of average male wages. Similarly, both participation rates and wages are lower for Black workers than for White workers. Women and non-White workers receive fewer vocational benefits from apprenticeships for several reasons.

Women and non-White workers have lower overall participation rates because apprenticeships are concentrated in male-dominated fields, like construction, which has a persistent history of discriminatory hiring and promotion practices. Similarly, female and non-White workers who seek apprenticeships in areas that require them to find a supervisor who will agree to train them, as is true in the real estate appraiser sector, often struggle to find supervisors if the industry is mostly male or all White. Moreover, apprenticeships that exist in female-dominated fields, like early childhood education, pay lower wages, given market-based discrimination. Even women who have apprenticeships in male-dominated fields, though, typically are paid less than male workers.[41]

One reason apprenticeship wages for Black workers are lower is that they disproportionately live in southern states, where overall wages generally are lower. In addition, because of their disproportionately lower college graduation rates, non-White workers do not qualify for apprenticeships in higher-wage industries that will only hire workers who have a bachelor's degree. Another reason overall apprenticeship wages for both female and non-White males are lower than wages for White males is that women and non-White men disproportionately participate in prison apprenticeships. These apprenticeships have lower pay scales, and wages for some apprenticeships in women's prisons can be as low as $1.00/hour.[42]

With fewer union-provided apprenticeships, workers must rely on their employers to provide skills training or must pay for it themselves. Some businesses will reimburse workers for the cost of a skills training course, but fewer are willing to provide on-the-job training opportunities at their workplaces. Businesses are less willing to invest in skills training for workers because of concerns that the workers might quit after receiving the training and leave to work for a competitor before the employer has recouped the value invested in training the worker. Competitive concerns are often cited as the reason employers force employees to sign noncompete agreements.[43]

Although employers have reduced (or completely eliminated) on-the-job training or apprenticeships for their employers, some offer a "new" type of workforce training: internships. While some internships are paid, many require interns (often college students or recent graduates) to work for free. Whether unpaid or not, or whether these work "opportunities" are adequate substitutes for free or low-cost job training, young workers covet internships. They willingly seek internships because they hope the (unpaid) work opportunity will lead to a full-time and permanent job, and this is often the case. They also are willing to work for no pay to gain skills that they hope will make them more competitive in labor markets. Likewise, many covet internships because these work opportunities provide a prestigious experience that students/workers can place on their résumés.

The number of unpaid internships peaked around 2012, and roughly 50 percent of all those opportunities for students were unpaid. By 2017, roughly 60 percent of surveyed college graduates completed an internship in school, compared to nearly 50 percent just ten years earlier. Some students receive college credit in exchange for their free labor, although, of course, the college credit itself is not *really* free because students are paying tuition to be eligible to participate in the internship. Unfortunately, some unpaid internships are exploitative, and the work experience they give students sometimes has no relationship to the student's educational background. There is a less subtle form of harm that unpaid internships do: they are largely beyond the reach of young LMI college students, *particularly* those with student loan debt.

Unpaid work opportunities privilege students whose parents (or grandparents) can afford to pay their living expenses while they labor in an unpaid job. The US Department of Labor has considered whether employers were using unpaid interns to displace paid employees and issued guidelines to ensure that internships give students useful and relevant training comparable to the educational benefits they would receive in a classroom setting. Although the number of unpaid internships has somewhat decreased, these work training opportunities disproportionately advance the careers of upper-income (and more than likely White) workers.[44]

With fewer opportunities for free skills training in high schools, on-the-job employer-provided training, or free apprenticeships, many young workers resort to borrowing money to attend high-cost for-profit schools. As discussed in more detail in the last chapter, these institutions historically offered students a sequence of vocational courses they could take part time over a relatively short period of time.[45] As Tressie McMillan Cottom chronicles in *Lower Ed: The Troubling Rise of For-Profit Colleges in the New Economy*, however, today's for-profits are expensive and exploit the desires of lower-wage workers, particularly women, who understand they need additional skills training to find better jobs. Although the Nashville Business School guaranteed my mother a job as a secretary once she earned her certificate, students now are often duped into believing that the credential they receive from a for-profit will be their ticket to the middle class. As discussed later in this book, students are now less likely to leave for-profits with a guaranteed job and more likely to leave with debt but no degree.[46]

SAVING THE ENDANGERED SPECIES: THE FINANCIALLY SECURE NONCOLLEGE LMI WORKER

After the New Deal, political leaders believed they had an obligation to enact bold and comprehensive legislation to help LMI workers become upwardly mobile. They no longer have that belief. Poor children today should assume that if they are born poor, they will remain poor *even if they work hard.* Middle-income children, particularly if they are not White, should prepare for backward mobility and assume they may never be financially stable. But children born to rich parents should assume that *even if they do not work hard* they likely will remain rich because of the structural biases in our educational and labor markets.

The stereotypical (White male) middle-class worker has reason to be angry and disappointed that he cannot find a full-time and permanent job that pays him enough to afford the markers of the middle class. These workers are wrong, though, to direct their anger at immigrants or DEI programs. White, male, noncollege LMI adults who may feel as if they are an endangered species need to understand, as Black and Latino workers have *always* known, that working hard and following the rules is no longer enough to become middle class in this country. Rather than blame women or non-White workers, White male noncollege LMI workers should direct their anger at political and business leaders who have created a labor market that warehouses them in jobs that do not pay them enough to afford the markers of the middle class.

LMI workers, *including* the stereotypical White male middle-class worker in the Midwest, should be angry that educational leaders let rich and lower-rich parents manipulate school boundary and zoning laws to exclude their children from going to school in the buildings that help children be more competitive in college admissions and labor markets. LMI workers also should be angry that local and state educational leaders gutted CTE and other vocational education programs. They should be angry that businesses replaced free or low-cost on-the-job training and apprenticeships with unpaid internships. Mostly, though, LMI workers should be angry that political leaders allowed businesses to use both global and domestic outsourcing to eliminate full-time and permanent jobs and replace those jobs with part-time or contracted work, and they should be furious that political leaders helped employers destroy the only entity that could have forced businesses to care about them: labor unions.

The "Middle-Class New Deal" presented in chapter 8 provides ways to comprehensively restore the middle class, but one thing policymakers must do now is find ways to ensure that LMI workers have access to reasonably priced skills training. Almost 40 percent of undergraduate students attend (or attended) community colleges, and these educational institutions educate the highest percentages of LMI and non-White (particularly Latino) students. Given the cost and mission of community colleges, policymakers should create more partnerships with them, *particularly* as community colleges have already demonstrated that they can provide low-cost vocational training. These institutions are also best equipped to offer middle-skills programs that could provide training to help credential students so they can secure higher-wage jobs or that they can use if they choose to transfer these credits to a four-year college to earn a bachelor's degree.

Partnering with community colleges and encouraging workers to attend these low-cost institutions would give workers short-term job skills training and also give them an economic incentive to avoid attending high-cost for-profit institutions. Community colleges have always provided vocational training for young workers and mid-career workers who have been affected by global or domestic outsourcing. To make skills training even more affordable, Congress should revise Pell Grant rules to allow students to pay for noncredit skills training courses or certificates at community college.[47]

In addition to encouraging workers to take skills training classes at community colleges, policymakers must also find ways to ensure that businesses invest in people—not just machines that replace people. Currently, businesses can receive tax deductions for technological research costs and development expenses. To give businesses incentives to retrain workers and not simply replace them with technology, legislators should revise applicable tax laws to provide credits or deductions for businesses that incur costs to provide skills training for entry-level workers or workers whose jobs have been (or may be) domestically or globally outsourced or replaced by automation.[48]

5 Finding Affordable Housing

Homeownership is perhaps the most defining marker of the middle class, and for that reason, political leaders ritualistically extol its virtues. As an example, a former US secretary of housing and urban development explained the benefits of homeownership by noting that it takes "a family out of the second-class citizenship that poverty so often inflicts upon people . . . gives them a chance to be in control of their own financial lives, and as such, to really rise in the way that America has for so many others provided that kind of opportunity."[1] Proclaiming the importance of home sales, both to families and the US economy, President Bill Clinton announced National Homeownership Week in 1995, and President George W. Bush later extended that to include the entire month of June.

The same politicians who claim to value homeownership have done little, however, to help LMI renters find affordable housing to buy, particularly in neighborhoods with high-performing schools. Instead, they have caved to NIMBY (not in my back yard) demands for regressive land use laws even though those laws increase the cost of housing and make it harder for developers to build (or localities to create) affordable housing. Rather than find ways to help LMI families find affordable housing, as they did after the Depression and World War II, today's political leaders seem content to scrutinize the affordable housing "problem" but do nothing to solve the problem.

HOME BUYING BEFORE THE 1980S

Before the Great Depression, homeownership rates were low, and most renters could not afford to buy homes. Buying a home was unattainable for most people who were not rich because pre-Depression mortgage loans typically required borrowers to have enough saved to make a substantial down payment, often as much as 50 percent of the value of the home. Homebuyers would then need to earn enough (or have enough saved) to repay the loan over a relatively short (five- to ten-year) period. In addition, Depression-era loans were complicated and risky, as they typically had adjustable interest rates that could cause a borrower's monthly payments to increase dramatically and that made monthly loan payments unpredictable.

Pre-Depression mortgage loans also did not self-amortize. Because of this, even borrowers who made all their monthly mortgage payments would be left with an outstanding balance at the end of the loan term. They would not own their homes outright until they made a final, often large, "balloon" payment, which few people could afford to do. At the end of the mortgage loan term, these borrowers would typically finish paying for their homes by taking out another mortgage loan. Lenders were willing to approve these loans until the Depression caused unemployment rates to rise and banks restricted lending. When homeowners could not finish paying for their homes, but banks stopped approving mortgage loans, foreclosure rates skyrocketed, and bank failures also reached historic highs.

To respond to these dual economic crises, federal leaders enacted a comprehensive and intertwined set of housing and banking laws. These bold actions helped LMI renters buy homes, helped existing homeowners remain in their homes, and in the process created the middle class as we knew it. Specifically, federal lawmakers and agency heads enacted legislation and regulations that simplified and democratized mortgage lending and made loans less costly and risky to borrowers.

To make it easier for renters to become homeowners, banks were allowed to offer longer-term (fifteen- to thirty-year), fixed-rate, self-amortizing mortgages that required smaller down payments. To further encourage lenders to make and approve low-cost and low-risk mortgages, Congress created an insurance program administered by the Federal Housing Administration (FHA) and the Veterans Administration (VA) mortgage program. The FHA insurance program helped boost home sales by assuring banks that if they approved a mortgage loan and the borrower defaulted, the government would guarantee repayment. Similarly, the VA mortgage program increased home sales by providing low-cost and low-risk mortgage loans to eligible veterans.[2]

Although these interventions democratized the home-buying process and helped LMI renters buy homes, political leaders had a clear view of *which* families should benefit from these programs. Indeed, while the federal government's "Everyman's Home" campaign promised that *everyone*—including the wage-earning plumber and electrician—could become homeowners, only White renters were included as "everyone." Until the 1960s, political leaders colluded with private entities (including lenders, home builders, subdivision developers, real estate agents, and appraisers) to virtually guarantee that few non-White borrowers would buy homes. These laws and policies also made it nearly impossible for Black families to own homes in all-White suburbs.

Overt discrimination in lending and housing markets by private entities, which I will refer to collectively as the real estate industrial complex (REIC), helped *overall* homeownership rates increase from approximately 44 percent in 1940 to 62 percent in 1960. Because of discriminatory lending and housing policies and practices, though, rates for Black families did not budge at all. For example, though federal policies and private actions by REIC actors helped White LMI families buy homes that would increase in value, they used an odious and overtly racist appraisal coding system, commonly known as redlining, to depress Black homeownership rates and Black household wealth.

With redlining, appraisers would rate neighborhoods based on their desirability, stability, and security, and this appraisal/rating would be used to determine whether a borrower would be approved for a low-cost, federally insured mortgage loan. While no credible empirical data then (or now) support the view that Black or racially mixed neighborhoods were inherently more unstable or dangerous than White neighborhoods, the former were regularly deemed to be unstable and unsafe. Buyers who sought approval for a mortgage loan to buy a home in a non-White neighborhood outlined in red on residential security maps (thus the term *redlining*) would be denied because the government would not guarantee any loan to buy a home or make repairs to a home in a redlined neighborhood, and banks would not approve loans that would not be federally insured.

As virtually no LMI buyers had enough cash to buy a home outright, redlining made it harder for non-White renters to become homeowners because, even if they found a nonbank lender, they would pay measurably more to buy a home.[3] Moreover, non-White buyers also would not qualify to buy homes in a White neighborhood with a federally insured bank loan, as their presence as a homeowner would transform the previously safe (White) neighborhood into an "unsafe" (racially mixed) one.[4]

REIC actors did more, though, than just make it harder for non-White renters to become homeowners. They also participated in a reprehensible practice, commonly known as blockbusting, that devalued the homes Black buyers bought in mixed-race neighborhoods. In the first step of a typical blockbusting scheme, real estate agents and investors approached White homeowners to "inform" them their neighborhoods were being "invaded" by low-income Blacks. Predictably, the White homeowners panicked and tried to flee the soon-to-be-invaded neighborhood. In the next step of the scheme, fleeing homeowners would sell their homes, almost always at rock bottom panic prices, to the blockbusters. After blockbusters bought the homes at fire-sale prices, appraisers then fraudulently inflated the value of the homes. In the last step, blockbusters sold these fraudulently inflated homes to unsuspecting Black buyers.

Lenders would not approve mortgages for Black borrowers to buy homes in mixed-race neighborhoods. But they were willing to approve the mortgage loans blockbusters used to buy homes from fleeing White homeowners. Because Black purchasers would not qualify for low-cost, federally insured mortgage loans, they typically used high-cost, predatory financing agreements (commonly known as installment sales contracts) to buy homes from blockbusters. These risky financing devices required buyers to make *all* installment payments before they built equity in their homes, which is why Black buyers regularly lost homes in blockbusting schemes well before they built equity in those homes.[5]

White renters during this timeframe could increase their household wealth by buying homes using low-cost and low-risk FHA-insured mortgage loans. In contrast, REIC actors—with the tacit approval of political leaders—virtually guaranteed that Black homebuyers would either lose wealth or would build significantly less wealth than White homeowners if they bought fraudulently inflated homes in blockbusting schemes. Blockbusting, though financially catastrophic for Black buyers, was an enormously profitable enterprise for the REIC participants. The blockbusters who sold homes to Black buyers, evicted them, then resold the homes to new, unaware Black buyers, made profits nearing $100,000 at the time, which is equivalent to roughly $1.2 million today. Most of the blame for this odious practice should be placed on blockbusters, but blockbusting would not have succeeded without the tacit approval of federal housing and lender policies. Stated differently, blockbusting succeeded only because lenders would *not* approve low-cost mortgage loans for Black buyers but *would* approve loans to blockbusters.[6]

Black renters also struggled to buy homes and increase their household wealth because of racist public and private land use laws. Early municipal zoning ordinances explicitly banned Blacks from buying homes in all-White or racially mixed neighborhoods. Once the US Supreme Court overruled these in *Buchanan v. Warley*, local politicians could not use public zoning laws to maintain neighborhood segregation.[7] White homeowners filled the gap by using private racially restrictive deed covenants that prevented White homeowners from selling, leasing, or giving their homes to non-Whites. Judges enforced these private agreements until the Supreme Court invalidated them in its decision in the 1948 case *Shelley v. Kraemer*.[8] A 1962 executive order and later the Fair Housing Act of 1968 finally banned all racially discriminatory housing policies. By then, though, there was already a sizeable racial homeownership gap in the country.

REIC actors continued to discriminate against non-White buyers despite antidiscrimination laws. As I noted in chapter 1, my parents became homeowners in 1963 when racial discrimination in housing markets was rampant and legal. Though they never fell prey to a blockbusting scheme, and they bought and sold three homes over their lifetimes, their path to homeownership faced obstacles. Why? Because until they bought their last home, they faced the burdens of "home-buying while Black."

My parents moved to Memphis to live with my Fenny grandparents after my father earned his bachelor's degree from Tennessee State. My grandparents had been renters for most of their lives and at one point lived in (legally) racially segregated public housing. Eventually my Fenny grandparents saved enough money to buy a 1,016-square-foot, three-bedroom, one-bathroom house in the only place open to Black families in Memphis in the 1950s: an all-Black neighborhood. My parents lived multigenerationally with my Fenny grandparents, my paternal great-grandmother, my brother, and (eventually) me in a house that was less than half the size of newly built homes today.

My parents chose this living arrangement because the Fenny home was within walking distance of George Washington Carver High School, the all-Black high school that hired my father as a math teacher. Their long-term goal was to buy a detached, single-family home in a stably integrated (by race and income) neighborhood whose homes were zoned to attend high-performing schools. In the interim, they peacefully coexisted in somewhat cramped living quarters. Despite the emotional support and encouragement my father received from his Black high school teachers, my parents understood that the best way to ensure their children graduated from high school and were prepared to attend and graduate from a four-year college was to enroll us in one of the high-performing public schools in Memphis. Then, as now, that essentially meant avoiding schools segregated by race or income.

Less than two years after they moved into the Fenny house, my parents used their savings and a $1,500 (roughly $13,000 today) interest-free loan they received from my father's oldest sister, Eva Mae Miller, to buy a three-bedroom, one-bathroom, 1,364-square-foot home.[9] Though they succeeded in buying a home, their path to homeownership was colored by the color of their skin. My father had a full-time and permanent job, and they had savings and minimal debt. Nonetheless, their housing goals were hindered by REIC actors, who flagrantly violated antidiscrimination laws well into the 1970s. Because my parents were financially stable, a bank approved their loan to buy their first home. Their first brush with REIC racism occurred when their real estate agent steered them *away* from stably integrated neighborhoods with high-performing schools and *toward* all-Black or unstably integrated neighborhoods (with high poverty and low-performing schools).

My parents explained their housing preference to the agent, but their preferences directly collided with the agent's determination to keep them *out* of stably integrated neighborhoods with high-performing schools. There was no internet in the 1960s. So, while real estate agents, city planners, and other REIC actors knew which neighborhoods were stably integrated by race and income, homebuyers like my parents did not. Instead, Black buyers were forced to rely on real estate agents to provide this information. If they were duped, as my parents were, they had two options: remain in a neighborhood that was not the one they wanted or participate in home buying while Black again. My parents' first home was in a neighborhood that included middle-class, college-educated public-school teachers and principals. Unfortunately, the neighborhood schools were low performing and were becoming increasingly low income and all Black.

My parents decided to sell their first home and buy one in a neighborhood whose homes were zoned for high-performing schools. They assumed their second home-buying venture would be a relatively quick and simple process because (1) my father's teaching job was stable and he would receive annual pay raises, (2) they had good credit and paid their mortgage loan and other bills on time, and (3) they could use the equity they had accumulated in their first home to make a sizeable down payment on their second home.

Only their first two assumptions were right.

All three assumptions my parents made were reasonable for comparable White homeowners in the 1970s who had stable jobs, had good credit, and were existing homeowners who could buy another home using the equity they had built in their current home. However, when my parents went house hunting for the second time, they discovered that their first home had barely increased in value. Why? Because then (as now) appraisers undervalue homes in predominantly or all-Black neighborhoods. This undervaluation then (and now) forces Black homeowners to pay what is sometimes referred to as a "Black homeownership tax." Because appraisers tend to undervalue homes in non-White neighborhoods, and White buyers generally resist buying homes in those neighborhoods (*unless* the neighborhood is gentrifying), Black homeowners build less equity in their homes.[10]

The Black homeownership tax caused my parents to accumulate significantly less equity in their home than they would have if the real estate agent had not steered them away from homes in all-White or stably integrated neighborhoods. When they went home shopping the second time, real estate agents could no longer legally steer Black homebuyers away from White neighborhoods, but this did not stop their new agent from steering them to homes in the up-and-coming, all-Black, middle-class neighborhood in Memphis—ironically named Whitehaven. This time, though, my parents avoided the steering. With their savings, an inheritance my mother received from the sale of my Leavell grandparents' farm, and my father's still stable teaching salary, they bought a four-bedroom, two-bathroom, 2,067-square-foot home in an all-White inner-suburban community in Memphis.[11]

This housing decision was financially beneficial for my parents and also helped them accomplish their goal of having their children attend a high-performing public school. It came with a steep emotional price tag, though, as some of our White neighbors made clear they did not want to have Black people living in their neighborhood.[12] Despite hostility from some of our neighbors, my parents remained in that home until we graduated from high school and college. They went home searching for the third time and assumed that, even though they were retired, they would be approved for another low-cost mortgage loan. They made this assumption because they had (1) savings, (2) stable and secure monthly retirement pension income, (3) good credit, and (4) little household debt.

This time, all their assumptions proved to be true. They made a sizeable down payment on the third (and last) home in a stable racially diverse neighborhood in Olive Branch, Mississippi. They sold this home (at a profit) during the early months of the 2020 COVID pandemic and used the sales proceeds to move into Kirby Pines, an upscale retirement community in Memphis.

One view of my parents' path to the middle class is that it is a clear "success" story because, despite multiple encounters with REIC racism, they triumphed and acquired the main marker of the middle class. But the crooked path they were forced to take helps explain the stubborn racial homeownership gap of roughly 25 percentage points between Whites and non-Whites (*especially* Blacks and Latinos). Their path also explains why there is a racial wealth gap and why it has become so hard for LMI families, particularly if they are noncollege, to buy homes. My LMI parents were able to triumph over racism and buy three homes in their lifetimes because they were college graduates who had full-time and permanent jobs with predictably increasing wages. The current path to homeownership for young married couples, *particularly* if they are not White, is more tortured and often measurably less successful.[13]

AMERICA'S STRUGGLING RENTERS

As discussed in the last chapter, LMI young adults are more likely to have part-time or temporary jobs, unstable income, and stagnant wages. Their job instability makes it harder for them to accumulate household savings, and their overall financial precarity makes it nearly impossible for most young LMI renters to buy homes. Their personal finances are not the only reasons they are struggling to find affordable housing to buy, or even to rent. They are struggling because political leaders have *always* cared more about rich and lower-rich homeowners than they do about LMI renters.

The policies federal leaders enacted after the Depression and World War II helped *some* renters buy homes, but most poor families, *particularly* if they were non-White, remained renters. Until the 1960s, renters were often relegated to living in high-density and often racially segregated public housing complexes or in privately owned rental units in deteriorating urban neighborhoods. Political leaders, in enacting the federal Housing Acts of 1937 and 1949, at least tried to eliminate substandard and unsafe housing, and the stated purpose of this legislation was to clear "slums" or blighted areas to ensure that every American family had "a decent home and a suitable living environment."[14]

Unfortunately, when localities destroyed substandard housing and displaced poor and usually non-White renters, political leaders did little to help them find suitable or affordable replacement rental housing. Indeed, lawmakers have never been willing to significantly increase the supply of public housing because of opposition from private real estate entities that fought attempts to increase the supply of public housing. These private entities opposed public housing because they did not want to compete with housing authorities for low-income renters. Thus, rather than expand the supply of federal subsidized housing, politicians instead enacted stringent income requirements that severely restricted the number of renters who would qualify to live in public housing.[15]

Housing options for White *renters* who were displaced in urban "slum" clearance programs were actually better than the options for displaced Black *homeowners*, primarily because Black families could not buy or even rent homes in White neighborhoods until the 1970s. As a result, Black residents who were displaced in clearance programs either (1) were pushed into racially segregated public rental housing in another part of the city, (2) bought or rented structurally unsound and often overpriced private housing in redlined neighborhoods, or (3) were duped into buying homes in wealth-stripping blockbusting schemes.[16]

When large public housing units became overcrowded, dilapidated, or unsafe in the 1960s, political leaders did not even consider constructing more public housing. Instead, federal leaders elected to create public-private partnerships with REIC actors and use devices like voucher programs and tax credits to increase the supply of safe and affordable housing for poor renters. Politicians consistently maintain that private-public partnerships can most efficiently increase affordable rental housing, but market-based rental-assistance programs have consistently failed to help most poor renters find affordable housing.

Housing voucher programs have failed principally because few (less than a quarter) low-income households are eligible to receive these federal housing assistance benefits, and data indicate that even renters who qualify for vouchers face a substantial wait time before they actually receive the voucher. Moreover, few renters can use the vouchers because the federal government refuses to mandate that REIC actors rent to poor tenants or accept vouchers as full or partial payment for rent. Even when some local political leaders enacted "source of income" (SOI) laws to prevent landlords from rejecting tenants who seek to pay their rent using vouchers, some states responded by forbidding localities from enacting SOI laws.[17]

In addition to vouchers, federal leaders enacted the 1986 Low-Income Housing Tax Credit (LIHTC) Program (a joint venture between the federal government, the states, and private REIC actors) to increase the supply of affordable rental housing. The LIHTC gives state agencies the authority to award tax credits to developers who build new (or renovate existing) affordable rental housing or who agree to reserve a portion of their rental housing for lower-income renters. While the LIHTC has helped increase the supply of affordable housing, that housing is concentrated in low-income, non-White neighborhoods. Because of zoning laws and NIMBY opposition to affordable housing, which I discuss next, private-public partnerships have not made it easier for lower-income renters to live in stably integrated (or all-White) neighborhoods, and certainly not in high-opportunity neighborhoods with high-performing schools.[18]

EXCLUSIONARY LAND USE POLICIES

Starting in the 1920s, the US Department of Commerce and the FHA encouraged cities to enact zoning laws to divide cities into districts. Since then, local leaders have separated neighborhoods with single-family structures from neighborhoods with multifamily structures. Almost one hundred years ago, the Supreme Court approved of zoning laws that exclude multifamily housing from single-family housing neighborhoods, in *Village of Euclid v. Ambler Realty*. The Court ruled in this case that because localities have the right to enact laws that protect the health and safety of their residents, they also have the power to enact laws that ensure the orderly development of neighborhoods, and that power includes keeping nuisances and other undesired property uses out of neighborhoods with single-family housing.

The Court in *Village of Euclid* held that localities' policing powers gave the authority to do more than just ban nuisances, like polluting factories or slaughterhouses, from residential neighborhoods. In finding that cities can overtly favor homeowners and single-family homes over renters and multifamily housing, the Court characterized apartments as "parasites" and proclaimed that

> the coming of one apartment house is followed by others, interfering by their height and bulk with the free circulation of air and monopolizing the

> rays of the sun which otherwise would fall upon the smaller homes, and bringing, as their necessary accompaniments, the disturbing noises incident to increased traffic and business, and the occupation, by means of moving and parked automobiles, of larger portions of the streets, thus detracting from their safety and depriving children of the privilege of quiet and open spaces for play, enjoyed by those in more favored localities--until, finally, the residential character of the neighborhood and its desirability as a place of detached residences are utterly destroyed.[19]

While conceding that constructing apartments in a single-family neighborhood might be the "right" thing, the Court nonetheless intimated that siting apartments in single-family neighborhoods was like putting a "pig in the parlor instead of the barnyard."[20]

Though the Commerce Department's Advisory Committee on Zoning proclaimed a century ago that zoning regulations should "treat all men alike," political leaders, municipal planners, housing and tax policies, and the judges who enforce those laws and policies continue to treat homeowners better than renters. Moreover, they consistently side with homeowners who claim that affordable housing increases traffic, eliminates open spaces, or otherwise changes the "character" of neighborhoods with single-family and owner-occupied homes. Indeed, Trump and former Secretary of Housing and Urban Development Ben Carson have gone on record quipping that building apartments in residential neighborhoods would destroy the suburbs by creating "stack and pack" high-density housing.[21]

The primary way LMI families are kept out of high-opportunity neighborhoods that consist mostly of single-family homes is through exclusionary zoning laws. All high-income neighborhoods and roughly 75 percent of neighborhoods in the largest cities in the United States are zoned exclusively for single-family detached housing. Exclusionary zoning policies increase the cost of building homes and also decrease the overall supply of buildable land by, for example, requiring large minimum lot or floor sizes for single-family homes. Exclusionary zoning laws also increase housing costs for LMI families by mandating minimum yard setbacks; requiring that there be a specified number of parking spaces per housing unit; and prohibiting property owners from (1) building additional but smaller rental units on their lots or (2) repurposing space in their homes to create garage apartments.[22]

Exclusionary zoning laws' near-total exclusion of lower-income families from higher-income neighborhoods caused the chairman of former President Barack Obama's White House Council of Economic Advisers to comment that these land use policies now serve as "modern-day Jim Crow through zoning."[23] But instead of acknowledging that these laws harm LMI renters and perpetuate and reinforce racially and economically segregated neighborhoods, political leaders (and current homeowners) regurgitate the same arguments they (and the US Supreme Court) have used to defend racist housing policies and to cast renters as parasites. That is, exclusionary zoning ordinances are justified based on the purported need to preserve the value of single-family homes. Likewise, political leaders oppose affordable housing projects (1) because of the importance of protecting open space and space for community gardens, hike and bike trails, or parks; (2) to ensure there are adequate parking spaces; and (3) to prevent an unwanted increase in neighborhood traffic.[24]

In addition, just as private homeowners entered into private agreements to exclude non-Whites from their neighborhoods when explicitly racist zoning laws were banned, homeowners now use homeowners' associations (HOAs) to exclude LMI residents from their communities even if there are no applicable public zoning laws. HOAs are private, owner-controlled, and owner-operated entities that let existing homeowners determine the type of resident who likely will be their neighbor. Rich and lower-rich homeowners gravitate toward covenanted communities even though some HOAs impose burdensome aesthetic regulations like when holiday lights can be displayed or where trash cans and recycle bins must be stored. Homeowners are willing to accept subjective aesthetic regulations because they recognize that belonging to a powerful HOA can help them achieve their goal of keeping LMI residents, particularly renters, out of their neighborhoods.

HOAs cannot explicitly exclude LMI and non-White residents from neighborhoods. But HOA regulations can legislate how homes in a neighborhood must look and what homeowners in those neighborhoods can do on or with their property. For example, HOAs can tell owners where they can park their cars, what structures (like fences or sheds) they can place on their property, and how they must maintain their lawns. Like public zoning laws, HOAs can also prevent property owners from subdividing their lots to build a smaller affordable housing unit, and HOA restrictions (like local land use laws) can limit the number of occupants who may live in one home or require all occupants to be related.[25] Of course, not all HOA members universally exhibit racist or classist conduct. Nonetheless, rich and lower-rich who choose to be governed by a powerful HOA that enforces rules that necessarily exclude LMI families epitomize "lip-service liberals" who may display politically progressive yard signs but who also embrace policies that keep affordable housing out of their high-opportunity neighborhoods.[26]

The residents of Marin County, which is part of the politically progressive San Francisco Bay area, epitomize how powerful and organized NIMBY homeowners can permanently exclude affordable housing from their communities. Marin County, built in the 1940s with race-restrictive covenants, has virtually no affordable housing because its rich and ostensibly liberal residents have systematically thwarted all efforts to help LMI families live in their community. The NIMBY residents initially blocked an affordable housing development that was proposed to be built on land that previously housed a seminary and on a blighted strip mall. Then they objected when George Lucas proposed to build an affordable housing development on his land. Lucas originally sought approval to expand his Star Wars production site but, after his neighbors objected, he submitted a proposal to build affordable rental housing for public employees and service workers. The Marin County NIMBYs objected to this proposal, but rather than acknowledge that they did not want to live near LMI renters, the residents relied on the familiar trope about the need to protect the environment and to preserve the beauty of the Marin County landscape.[27]

A lower-profile but equally vitriolic clash involving an affordable housing development occurred in America's heartland, Cedar Rapids, Iowa. As is true in most NIMBY fights, a developer's proposal to build affordable housing pitted the views of existing neighbors against the needs of renters. While some existing residents advanced the well-trodden pretextual concerns about traffic congestion, others did not even try to hide their racist or classist views. Some proclaimed that they did not want to live with drug dealers, and one resident crassly declared that they did not want "those little monkeys climbing up my trees." City leaders ultimately approved the proposal, but only after the developer agreed to make infrastructure upgrades, including constructing a turn lane into the complex and adding sidewalks, a playground, and an underground storm water system.[28]

While the antics of rich, lower-rich, or White homeowners may be unseemly and distasteful, NIMBYism works. Political leaders consistently cave to their desires and allow them to enforce exclusionary private deed covenants, even though this requires elected or appointed officials to cede some of their regulatory powers to private entities. If political leaders continue to favor the housing *desires* of rich and lower-rich families more than the housing *needs* of LMI families, LMI families will always face an affordable housing crisis.

HOME BUYING WHILE BLACK OR BROWN

Although unstable employment, stagnant household income, zoning laws, and powerful HOAs make it difficult for *all* LMI families to find affordable housing, the current housing crisis is not a new one for non-White families. It has always been harder for non-White households to find safe and affordable housing, whether they are seeking to rent or to buy.

Poor Black renters had abominable housing options before World War II. The "slum" or "blight" removal programs noted earlier helped improve their housing conditions by destroying unsafe and rundown buildings that were largely uninhabitable. However, local political leaders often used clearance programs for reasons that ultimately harmed the existing Black residents. That is, urban "renewal" programs did more than just destroy blighted structures; they have been used to destroy habitable housing and thriving businesses in non-White communities under the guise of "economic redevelopment."

The government has long used its eminent domain powers to condemn private property to build bridges, roads, or other infrastructure projects or to build colleges. For example, the City of Memphis destroyed a stable Black community in the 1930s and 1940s even though the residents of the community included college graduates, Black-owned businesses, schools, and churches. The city used the then-vacant land to build a segregated all-Black public housing project, Foote Homes, and city leaders made no attempt to replicate the stable community they had destroyed, nor did they make any effort to help rebuild the homes destroyed in the removal program. Later, under the guise of "urban renewal," city leaders in Memphis condemned and destroyed properties in another Black neighborhood. They destroyed that neighborhood because they wanted to develop what is now the Beale Street tourist destination. Beale Street continues to provide economic benefits for Memphis, but city leaders never tried to provide affordable housing for the Black residents they had displaced when they destroyed a poor but functional Black neighborhood.

Similarly, in the 1950s and 1960s (and then again from the end of the 1980s until just before the 2020 pandemic) city leaders in Newport News, Virginia, used federal funds to expand a regional college. In the process, they destroyed a middle-class Black neighborhood just as institutions like the University of Pennsylvania, University of Georgia, and University of Oklahoma did in their respective cities. These projects were not unusual, unfortunately, as state and federal political leaders routinely use their police powers and urban renewal programs to *displace* low-income LMI residents in non-White and LMI neighborhoods for infrastructure projects that primarily *benefit* White residents.[29] For example, federal transportation laws in the 1940s destroyed Black housing for "the greater good" to create the four-lane, nationally integrated highway system. These urban renewal projects expelled existing residents after condemning the homes and businesses and deeming them to be "blighted."

While those projects ostensibly can be viewed as successful because they built an interstate highway system that helped workers who had purchased suburban homes have a quicker commute to their jobs in city centers, and the shorter, easy commute increased the desirability (and value) of suburban homes. The only people who could buy those suburban homes, however, were White. Thus, these transportation policies imposed negative externalities on poor and non-White neighborhoods and gave all benefits to higher-income, White suburban homeowners. In almost all cases, when the owners of condemned property were "compensated" for the land the government destroyed, the condemnation proceedings stripped wealth from existing owners because they rarely received the true fair market value of property deemed to be "blighted."[30]

In addition to displacing residents and stripping wealth from the owners of condemned property, urban renewal projects have been used to transfer wealth directly to REIC actors who want to develop lands seized during clearance programs. A particularly egregious example involves a massive New York City apartment complex (Stuyvesant Town), which Metropolitan Life Insurance Company (MetLife) built in the 1940s. Specifically, the city used its eminent domain powers to "clear" land and destroy buildings in a racially integrated area of Manhattan. The land was then transferred to MetLife, which received tax exemptions to build an affordable rental housing complex on the now clear land. Despite its history of discriminating against Black tenants, MetLife had the sole authority to select tenants for the complex and (predictably) chose only White renters though some of the displaced residents were Black. Eventually, MetLife caved to political pressure and made a few affordable units available for Black tenants.[31]

Even when not overtly sanctioning discrimination against poor, non-White renters, political leaders have routinely neglected their housing needs and only seemed interested in helping them become homeowners during housing market downturns. For example, when White home-buying rates slowed in the 1980s, political leaders and REIC actors concluded that helping Black and Latino renters buy homes would be in the country's/housing market's best interests. To spur home sales, both the Clinton and George W. Bush administrations encouraged lenders to create innovative mortgage loan products to help renters quickly and cheaply buy homes. Lenders eagerly responded by creating no downpayment mortgage loans, loans that let borrowers make only monthly interest (not principal) payments, mortgages that let borrowers choose how much to pay each month, and loans that did not require them to document their income or wealth or that encouraged applicants to inflate their incomes to qualify for larger loans.[32]

Just as the government interventions in housing and lending markets succeeded in increasing homeownership rates after World War II, these innovations also succeeded in getting more renters (particularly non-White families) into homes. For example, the Clinton White House strategy helped increase overall homeownership rates from 64 percent to more than 67 percent between 1993 and 2000, and the Bush strategy helped overall homeownership rates hit an all-time high of more than 69 percent% in 2004.[33] Homeownership rates for Black and Latino (especially college-educated) households soared during this period and constituted approximately 40 percent of the net growth in new homeowners. Black homeownership rates rose by 25 percent, nearly double the overall homeownership increase of 14 percent and more than three times the 7 percent increase in White homeownership. Latino homeownership saw an even more dramatic rise of 60 percent.[34]

Unfortunately, a significant problem with these mortgage innovations is that they created what has been called "reverse redlining." Specifically, lenders steered Black and Latino potential borrowers to higher-interest loans or charged them fees that White borrowers with similar financial characteristics were not required to pay.[35] Similarly, while lenders approved high-cost nontraditional mortgage products for non-White borrowers, lenders disproportionately rejected their applications for traditional low-cost mortgage loans. Like the now-banned redlining, reverse redlining increased borrowing costs in ways that cannot be explained solely by credit risk factors.[36]

Research from the Harvard Joint Center for Housing Studies found that higher-income Black homeowners (earning $75,000–$100,000) paid higher mortgage interest rates than White homeowners with comparable incomes. They also were assessed higher interest rates than White borrowers with significantly lower household incomes ($30,000 or less). One model suggests that reverse redlining increased buying costs by as much as $3,000 and that these amounts, if invested at a 5 percent rate of return, could have increased household wealth for Black and Latino households by more than $11,000.[37] Despite reverse redlining and real estate agent steering, the Clinton and Bush initiatives succeeded in increasing overall homeownership rates. But like all middle-class households, LMI and non-White families lost household wealth when foreclosure rates soared during the 2007–2009 Recession.

Black and Latino households had disproportionately high foreclosure rates due to the high-risk and higher-cost "innovated" mortgage products they used to buy homes. The housing crash caused them catastrophic long-term harm because housing equity constitutes a disproportionate amount of Black (almost 60%) and Latino (approximately 65%) overall wealth compared to overall White household wealth (roughly 44%). As a result, while the innovated products helped some Black and Latino renters buy homes and build housing equity, many of these homeowners ended up no better off than the renters who were duped into buying homes during blockbusting schemes.[38]

A more recent practice, which has characteristics eerily similar to post–World War II blockbusting schemes, presents additional roadblocks for poor and non-White renters who seek to become homeowners. After the 2007–2009 Recession, institutional investors bought homes at rock bottom prices in foreclosure or tax sales, made cosmetic repairs to homes that often needed major improvements to electrical or plumbing systems, then sold these homes to lower-income renters. The renters often purchased the homes using high-interest-rate loan agreements, generally referred to as installment land contracts, contracts for deeds, or "rent-to-own" (RTO) contracts. Most RTO contracts required the party who occupied the home to pay for home repairs, whether relatively inexpensive routine maintenance or significant structural and expensive repairs. Other contracts required buyers to correct outstanding housing code violations, pay property taxes, or provide property insurance for the home.

By the mid-2010s, installment contract transactions had become more common than sales or leases in lower-income, predominantly non-White or immigrant communities. As these contracts are not true mortgages that require recorded deeds, the homes that were "sold" in these transactions had not been appraised or inspected. As a result, buyers typically did not know that the homes were structurally defective until well after they had signed the contracts and moved into the homes. Because the renters who bought these homes could rarely afford to make the repairs required by the contract, like the Black buyers in now-illegal blockbusting schemes, many were evicted.

Some buyers voluntarily abandoned their often uninhabitable homes, but others were forced to leave by city officials who declared the homes to be uninhabitable. As was true with blockbusting, after investors stripped any housing equity from the first buyer, they typically flipped the same structurally unsound home and sold it to another unsuspecting buyer. But even buyers who made repairs to the homes and remained in them were at constant risk of losing them because the sellers retained all ownership interests in the homes until the buyers made all installment payments. Indeed, because the sellers remained the owners of record, they retained the right to borrow against the homes *even after the buyers moved in.*[39]

RTO contracts, while odious, are legal. In addition to legal ways to strip wealth from non-White homeowners, REIC actors continued to engage in illegal discrimination. For example, investigations and lawsuits revealed that as recently as 2021 lenders were still offering Black and Latino potential mortgage loan applicants significantly fewer loan options (including different rates, fees, and structures) than White potential buyers, or discouraged non-White testers from applying for mortgage loans.[40] A 2022 report prepared by the National Association of Real Estate Brokers documented ongoing lending discrimination and revealed that Black loan applicants are denied mortgage loans at more than twice the rates of loan denials for White mortgage loan applicants. This report further disclosed that Black borrowers are three times more often than comparable White borrowers to buy homes with high-cost mortgage loans. Even more recently, the Navy Federal Credit Union (the largest credit union in this country) was named a defendant in a 2024 class action lawsuit that alleged that the credit union had the widest disparity (29 percentage points) in mortgage approval rates for White and Black borrowers in 2023 and approved White mortgage applicants at disproportionately higher rates than Black and Latino applicants.[41]

Real estate agents also continue to illegally discriminate against non-White buyers. For example, some agents who perceive a buyer to be non-White based on the potential buyer's ethnic-sounding name or voice will deny or cancel their appointments, show them fewer houses, or give them limited (or misleading) information. Likewise, some agents refer to the quality of the neighborhood public schools in ways that appear designed to steer Whites away from non-White areas. For example, a recent study examined discriminatory real estate agent practices in Long Island, New York—one of the most racially segregated areas in this country. The study found that Long Island agents consistently warned White clients to do research on gang activity in certain neighborhoods while regularly steering Blacks and Latinos *to* those neighborhoods *even though* agents cannot legally discuss the characteristics of people who reside in neighborhoods when they show homes to potential clients. Likewise, despite antidiscrimination laws, White sellers continue to refuse to sell their homes to buyers who are Black.[42]

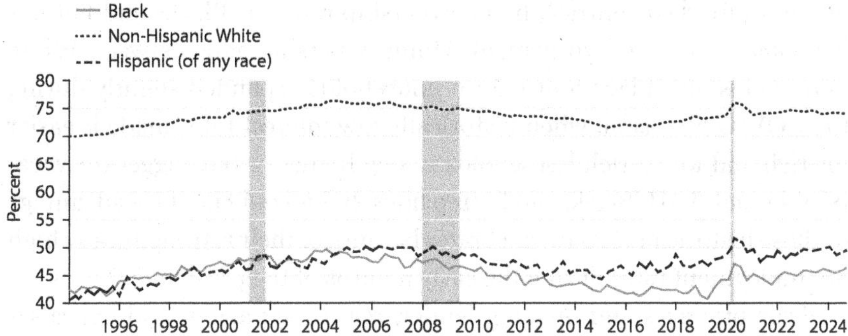

Figure 6. Homeownership rates by race/ethnicity, 1994–2024. Shaded areas indicate US recessions.

SOURCE: US Census Bureau, retrieved from Federal Reserve Bank of St. Louis, "FRED," accessed June 25, 2025, https://fred.stlouisfed.org/series/BOAAAHORUSQ156N.

Finally, appraisers also continue to make it harder for non-White LMI homeowners to build housing wealth. As they did when my parents went home buying in the 1960s, appraisers continue to undervalue homes in non-White neighborhoods. Homes in White neighborhoods are sometimes appraised at *roughly triple* the value of comparable homes in non-White neighborhoods, and some research suggests that Black homeowners were affected more by racially biased appraisals in 2015 than they were in 1980.[43] One reason appraiser discrimination persists is that the industry operates based on an apprenticeship model that requires potential appraisers to find a supervising appraiser. Few (roughly 1%) appraisers are Black, and this makes it harder for Black people who want to become appraisers to find a supervisor. With little diversity in the appraisal industry, appraisers—either intentionally on unwittingly—continue to unfairly devalue homes owned by non-Whites, whether those homes are located in non-White or White neighborhoods.[44]

Despite lingering vestiges of discrimination and more recent versions of real estate agent, seller, or appraiser biases, non-White homeownership rates have increased since the 1960s, when my parents bought their first home. Even with these gains, the racial homeownership gap has consistently remained at or above 25 percentage points. As figure 6 shows, White homeownership rates have held steady at at least 70 percent since 1995, reaching a record high of 76 percent in 2004 at the height of the housing boom. In marked contrast, homeownership rates for Blacks and Latinos have *never* exceeded 70 percent. Homeownership gaps between White households and Black and Latino households expanded slightly during the COVID recession, when historically low interest rates made it easier for rich and lower-rich households to buy homes or buy bigger (or vacation) homes. LMI, Black, and Latino households could not take advantage of those historically low interest rates because of their astronomically high unemployment rates during the early months of the pandemic.[45]

Prior practices and ongoing lender, real estate agent, and appraiser discrimination primarily harm individual renters or homeowners. But forcing families to live in segregated neighborhoods also appears to have harmful generational consequences. Children who grew up in a redlined neighborhood have lower credit scores as adults and, according to a recent American Medical Association study, may also face greater health risks. Recent research also found that children reared in formerly redlined neighborhoods were (1) less likely to reach the top income quintile, (2) more likely to be reared in single-parent households where no father was present, and (3) more likely to be incarcerated than children who did not grow up in redlined neighborhoods.[46]

It has never been easy for non-White workers to buy homes, and their disproportionately low homeownership rates are due in part to their lower college graduation rates and lower overall household income. But as the secretary of HUD during the George W. Bush administration aptly noted, the primary reason the racial homeownership gap exists is that racial discrimination and segregation in housing and lending markets exist as well.[47]

MAKING HOUSING AFFORDABLE FOR LMI FAMILIES

After decades of stagnant income, unstable employment, and skyrocketing housing prices in some localities, many LMI families have abandoned the American Dream of homeownership. In fact, many now question whether they will even be able to achieve the dream of a safe and affordable place to rent. Although political leaders understood that they needed to intervene in banking and housing markets to help make homeownership possible for cash-strapped families after World War II, the current affordable housing crisis exists because of the *unwillingness* of political leaders to enact laws to help keep this primary marker of the middle class within the reach of LMI families, combined with their *willingness* to embrace exclusionary zoning laws and cater to the whims of rich and lower-rich NIMBYers.

As discussed earlier in this chapter and in chapter 2, political leaders have done little to help LMI families find affordable housing in neighborhoods with high-performing public schools that would help their children graduate from college and experience upward mobility. Chapter 8 includes comprehensive proposals that would help make upward mobility more likely for LMI families, but there are things state and local leaders can do now to help increase the supply of affordable housing. One thing states and local leaders have already started to do is eliminate or relax exclusionary zoning policies that increase housing prices and reduce housing supply. Local political leaders should also relax or amend their land use laws to let homeowners add smaller secondary residences, including garage or attic apartments, to their lots.

Accessory dwelling units (ADUs) can provide affordable rental housing for childless young LMI workers or older LMI adults who want or need to live close to family members. Fortunately, local leaders throughout the country in places ranging from Ann Arbor, Michigan, Arlington, Virginia, Barnstable, Massachusetts, Durham, North Carolina, and Fresno, California, to Spur, Texas, have already relaxed zoning laws to permit owners to create smaller units on their property. While laws vary, localities typically let owners construct ADUs on their property if they agree to rent the units at prices that would be affordable for middle-class renters. Local leaders should also consider ways to give owners economic incentives to build ADUs that the owner intends to rent to tenants who use housing choice vouchers or who have been displaced by gentrification.

These local efforts are a great start, but federal leaders must also do their part. For over a century, federal laws have allowed homeowners to deduct the interest they pay on mortgage loans. When Congress revised tax laws in the Tax Reform Act of 1986 and eliminated all personal interest deductions *except* the mortgage interest deduction (MID), the MID became particularly valuable. The taxpayers who benefit from this tax break narrowed significantly after 2017 revisions to the tax code roughly doubled the amount of the standard deduction. Congress should modify or eliminate this enormous housing expenditure, as it benefits the people who least need it: rich and lower-rich taxpayers.[48]

Rich and lower-rich taxpayers (who are disproportionately White) benefit most from the MID because (1) they have the highest homeownership rates, (2) they buy the most expensive houses, and (3) those most likely to itemize deductions are in the top 10 percent of households. Particularly since the 2017 tax code revision, few LMI households benefit from the MID, but Congress continues to protect the MID even though it does little to help taxpayers who otherwise could not afford to buy a home become homeowners. Instead, it subsidizes housing costs for taxpayers who can and would buy homes even without the deduction or who could find suitable rental housing if they chose not to buy homes. Moreover, the MID and other homeownership subsidies *harm* LMI households by encouraging rich and lower-rich homeowners to take out large mortgages to buy larger, more expensive homes. The cost of homeownership tax expenditures is roughly twice the *combined* cost of federal rental assistance programs for LMI families, even though there are significantly more LMI households in this country than rich and lower-rich households, and upper-income taxpayers do not need housing subsidies.[49]

Another reason Congress should substantially reduce homeownership tax subsidies is that they simultaneously burden LMI households and insulate rich and lower-rich households from the impact of rising housing prices. That is, the MID and other housing deductions give higher-income households incentives to borrow to buy large, expensive homes because they can deduct some of the interest they pay on their mortgages or state and local taxes. These tax subsidies, in turn, *encourage* developers to build the McMansions that appeal to these households but *discourage* local leaders from repealing exclusionary zoning regulations (like maximum lot or house-size requirements) that make it harder for LMI households to find smaller affordable housing.[50]

Homeownership subsidies drive up housing costs for both potential buyers and renters by fueling bidding wars. The homeowners who are the most likely to win bidding wars are rich or lower-rich renters who have significant savings or can borrow (or be gifted) money from family members. Armed with the knowledge that they can deduct part of their mortgage interest, rich and lower-rich homebuyers are little harmed if they bid up the price of their desired houses, and many are confident that they will win bidding wars because they can make all-cash offers. Given how homeownership tax subsidies cause detrimental harm to LMI families, Congress should either repeal the MID or, at a minimum, limit the deduction to taxpayers who own modest homes that are, for example, no larger than 2,500 square feet.[51]

Federal, state, and local political leaders also should revise housing policies to ensure that those policies reflect demographic trends and the economic and social realities homebuyers now face. The housing unaffordability crisis has dramatically altered the fabric of this county. We are becoming a nation of renters. Young people who are struggling to find jobs that pay them enough to afford any of the markers of the middle class are delaying marriage, avoiding having large families, and even avoiding having one child. Homeownership no longer seems to be viewed as a desirable marker of the middle class for most young LMI workers because so few of them can afford to buy a home. Some no longer even want to be homeowners, and younger adults are now less likely to live independently and more likely to live at home with their parents.

Young rich and lower-rich adults have higher homeownership rates than their LMI peers, but all young adults question whether they will ever achieve traditional adult milestones (marriage and children), because many believe those milestones are out of reach for them financially. Indeed, even young adults who buy homes often must rent for longer periods or compromise on the type of home they buy. These demographic trends and realities are not, however, reflected in the types of homes that are being constructed. Moreover, these demographic realities are not reflected in zoning laws that favor single-family homes and prevent builders from constructing more affordable duplexes, triplexes, or accessory dwelling units like tiny houses.[52]

The *number* of bedrooms and rooms in single-family housing has remained stable since the 1980s, but the average *size* of houses has increased by roughly 1,000 square feet (peaking at more than 2,500 square feet a decade after the Great Recession). Just as federal tax laws and local zoning laws should discourage developers from building McMansions, given the mismatch between house sizes and the types of houses young people need (or can afford), federal, state, and local housing officials must give developers incentives to build smaller or higher-density housing units, like duplexes, triplexes, modular housing, or tiny homes, to increase the supply of affordable housing for young people. Moreover, as they did after the Great Depression and again when housing became unaffordable in the 1990s and early 2000s, federal leaders should reevaluate all mortgage lending laws and encourage lenders to innovate financing options for developers or owners who seek to build or renovate smaller affordable units.[53]

One thing federal leaders can do is enact legislation like the Neighborhood Homes Investment Act (the NHIA). The NHIA, introduced in the Senate in 2021, would give tax credits to developers who create one- to four-family housing units in distressed urban, suburban, and rural neighborhoods.[54] Giving developers a higher return on their investment if they build or renovate (rather than destroy) deteriorating structures in LMI neighborhoods would increase the supply of affordable housing and also help prevent gentrification, which pushes LMI families out of their housing. Likewise, federal leaders should also find ways to encourage banks to lend to people who want to build smaller ADUs and should provide federal tax subsidies that help unrelated homeowners or those co-owning homes as tenants in common receive homeownership tax benefits just as single or married homeowners already do.[55]

The housing unaffordability crisis affects more than just shelter. Stagnant income and unstable employment combined with the housing crisis now force LMI families to make heartbreaking trade-offs and sacrifices. A January 2020 report reveals that housing costs force both renters and homeowners to reduce their spending on nonessential but stereotypical middle-class activities, such as entertainment. Housing costs are also forcing LMI families to reduce their spending on essentials like food and utilities. Because home equity historically constituted the bulk of wealth for middle-class households, the next chapter shows how the combination of stagnant income and the inability to find jobs that pay them enough to become and remain middle class has caused LMI families to drown in debt.[56]

PART 3 Falling out of the Middle Class

6 Drowning in Debt

Until the 1980s, middle-class families had a relatively harmonious relationship with credit and debt. Like my parents, most middle-class families used savings and sometimes an inheritance or money they borrowed from family members to pay for the major marker of the middle class, a home. Most could not pay for their homes in cash, so they would borrow money from a bank in the form of a mortgage loan. Many also borrowed from banks (or automobile dealers) to pay for cars, though some bought cars using cash. Middle-class families typically used savings, cash gifts, or wages from part-time jobs to pay for their college expenses, though starting in the 1980s parents and students often used student or parent loans to pay for college. These families also used credit cards or store credit to pay for major appliances and major home repairs, but not for smaller items.

Being in debt rarely derailed middle-class households, who could use their current income to repay the debts. In fact, a lifetime of job and income stability meant that the only major debt most middle-class families had as they approached retirement would be a small balance on their mortgage loan and maybe a small outstanding balance on their credit cards. Finally, as the next chapter shows, until the 1980s retired LMI workers generally could expect to use Social Security or income from a pension to pay their living expenses once they stopped working.

That scenario is no longer true for most LMI families: they are drowning in debt.

For more than two decades, academics and progressive politicians have chronicled how LMI workers came to view and treat credit as a wage replacement.[1] As these workers struggled to pay their bills, they also became willing to drown themselves in debt to maintain the façade of having a middle-class lifestyle. They view credit as an income supplement because they often cannot find full-time and permanent jobs with benefits and wages that will pay them enough to afford the markers of the middle class, pay their basic living expenses, or build household savings.

With stagnant income but soaring medical expenses, even LMI workers with jobs that provide health insurance are now drowning in medical debt, in part because of high copayments or deductibles. Likewise, while middle-class families with stable jobs historically avoided high-cost consumer installment, payday, or pawnshop loans, they now use those credit products to try to maintain the façade of a middle-class lifestyle. And, as the end of this chapter shows, a newer form of pernicious debt now threatens the financial stability of LMI workers, particularly if they are non-White: the court and judicial fines and fees that localities use to balance their budgets.[2]

STUDENT LOANS

As discussed in chapter 3, federal leaders created the GI Bill to help returning World War II veterans obtain postsecondary skills training or earn a bachelor's degree. At that time, the benefits were so generous that veterans could have paid for all but $25 of tuition at Harvard. Similarly, when Congress created the Pell Grant program, it set benefits at a level that covered roughly three-quarters of the total cost to attend a four-year public college degree. That is no longer true, and political leaders do not seem to care that LMI students are now plunging into debt to get the educational training they need to become and remain middle class.[3]

Tuition and fees have been steadily increasing since the 1980s, often because college and university leaders needed to find additional funding to offset budget shortfalls that were created when states reduced funding for public schools. In addition to slashing funding for public universities, state leaders were also creating (or endorsing) programs that provided "merit-based" scholarships for students with no demonstrated financial need. In perhaps the clearest signal that state educational leaders no longer care whether LMI students can afford to go to college, many public and private colleges have now abandoned "need-blind" admissions policies and openly signal that they prefer students who do not need financial assistance. For their part, federal leaders have done nothing to ensure that Pell Grants remained at levels that even come close to covering the costs of a bachelor's degree.

Because of the inaction of federal and state leaders, the total number of indebted students and the amount of outstanding student loan balances started to soar in the early 2000s, and borrowers now owe more on student loan debt than they owe on credit cards. When the COVID pandemic hit, borrowers were shouldering almost $1.5 trillion in student loan debt. Although the Biden administration forgave billions in student loan debt for eligible borrowers, including many who attended for-profits, court decisions thwarted programs that would have provided more extensive debt relief. As chapter 3 explains, student borrowers and their parents are facing a student loan debt crisis, though most student and parent borrowers have small outstanding loan balances, and most make their student loan payments on time.

Most student loan borrowers owe between $20,000 and $25,000 in outstanding debt, and 25 percent owe less than $10,000. The borrowers with high balances held more than half of total aggregate outstanding debt, and the share of borrowers with large (more than $50,000) outstanding balances has steadily increased. The borrowers who are most likely to have large outstanding balances and who have high default rates, however, generally cluster in two distinct groups.[4]

Despite being a relatively small percentage of the US population, students with graduate school loans hold roughly 20 percent of outstanding educational debt. That graduate student borrowing is disproportionately high is not terribly surprising, as graduate programs typically are more expensive than undergraduate programs. While the amount of graduate debt soared after the 2007–2009 Great Recession, default rates for graduate students have always been low relative to default rates for undergraduate borrowers. Indeed, graduate and higher-income borrowers (including those with graduate degrees) are responsible for almost 75 percent of all loan repayments. This, again, is not surprising, particularly since graduate borrowers earn more, particularly if they borrowed to attend medical or law school.[5]

Although most graduate borrowers earn more than undergraduate borrowers and have higher repayment rates than undergraduate borrowers, there is a subset of graduate borrowers who have large outstanding loan balances *and* high default rates. These are borrowers who attended a for-profit institution. Indeed, the borrowers who are the least likely to repay their student loans, whether they borrowed to earn a graduate or an undergraduate degree, are people who attended for-profits. Given their low graduation rates, large outstanding loan balances, higher default rates, and dismal job prospects, it is not surprising that the student loan crisis can fairly be viewed as the "for-profit dropout" crisis.[6]

Today's for-profits are nothing like the low-cost "trade schools" that existed when my mother earned a secretarial certificate in the 1960s. For one thing, students who attended trade schools before the 1980s typically attended in-person classes. Even before the COVID pandemic normalized online educational offerings, students who attended for-profits were significantly more likely to attend online-only colleges, which saves for-profit owners money but makes it less likely students will actually graduate. My mother and other students who attended trade schools typically paid for those their classes with wages they earned working part time, whereas students borrow heavily to attend for-profits.

Before the 1980s, for-profits focused on providing students short-term certificates they could use to secure a full-time job. Now, for-profits compete with public and nonprofit private schools for students who are seeking a four-year or graduate degree. Moreover, unlike trade schools like the Nashville Business School and public and nonprofit colleges and universities, generating revenue for the owners of for-profits is the main goal of for-profits, *not* providing a low-cost education for students. Because of the profit-driven business model, for-profits invest more in marketing and advertising to recruit students than they invest in academic courses or career services that would help students find good jobs.

For-profits provide a terrible return on investment (ROI) for the students, who often leave the for-profit with debt but no degree, and most students borrow more to take classes at a for-profit than they would if they attended a community college or regional university. For-profits do not receive state funding and receive minimal (if any) alumni donations. Instead, they primarily rely on federal aid, including student loans and Pell Grants, for their revenue. In fact, while they enroll only about 10 percent of college students, for-profits receive a disproportionate percentage of federal educational funding, including Pell Grants and student loans. Because their profit-driven business model relies heavily on federal funding, the average outstanding debt for students who attend for-profits is generally 25 percent higher than debt for students who attend public or private nonprofit universities.[7]

One reason the ROI for students who borrow to attend for-profits is lower, while their outstanding student loan balances and default rates are higher, is that their graduation rates are low, particularly compared to students who attend public flagship and private nonprofit colleges. Students who borrow to attend for-profits also have more debt than other student borrowers because they are (1) more likely to be lower income, first generation, non-White, and older and (2) less likely to receive financial assistance from their parents. In addition, students who attend for-profits are less likely to find full-time and permanent jobs even if they graduate, because employers routinely discount the value of those degrees.[8]

The other group with disproportionately high student loan debt and default rates are non-White, particularly Black, borrowers. Black borrowers owe approximately $25,000 more than White borrowers at graduation and are significantly less likely to have reduced their student debt four years after graduation than White student borrowers. One recent report shows that more than a decade after they started college, White borrowers had reduced their student debt by 35 percent, while loan balances for Black borrowers *increased* by 13 percent.[9] One reason non-White (particularly Black) borrowers have large outstanding student loan balances, higher default rates, and lower overall educational attainment than White borrowers is that they are overrepresented at for-profit institutions, especially in graduate programs. Because many attend college but fail to graduate, they are more likely to have debt but no degree, and even if they graduate from a for-profit, the degree they receive often does not help them find a job that pays them enough to repay their loans.[10]

Despite the risks and costs of attending a for-profit graduate school, non-White students often elect this educational path because of their need to earn an additional educational credential. Black *college* graduates earn more than White *high school* graduates, but Black and Latino workers generally need a graduate degree to achieve income parity with White college graduates. As an example, for Black and Latino men to earn more than White males who have an associate's degree, these non-White workers need a master's degree. Another reason non-White workers may participate in high-cost "credentialing" is that they are overrepresented in public-sector jobs (like education or social work), for which workers typically need an advanced degree—even if it is from a for-profit—if they hope to receive anything more than minimal annual pay raises. Ongoing discrimination in labor markets, occupational segregation, and the actual or perceived need for "credentialing" causes Black college *graduates*—regardless of their parents' income or the type of school they attended—to have higher outstanding debt and default rates than White college *dropouts*.[11]

Educational redlining is another reason Black and Latino borrowers (and their parents) have more outstanding student loan debt. Recent research revealed that interest rates for students who attend HBCUs or HSIs are almost 5 percent higher than rates lenders charge students who attend elite PWIs. Like mortgage loan redlining, these higher interest rates do not appear to be justified by risk factors, given that income for Black HBCU graduates is roughly the same as income for Black graduates of PWIs.[12]

Another small, but fastest growing, segment of student loan borrowers who are struggling to repay their educational debt are adults over the age of sixty-five. Since the 1980s, student loan debt has increased for older adults because they are borrowing more to help their children (or grandchildren) pay rising college costs. Others increased their student loan debt to return to school after the Great Recession to get a college degree or additional skills training to qualify for a new (or a better) job. Most older borrowers, like most graduate borrowers, repay their loans on time. But parent "PLUS" loans have disproportionately high default rates for reasons that are similar to the reasons the innovated mortgage loans approved during the housing bubble had high default rates.[13]

The reason? Lenders approve PLUS loans based on the borrower's credit history, *not* their ability to repay the loans. Because lenders let parents borrow up to the total cost of attendance (minus any financial aid their child receives), older borrowers who use these loans to help pay college expenses have disproportionately higher loan balances and default rates. Like students, parents must repay the loans even if their children fail to graduate. Unlike students, parents are not entitled to participate in student loan forgiveness programs.[14]

Scholars are now questioning whether student loans should continue to be viewed as "good" debt. Some have concluded that predatory inclusion practices that extend high-cost loans to "help" certain borrowers do not increase social or economic mobility for poor students. Instead, the combination of stagnant wages for all but the highest earners, high-cost borrowing, and high default rates has transformed student loan debt from good to bad debt. It has become another factor—alongside limited job opportunities, *particularly* for students who attend for-profits—that now causes so many lower-income borrowers to experience downward (*not* upward) mobility.[15]

HOUSING AND HOUSEHOLD DEBT

Like educational debt, mortgage debt has historically been viewed as "good" debt because it helps families achieve the American Dream of homeownership. It is also viewed as "good" debt because it helps borrowers acquire a valuable asset (a house) that can increase their net worth or be used as collateral for a loan to start a new business or pay for college expenses. Other reasons mortgage debt is viewed as a good investment for borrowers is that they get to live rent-free in their homes once they repay the mortgage, they can sell the home and use the proceeds to pay their retirement expenses, and the housing equity they build can create intergenerational wealth for their children. Unfortunately, because the "innovated" and nontraditional mortgage products lenders created to boost home sales in the 1990s were high risk and high cost, this "good" debt soared to almost $10 trillion before the Great Recession. Mortgage debt inched to over $14 trillion just before the 2020 COVID recession, and now constitutes almost 70 percent of total consumer household debt.[16]

While mortgage debt remains the largest type of consumer debt, credit card debt is also making it harder for LMI families to become financially stable. Unlike student or mortgage loans, credit card debt has never really been viewed as "good" debt. This type of consumer debt can be good, as it helps buyers spread out payments for larger items (like appliances) over time, though credit cards were originally created to help wealthy people avoid the risk, inconvenience, and often danger of carrying large amounts of cash while when traveling. Charge (now credit) cards likewise helped merchants avoid the risk of accepting a check drawn on an out-of-state bank.

Until the 1980s, lenders generally would only approve credit for borrowers who completed a burdensome and intrusive application that asked about their income, wealth, and general ability to repay the credit. That has all changed. As then Chairman of the Federal Reserve Alan Greenspan famously quipped in 2000, almost anyone, including "children, dogs, cats and moose" can get a credit card.[17] The reason that it is easier for borrowers to drown themselves in credit card and other consumer debt is that federal leaders chose to deregulate credit markets and relax banking laws, and state leaders essentially repealed usury laws.

Relaxed lending standards resulted in the "democratization" of credit and created the impression that borrowing money for consumption would give people greater choice and freedom. No one could have imagined, though, that (1) point-of-sale terminals in brick-and-mortar or online stores would allow lenders to approve debt almost instantaneously; (2) borrowers would be able to buy things in person or online with a click, swipe, or tap; or (3) people would pay for things like tickets to a high school football game or bets at a casino using a credit card.

While political leaders castigate borrowers who fail to repay their credit card debt or attempt to discharge their debts in bankruptcy, these leaders have done nothing to discourage them from drowning themselves in credit card debt. Indeed, lenders and political leaders alike encourage borrowers to "spend, spend, spend" and bury themselves in debt because they know that consumer spending drives the US economy. Moreover, though lenders control who can be approved for a credit card, they have made it easier, *not* harder, for LMI families to use credit cards given the profitability of credit card fees and penalties. Indeed, lenders deliberately design frictionless payment systems because they know that the easier it is for people to spend—whether by tapping a credit card or using apps like PayPal, Venmo, or Apple Pay—the more people are likely to drown themselves in debt.

Credit card debt and default rates have soared since the democratization of credit. By the 2020 COVID pandemic, roughly 83 percent of American adults had at least one credit card. Credit card debt surpassed mortgages and student loans and became the most popular and common *type* of household debt, though the overall *amount* of mortgage and student loan debt exceeds the total amount of outstanding credit card debt. LMI and young borrowers continued to struggle with credit card debt even after the pandemic recovery, as evidenced by 2024 Federal Reserve data that reveal that serious credit card delinquencies have now surpassed prepandemic levels.[18]

While it is easier for everyone to bury themselves in debt, the type of credit card debt a borrower has often varies. The Equal Credit Opportunity Act (ECOA) of 1974 forbids credit card companies from making decisions based on the borrower's race. Despite this, Black credit card applicants have lower approval rates, and Black credit card holders pay more interest on their outstanding balances even if they have lower account balances than comparable White cardholders. Moreover, as some subprime mortgage companies did during the housing boom, some credit card issuers appear to engage in "reverse redlining," which occurs when lenders disproportionately approve lower-cost credit cards for certain borrowers but push other borrowers toward higher-cost and higher-risk cards.[19]

As is true with mortgage lending, lenders approve college-educated, White, and male borrowers for lower-cost credit cards at rates that exceed other groups and for reasons that do not appear related to risk factors. For high-income borrowers, credit cards actually could be a form of "good" credit because their credit cards often include perks like airline miles or hotel stays. The same is not true, though, for borrowers in low-income neighborhoods, which are saturated with preapproved credit offers for cards that have higher interest rates and less favorable terms. For these borrowers, credit card debt remains bad (and indeed predatory) debt that typically does not provide either short- or long-term financial benefits.[20]

Subprime automobile loans may be a necessary evil for LMI workers but, like credit card debt and subprime mortgage loans, this type of debt also threatens their financial stability. Just as mortgage lenders did in the early 2000s, auto lenders innovated financial services products to help cash-strapped borrowers who would not qualify for a traditional automobile loan buy cars. Innovated subprime auto loans, like subprime mortgage products, have higher interest rates. The average size of a new car loan increased by more than 10 percent over the last decade because of pandemic-related inventory shortages and because borrowers have used the proceeds of subprime auto loans to pay off existing auto debt.

Just before the pandemic, auto loan delinquencies and default rates had approached historic highs, often because borrowers were defaulting on subprime auto loans within months of being approved for those loans, likely because some auto lenders approved loans for people who did not have the ability to repay them from their current income. Young debtors are especially likely to default on auto debt and have their cars be repossessed. Outstanding automobile loans constituted almost 10 percent of household debt; they hit a record high of $1.43 trillion by 2022, and by 2024 roughly one in four borrowers owed more on their vehicle than it was worth.[21]

While auto loan debt increased for all LMI adults, and young debtors are especially likely to default on auto debt and have their cars repossessed, a borrower's race often determines how much they will pay to buy a car using an auto loan. Even with similar credit scores and income, Black and Latino car owners pay more to finance cars than comparable White buyers, and they also are charged a higher markup for auto service contracts. As revealed in recent settlements between Honda, Toyota, the US Consumer Financial Protection Bureau, and the Department of Justice, Black and Latino car buyers paid between $100 and $200 more in interest rates on car loans than White customers, regardless of their creditworthiness. Similarly, although auto insurance "redlining" is banned in almost all states, a recent study found that borrowers in non-White neighborhoods spend almost twice as much on auto insurance as borrowers in majority White neighborhoods who have similar credit profiles.[22]

Another form of debt, alternative financial services (AFS) products, has trapped LMI families in a debt cycle since the 1980s. AFS borrowing is high risk and often predatory, and products include check cashing and rent-to-own services and payday, pawnshop, auto title, and tax refund loans. These products strip wealth from customers by charging them excessive banking fees and historically were viewed as "fringe" credit products, though they have gone "mainstream" now, as there are more payday loan stores than McDonald's or Starbucks.

AFS products initially were marketed to lower-income, noncollege borrowers who did not have a checking or savings account ("unbanked" borrowers) or borrowers whose credit history did not satisfy traditional lending standards. Sociologists and organizations like the National Consumer Law Center and Shelterforce have stressed that this form of marginalized debt has exacerbated the racial wealth gap and disproportionately harms lower-income and non-White borrowers, who are more likely to be unbanked. These customers disproportionately use AFS services because the borrowing experience is easy, and AFS providers are conveniently located in low-income and non-White neighborhoods. For various reasons (including bank mergers), since the 1980s traditional lenders have largely abandoned non-White communities and closed or reduced services in branches in those neighborhoods at rates exceeding the rates at which they close accounts (or branches) in predominantly White neighborhoods.[23]

Many LMI communities are now banking deserts that lack an independent bank or close proximity to a branch of a traditional bank, and this makes it more likely that the residents of those communities will rely on AFS providers. Unfortunately, some of the traditional lenders that remain in non-White LMI neighborhoods have behaved in ways that give residents good reason to avoid being banked. Black families have been skeptical of traditional banks for almost a century, since lenders at the Freedmen's Savings Bank squandered the modern equivalent of $1.5 billion in deposits from formerly enslaved depositors. Bank failures during the Great Depression further eroded the trust Black families had in banks and even Black-owned institutions that failed when they could not obtain adequate funds to survive the 1929 stock market crash.[24]

Some lenders in LMI neighborhoods continue to engage in abusive and at times fraudulent acts, including charging customers dormant account fees for accounts the banks opened without their knowledge. For example, investigations have revealed that some lenders increased overall banking costs for customers in lower-income and non-White neighborhoods by using third-party screening agencies to help identify or "evaluate" potential customers and passing the costs of that process on to their customers.[25] Lenders also increase borrowing costs and risks for these customers by disproportionately placing holds on their accounts, which effectively denies the customers access *to their own money*. Lenders in Black and Latino neighborhoods often require potential customers to make larger initial deposits to open basic checking accounts or to demand that existing customers keep higher minimum balances. The combination of questionable lending practices that make it hard for customers to qualify for lower-cost financial services, the physical convenience of AFS providers, and the shoddy treatment some non-White LMI borrowers receive when they attempt to bank with traditional lenders makes AFS and financial technology (FinTech) providers more attractive to some borrowers despite higher costs and greater risks.[26]

Since the mid-2010s there has also been an uptick in the number of middle-income households that earn at least $75,000 or are headed by college graduates who use AFS products. Younger adults, in particular, use higher-FinTech platforms, like Venmo and Square, that replace traditional banking and credit services. FinTech digital payment systems like Buy Now Pay Later help spread out purchases evenly over multiple payments. The employment uncertainty and instability and overall financial precarity young LMI workers have faced since the Great Recession resulted in an almost tenfold increase in their use of FinTech between 2019 and 2021.[27]

MEDICAL AND INVOLUNTARY DEBTS

Chapter 4 showed how hard it is for LMI workers to find permanent and full-time jobs with stable wages that provide health insurance. Soaring health-care costs are now burying LMI families, *particularly* if they are non-White, in medical debt. Medical debt has been soaring since the 1980s, and while it is not the largest type of *debt*, it is now the most common type of *unpaid bill*. The 2010 Patient Protection and Affordable Care Act (commonly known as ObamaCare) helped workers obtain health insurance through marketplace plans, but premiums for those health insurance plans are high and, as is true for households with employer-provided health insurance, copayments and deductibles burden LMI families with medical debt. Medical debt constitutes roughly half of all debts sent to collection agencies, and, as a 2022 report by the Consumer Financial Protection Bureau found, the amount of medical debt in collections proceedings is staggering, ranging from $81 to $140 billion.[28]

The average nonelderly American family spends roughly more than $8,000 on health-care costs, and the percentage of American adults with medical debt ranges from roughly 18 to 40 percent. Families are now devoting approximately 11 percent of their annual income to pay for medical expenses, and roughly 12 percent of families have at least $10,000 in medical debt. Some families who are drowning in medical debt lack health insurance, while others with debt are underinsured, cannot afford to pay out-of-pocket medical costs, cannot afford to pay copayments or "surprise" out-of-network medical bills, or incur additional expenses because of their health conditions. More than twenty million households owe more than $250 in medical debt, even though most (90%), Americans have some form of health insurance. Outstanding medical debt now exceeds $220 billion and is exacerbating the credit card crisis. Though medical credit cards originally were designed to pay for elective procedures insurance companies would not cover, LMI households increasingly use these high-interest-rate cards or other high-cost financing plans to pay for basic medical treatment.[29]

Medical debt and the cost of health care are literally making people sick. Americans, particularly young adults and lower-income households, are sacrificing their health care due to costs and are choosing not to see a doctor, are delaying or avoiding medical treatments or procedures, or are otherwise deciding not to follow through with their doctors' recommendations. They also are failing to fill prescriptions, or rationing what they spend on medical care and prescription drugs because they worry that they cannot afford to pay for both health care and their other living expenses, including housing.[30] The health-care challenges some people (especially men) face appear to be increasing "deaths of despair" from drug overdoses, suicides, and alcohol-related mortalities.[31] The pandemic brought into plain view what happens when workers whose wages have not kept pace with inflation face a global economic and health crisis. During COVID, some LMI essential workers who were told to return to in-person work avoided seeking medical treatment—even when they suspected they might have COVID—because they could not afford to see a doctor or because they already had medical debt. Moreover, despite the potentially lethal health risks they posed to coworkers, some LMI workers who suspected they might have COVID chose to go to work because they simply could not afford to lose income. After the pandemic, medical debt spiked for workers who had long COVID because some insurers refused to cover the costs to diagnose and treat this new medical condition.[32] The Consumer Financial Protection Bureau announced rules in 2024 that would block credit reporting agencies from using medical debt to calculate credit scores or eligibility for certain loans, but though these rules do not erase the medical debt itself.

As is true of almost all types of consumer debt, medical debt disproportionately burdens Black and Latino households. These workers are more likely to be uninsured than White workers and, as chapter 3 explains, are less likely to be college graduates or have permanent and full-time jobs with employers who provide health insurance. Non-White workers, particularly if they are noncollege, also are disproportionately employed in dangerous or physically taxing jobs.[33] Another form of debt that is less frequently discussed and often not viewed as "consumer" debt also disproportionately burdens non-White LMI families and often has catastrophic consequences: nonconsensual judicial debt.

For decades, state and local governments have relied on the revenues they receive from criminal or civil court fines and fees or assessments from unpaid traffic tickets or minor traffic violations to fund their courts and close budget shortfalls. Cities with large Black populations derive a significant portion of their revenue from judicial debt, though some might explain this disparity by suggesting that Black and Latino people have more judicial debt because they are inherently crime prone. This suggestion is false, however.

The residents of cities with large Black popularions have more judicial debt because the police departments in those cities disproportionately target them.[34] Research shows that local law enforcement officers and judges are more likely to assess municipal court fines and fees (often as high as $300 or $500 per occurrence) against Black defendants for relatively minor traffic crimes and for nonviolent misdemeanors. Black people who have unpaid fines and fees are also more likely to be imprisoned if they fail to pay those debts. Likewise, Black debtors are more likely to be (1) held in contempt or arrested for outstanding warrants for unpaid fines or fees or (2) forced to post bond as a condition of being released after arrest or to "rent" an electronic ankle monitor while they await trial.[35]

In addition to the debt itself, non-White debtors face significant financial and emotional consequences from debt collection efforts. Medical debt is the largest percentage of debt held by collection agencies, but Black debtors with judicial debt are significantly more likely to be defendants in debt-collection judgments than White debtors with similar financial attributes. Before the pandemic, roughly 40 percent of consumers reported being contacted by a debt collector four or more times a week, and roughly 15 percent of middle-income families report that they are regularly contacted by debt collectors. Black debtors, however, are more likely to have their wages garnished or their bank accounts seized. Without cash, it becomes harder for them to repay that debt.[36]

A growing concern for people with judicial or other forms of involuntary debt is that these debts may make it impossible for them to pay *any* debt or pay for their regular living expenses. These debtors are also at risk of losing their jobs if they are forced to miss work for court dates, their cars are towed, their driver's licenses are revoked, or they are thrown in jail because they cannot post bond. Moreover, as we have seen repeatedly over the last decade, the debt collection process itself can have deadly consequences.

Walter Scott was shot in the back in 2015 while he was running from police in South Carolina after they stopped him for a malfunctioning brake light. The reason he appears to have taken off running? He had an outstanding arrest warrant for unpaid debts. Scott, like others with judicial debt, had already lost jobs because of unpaid debts. He reportedly ran to avoid losing yet another job and potentially incurring more judicial debt. In an eerily similar set of circumstances during the pandemic, police killed Rayshard Brooks in 2020 after he fell asleep in his car in a Wendy's drive-through in Atlanta, then ran away from the police. The reason he likely ran? He was on probation for credit card fraud.[37]

WHY ARE LMI FAMILIES DROWNING IN DEBT?

Debt can be a financial equalizer that gives LMI families access to lifesaving credit. For most LMI families, however, debt is not a lifesaver; it is an anchor that is causing them to drown financially. There is no dispute that LMI households are struggling to pay their bills, but there seems to be some dispute among political leaders, policymakers, and maybe even the general public about *why* so many people are struggling to pay their debts. The most common narratives include financial illiteracy or the lack of discipline or willpower to resist buying unnecessary goods and services. Another narrative that is frequently used to explain why non-White households are so indebted is the well-worn trope that they refuse to accept personal responsibility for their spending choices and are unwilling to "pull themselves up by their bootstraps" and work harder to pay their bills.[38]

Many LMI families have woefully low levels of financial literacy, and some of them no doubt make impulsive purchases, just as rich and lower-rich families do. But the notion that individual behaviors rather than structural barriers trap LMI families in debt is disingenuous and misleading. People who blame LMI families for drowning in debt choose to ignore that political leaders and the financial services industry encourage the drowning by actively promoting impulsive and irresponsible spending. If lenders truly wanted to make sure families are not overindebted, the financial services industry could easily tighten credit standards. It refuses to do so, because this industry profits from having families drown in debt.[39]

As an example, when home sales to White buyers stalled in the 1990s, both Presidents Clinton and George W. Bush encouraged lenders to create "innovative," nontraditional mortgage loans to help LMI and non-White renters buy homes they otherwise could not afford. When home values skyrocketed in the 2000s, the financial services industry cleverly marketed "second mortgages" as "home equity loans" and encouraged homeowners to "unlock" the equity in their homes and take out second loans to pay for college, to start small businesses, or to pay medical expenses.[40] When President George W. Bush addressed the nation after the 9/11 terrorist attacks, he appealed to patriotism and urged Americans to "stimulate" the economy . . . by going shopping.[41]

As Jacob Hacker details in *The Great Risk Shift*, since the 1980s, political leaders, employers, and financial institutions have weaponized the trope of "personal responsibility" to justify transferring economic risks from the state or large businesses to individuals, particularly LMI workers. It is both cruel and nonsensical, however, to suggest that LMI workers are *choosing* to live on the edge financially and drown themselves in debt. Indeed, people regularly and consistently report feeling shame and guilt when they cannot pay their bills and file for bankruptcy.[42] If given a choice, LMI families would choose financial stability, not financial precarity.

For example, if personal choices were all that is needed to help LMI adults become financially stable and find jobs that pay them enough to afford the markers of the middle class, they would choose to attend the same type of K–12 schools and would choose to have the shadow education that rich and lower-rich children receive. Then, if their employers chose to offshore or domestically onshore their jobs, LMI workers would choose to avoid for-profits (and ruinous student loan debt) and instead would pick low-cost skills training to ensure they would not be stuck in lower-wage, temporary, or part-time jobs. And if given the option, LMI workers would choose to pay their bills on time rather than place themselves in the untenable position of having to make painful life-altering decisions, like whether to have a roof over their heads, place food on their tables, or take prescription drugs to keep themselves healthy or alive.

Blaming LMI workers for drowning in debt also lets political leaders conveniently ignore that being in debt in one area of life often triggers a chain reaction of cascading and potentially catastrophic consequences. For example, because employers now routinely run credit checks on potential employees, having unpaid student loan could result in a debtor not securing a permanent, full-time, or higher-wage job that could help them pay their debts and living expenses. Likewise, as we saw during the COVID pandemic, people with too much debt (or who have defaulted on loan repayments) may be denied access to financial lifelines like additional federal student aid to return to school, small business loans to start a business, or loans like the forgivable Paycheck Protection Program that would help their existing businesses remain afloat during the pandemic.

In addition to being denied access to financial lifelines that could help them become and remain middle class, borrowers who have defaulted on student loans often cannot get or renew state-issued licenses, like driver's licenses and professional or occupational licenses. Moreover, until recently, some students/former students could not get their college transcripts if they had defaulted on their student loans or they owed their colleges money for library fines or parking tickets. The inability to get a license or a transcript may be the difference between a worker keeping their current job or finding a new one.[43]

Outstanding student loan debt is also causing seismic changes in the financial and social lives of young adults. Many are delaying or avoiding (1) marriage, (2) having children, and (3) buying homes, and some list being debt free as the number one indicator of financial success. Debt is also having devastating effects at the other end of the age spectrum, as older LMI workers can no longer assume they will have a modest but comfortable lifestyle in retirement. Some older workers approach retirement age with mortgage debt that is roughly double the debt of borrowers their age in the 1980s. Others are taking out reverse mortgages even before they reach retirement age. And older adults who want to help pay for their children's college expenses (or who need to repay their own PLUS loans) often choose to borrow against their homes, which increases their housing debt and places them at greater risk of losing their homes.[44]

LMI Americans, particularly retirees, increasingly find themselves facing the painful choice of paying their mortgage debt, paying for health care, or repaying student loans. Borrowers who opt to repay their mortgage debt to keep their homes may be placing their ability to retire comfortably—long been viewed as a marker of the middle class—at risk. Older individuals with credit card, student loan, or medical debt do not enter into retirement with a balanced budget, and debtors with unpaid federal student loans could lose their federal tax refund and up to 15 percent of monthly disability benefits or retirement savings if the federal government exercises its right to garnish those payments. An increasing number of older workers cannot afford to stop working, and another troubling signal of the perils older indebted individuals now face is the increase in bankruptcy filings for people over the age of 55.[45]

Soaring levels of household debt makes it nearly impossible for LMI workers to pay their bills, engage in routine middle-class activities (like eating out or taking a vacation), or stop working when they are older. As the next chapter shows, paralyzing debt also makes it all but impossible for LMI families to save. Without savings, there is little hope that an LMI worker will ever become or remain middle class.

7 Trying to Save

Chapter 6 showed how stagnant wages now cause LMI workers to view credit as a wage supplement. The flipside of too much debt, of course, is too little savings. Most middle-class households do not have sufficient short- or long-term savings, and credit increasingly is replacing savings as a safety net for adults who are not born rich or lower rich. The financially lethal combo of no emergency and retirement savings has caused wealth disparity gaps to expand, and is why many LMI workers assume they will *never* be able to retire.

HOUSEHOLD SAVINGS

The Federal Reserve and private financial planners recommend that households have enough saved to pay for three months of expenses just in case they lose their jobs or need to stop working because they get sick or need to provide care for a family member. Having even minimal savings of $250–$750 can help LMI families, and those with modest savings can more easily withstand a financial emergency than higher-income households without savings. Unfortunately, roughly 30 percent of households in this country have inadequate savings and cannot afford to pay for a hypothetical $400 emergency or unexpected expense without using a credit card (and paying off the balance over time), borrowing (from family, friends, or an AFS lender), or selling or pawning personal items.[1] The consequences of not having emergency savings were on full display during the COVID recession, when nearly one-third of adult workers were laid off either permanently or temporarily or had their work hours reduced. Some LMI families survived only because of the financial assistance they received from federal relief programs or mortgage and rent moratoria.

Whether, how, and how much people save now is different from whether, how, and how much people saved before the 1980s. Thus, while COVID demonstrated why savings are important, the pandemic did not cause the household savings crisis. The household savings crisis has been mounting since the 1980s because there are fewer permanent and full-time jobs that pay workers enough to pay their bills and build household savings. That is, from the 1960s through the mid-1970s, the personal savings rates for households ranged between 10 and 15 percent, before dropping to single digits by the mid-1980s.

As shown in figure 7, savings rates ranged from 4 to 9 percent until the 2000s, when rates dipped to 2 percent. Household savings skyrocketed in 2020, but only because people essentially stopped spending during the early months of the COVID pandemic. Overall household savings rates plunged during the post-COVID economic recovery, then returned to rates similar to those in the period after the 2007–2009 Great Recession.[2]

Aggregate savings rates and patterns are deceptive, however, as they hide demographic disparities that have existed for decades. Whether, how, and how much people save varies significantly by income, race, and educational level. For example, just less than half (47%) of White adults do not have enough saved to cover three months of expenses. In contrast, almost three-quarters of Black (73%) and Latino adults (70%) lack sufficient emergency savings. White adults are more likely to have bank savings accounts than Black or Latino adults, and their average savings account balance is roughly four times the amount of bank savings for Black or Latino adults, who, as the last chapter noted, are more likely to be LMI households who are unbanked.[3]

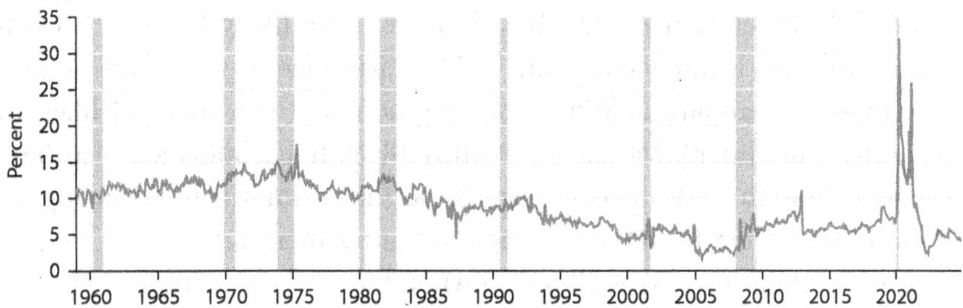

Figure 7. US personal savings rate, 1959–2024. Shaded areas indicate US recessions.
SOURCE: US Bureau of Economic Analysis, retrieved from Federal Reserve Bank of St. Louis, "FRED," accessed June 25, 2025, https://fred.stlouisfed.org/series/PSAVERT.

Black, Latino, LMI, and noncollege households are also less likely to be stock owners. For example, Gallup polling reveals that roughly 61 percent of Americans own stock directly or indirectly through retirement savings accounts. But virtually all of the top 1 percent own stock either directly or indirectly through a retirement account or mutual fund, and rich and lower-rich families own roughly 90 percent of the total share of corporate equities and mutual funds. Likewise, college graduates (who are disproportionately rich and lower rich) collectively hold more than 75 percent of stock market wealth despite accounting for less than 40 percent of adults in this country. In contrast, less than 5 percent of the overall household wealth of noncollege workers is held in direct stock holdings. The bottom 50 percent of families (who are disproportionately noncollege) own a negligible share of corporate stocks or mutual funds.[4]

Black and Latino households (regardless of income or educational attainment levels) are significantly less likely to own stock than White households. Ownership rates have increased (particularly for Black households) since the 1980s, but the average value of stock holdings Black and Latino families own is less than half the value of stock holdings by White families. A recent report prepared by the Pew Research Center analyzes Federal Reserve data and notes that nearly two-thirds of White households (66%) own publicly traded stocks, either directly or indirectly, compared to only 39 percent of Black households and 28 percent of Latino households.[5] Black college graduates have higher stock ownership rates than noncollege Black households, but they are more likely to save through lower-risk and lower-yield vehicles like insurance, savings bonds, and CDs than are comparable White college graduates (who are more likely to have stock holdings). Moreover, wealthy Black households are also "less wealthy" than their White counterparts, as they primarily build savings in their homes rather than the stock market or businesses.[6]

Despite their lower overall homeownership rates, housing wealth constitutes a larger percentage of savings for Black and Latino households in all income groups than for White and rich households. Though housing wealth is more important to non-White homeowners than to White homeowners, non-White households accumulate less housing equity, and these racial gaps in housing have significant effects on retirement savings and retirement security. Non-White homeowners have less housing wealth because ongoing biases in lending markets increase their homebuying costs, appraisers continue to undervalue their homes, and local governments underinvest in their communities.[7]

My parents were fortunate to be able to buy homes with a loan from my father's sister and an inheritance from my mother's parents. Having access to capital or wealth has never been the norm for Black and Latino renters who want to buy homes, however. Black and Latino homebuyers are two to five times less likely than White adults to receive an inheritance, gift, or loan that they could use to make a down payment. Indeed, controlling for age and educational or marital status, Black and Latino adults are less likely to receive an inheritance, the inheritances and gifts they receive are significantly smaller than the amounts White adults receive, and some do not even *expect* to receive an inheritance.[8]

LMI and non-White parents are also less likely to have college savings accounts they can use to help pay their children's college expenses. Chapter 3 explained that rich and lower-rich parents assume they will help pay for their children to go to college, and these parents are less likely to have student loan debt than LMI and non-White parents. One reason they have less debt is that they are more likely to save money in tax-preferred 529 college savings accounts while their children are young. These accounts let parents build college savings by investing in mutual funds or other market-based devices that plan sponsors select. Parents can contribute to 529 accounts as soon as their children are born, then withdraw funds from those accounts tax-free when it is time to pay for their children's qualified higher education expenses.

529 savings plans are enormously popular with rich and lower-rich parents (and grandparents), and these groups are significantly more likely than LMI parents to use these tax-favored devices to save for their children's college expenses. For example, research indicates that while less than 3 percent of families overall invest in 529 plans, roughly 15 percent of the richest top 5 percent of households have these plans. In contrast, only 20 percent of families earning less than $75,000 *and less than 1 percent* (.3%) of families in the bottom 50 percent saved for college using these tax-favored plans. Participation rates may be lower for LMI parents because they are not familiar with 529 college savings plans, but even LMI parents who participate have smaller account balances. The average balance in 529 plans for the wealthiest 5 percent of Americans ($152,300) is almost three times the size of overall account balance averages. The average account balance for the bottom 50 percent of households is only $3,800.[9]

Black, Latino, and LMI households are also less likely than White or Rich households to have savings in small businesses or other business assets. Before the pandemic, only 5.6 percent of small businesses were Latino owned and just over 2 percent were Black owned despite Latinos and Blacks constituting approximately 17 and 12 percent of the US population, respectively. The individual characteristics (including educational attainment and their involvement in the business) of Black entrepreneurs are similar to those of White entrepreneurs. Yet the businesses Blacks and Latinos own are smaller than comparable White-owned businesses and fail at higher rates. The main reason their businesses fail at higher rates is that they have, on average, less than one-third of the capital White entrepreneurs have when they start their businesses.[10]

Black and Latino entrepreneurs start small businesses (and seek financing) at higher rates than White entrepreneurs, and successful Black-owned businesses provide wealth gains that are comparable to the gains successful White businesses provide. Still, these non-White entrepreneurs struggle to maintain successful small businesses because of factors discussed throughout this book. That is, non-White owners overall have less capital to start and continue small businesses because they are less likely to have (1) full-time permanent high-wage jobs, (2) access to housing equity, (3) cash savings, or (4) access to family members who can lend (or bequeath) them money.[11]

Structural factors—not just personal financial characteristics—also make it harder for non-White entrepreneurs to start and maintain small businesses. Discussed in more detail later in this chapter, traditional lenders have closed branches or reduced services in branches in non-White communities at rates that exceed the rates at which they close accounts (or branches) in predominantly White neighborhoods. Just as some lenders give less favorable treatment to non-White customers who apply for mortgage loans or personal loans, matched paired testing studies and other research reveal that lenders also give non-White entrepreneurs less advice or assistance when they apply for loans to start a small business.

Paired testing that occurred roughly a decade after the Great Recession revealed that when non-White testers with similar credit and asset characteristics as White testers attempted to apply for a business loan, banks asked them for more personal financial statements than they requested from White applicants. Non-White testers were also discouraged from seeking financing, were offered less favorable products, and were provided different (and less favorable) lending information than White testers. Non-White testers also were asked to provide more information about their marital status even though lenders cannot legally base credit decisions on a borrower's marital status. The negative responses non-White entrepreneurs get from lenders when they seek financing, a desire to avoid a demeaning loan application process, and the assumption that their loan applications will be rejected all combine to discourage them from even applying for financing.[12]

Structural barriers to obtaining capital to start and maintain small businesses were on vivid display during the early weeks of the COVID pandemic. When government-mandated shutdowns forced nonessential businesses to close, and sales revenue for these businesses plummeted, the Trump administration quickly authorized and structured a pandemic relief program, the Paycheck Protection Program (PPP). The PPP provided forgiveable loans to help small businesses cover payroll, utilities, mortgage, or rent expenses. The program can be deemed a success, as roughly 75 percent of the businesses that requested PPP loans received them, and small businesses failures did not cripple the economy or lead to a deep recession. Unfortunately, the program was a success only for the businesses that were able to access the lenders who were allowed to approve the loans.

Intially, the Trump administration only allowed large institutional banks to grant PPP loans, and these lenders were given the right to favor their existing customers. Because the customers of large institutional lenders were disproportionately White-owned businesses, during the initial round of the PPP process non-White applicants were rejected at rates that were at times 50 percent higher than loan rejections for White applicants. Loans for non-White businesses were not denied because they were deemed to be bad credit risks or because the owners failed to apply for this pandemic relief. Instead, lower loan approval rates were due to structural factors: the owners did not have preexisting relationships with the institutional lenders that were allowed to approve loans.[13]

Because non-White-owned businesses struggled to obtain operating capital, failure rates for Black- and Latino-owned businesses reached as high as double the failure rates for White-owned small businesses. Once smaller community development financial institutions and minority-owed financial institutions were allowed to approve PPP loans, more non-White businesses received funding. By then, though, it was too late for some businesses, and some non-White-owned business owners reported that they gave up even trying to obtain a PPP loan after being denied by so many lenders.[14]

Given how some traditional lenders have treated them, non-White businesses have turned to online lenders to raise capital to finance their businesses, despite the risks and costs associted with this form of lending. Other entrepreneurs borrow against their homes to fund their businesses. Using home equity to start or maintain a business is risky, though, as this type of financing increases the risk that a non-White entrepreneur might lose their shelter, their business, and the entirety of their household savings if their business fails.[15] Overall, while Black wealth (including housing and small business equity) has increased since the pandemic, the ongoing racial savings disparities continue to increase the racial wealth gap.[16]

RETIREMENT SAVINGS

Financial advisers recommend that workers save at least 70 percent of their preretirement income to live comfortably when they retire. A recent study indicates that most preretirees are somewhat confident that

Social Security will pay them enough for them to live comfortably once they retire. Confidence levels vary by gender (with men expressing more confidence), and the amount many Americans believe they will need in retirement is *significantly more* than what they actually have saved. Unfortunately, by all subjective and objective measures, LMI workers are facing a retirement savings crisis.[17]

Baby boomers (born 1946–1964) and members of the Silent Generation (including my parents; born 1928–1945) have depended on three pillars of retirement income (personal savings, Social Security payments, and employer-provided retirement savings) to pay their expenses when they stopped working. This three-legged retirement stool is wobbling. For many LMI workers, the stool has all but collapsed. The only leg of the stool that is intact for most LMI older adults is Social Security, but given the hostility some members of Congress direct toward this guaranteed payment stream, that leg also is also on shaky ground.

SOCIAL SECURITY

Congress enacted the Social Security Act during the Great Depression, when poverty levels rose for older adults and federal leaders feared poor workers would need to rely on public assistance or money from their families once they had to stop working. The program operates essentially using a pay-it-forward model in which employers deduct money from the paychecks of current workers who are eligible to participate in the program and contribute those funds to a trust fund that is used to pay benefits for current retired workers.[18] The amount of a worker's future retirement benefit is based on their lifetime earnings and how long they worked. The program uses a progressive formula that awards lower-wage workers a higher percentage (roughly 50%) of their preretirement wages relative to higher-paid retirees (roughly 30%).

Retirees can start receiving Social Security payments once they reach age sixty-two, though most try to wait until they reach their full retirement age (FRA) to avoid paying an early retirement penalty that permanently reduces monthly payments. The FRA is sixty-five for most current retirees but is sixty-six or sixty-seven for workers born after 1960. Workers who can (and choose to) work past their FRA would receive larger monthly payments because they would earn more retirement credits.[19] People born before 1960 have typically retired at the FRA age of sixty-five, though some noncollege workers now assume that they will never be able to afford to retire.

Surveys indicate that the main reason most older workers retire later than planned is that they need the income or benefits their jobs provide. Though lower-income workers receive a higher percentage of their wages, they retire earlier than higher-income workers. Lower-income workers retire earlier than higher-income workers, even though most lack other sources of retirement income, and they will face a reduced monthly payment due to the Social Security early retirement penalty. LMI and noncollege workers often retire sooner than planned because they physically cannot continue working; as chapter 4 shows, they are disproportionately employed in manual labor jobs or have jobs that are environmentally hazardous. Thus, while working past the FRA or even well into the eighties is feasible for people like Donald Trump, Joe Biden, Michael Bloomberg, and Warren Buffet and other workers with jobs that are not physically taxing, and for workers who are not likely to confront ageism in their jobs, working even until the age of sixty-five is not feasible for some lower-income workers.[20]

Even without the early retirement penalty, benefits for LMI workers will be less than those for higher-wage workers because Social Security benefits are calculated based on lifetime earnings. LMI workers earn less and also have shorter life expectancy (particularly for men) relative to higher-wage workers. With longer life expectancy and jobs that typically are not physically taxing, rich and lower-rich workers can work longer to build emergency savings. Because working longer means they can earn more retirement credits, people who can work past their FRA can defer using their retirement savings and will have a larger monthly payment when they do choose to retire.[21]

Social Security benefits were never intended to be the sole source of retirement income, and this income is often not enough for retirees to maintain their preretirement lifestyle. Most workers expect Social Security benefits will be the top source of their retirement income, and for LMI workers, the Social Security program is the *only* stable leg of the stool for them, as most lack household savings and, as the next section shows, are less likely to work for employers who provide retirement plans.[22] Unfortunately this leg is becoming less steady as the Social Security trust fund has faced shortfalls for decades, and the fund's reserve funds may be depleted in less than a decade. The trust fund risks depletion due to low US fertility rates, stringent immigration policies that limit the number of workers available to contribute to the trust fund, and retirees' longer life expectancies.

While the funds that are deducted from workers' paychecks are not placed in separate accounts for each worker, Americans view the social security program as an entitlement (not a welfare) program because their taxes are used to fund the program. They adhere to this belief even though life expectancy for Silent Generation and older boomer retirees is almost twenty years longer than the typical life expectancies for workers when Congress created the program in the 1930s, and the amount many receive overall exceeds the amount of taxes deducted from their paychecks.[23] Some Republican members of Congress who seek ways to cut government spending scoff at the notion that Social Security payments are a lifetime-guaranteed "entitlement" for retired workers, but the program's popularity with seniors (who vote in vastly larger numbers than younger adults) and powerful lobbies like the AARP has prevented political leaders from gutting this program. If Congress ultimately dismantles or privatizes the program or increases the FRA, the retirement savings gap between LMI, Black, and Latino retirees and rich, lower-rich, and White retirees will be wider than it already is. Dismantling this stable leg of the retirement stool could be catastrophic for LMI retirees since, as the next section shows, businesses have all but abandoned any duty to help their workers save for retirement.

EMPLOYER-PROVIDED RETIREMENT PLANS

Even before Congress created the Social Security program, some employers were providing retirement plans for their workers. Early plans included one created by the Continental Congress in response to an appeal from George Washington to provide a pension for military veterans.

Private pension plans created after the Civil War included one offered by American Express and one created by an owner who believed that his company had a duty to provide for the "depreciation" of older workers just as it provided for the depreciation of the old machinery.[24]

Pension plans became popular during World War II when federal wage freezes prevented businesses from attracting or retaining workers during the wartime labor shortages with promises of higher pay. Because businesses could not entice workers with higher wages, they used *nonwage* compensation, like retirement plans, health insurance, and holiday and sick leave, to attract and retain workers because this form of compensation was not subject to federal wartime wage controls. To give businesses incentives to help their workers have retirement security, the Internal Revenue Service views the costs businesses pay to provide pensions as deductible necessary business expenses.

While businesses still offer plans, the type of plans they offer has changed dramatically since the 1980s. Specifically, until the 1980s most public and large unionized private manufacturing employers offered a pension plan commonly referred to as a defined benefit (DB) plan. DB plans provide guaranteed and fixed income based on the worker's income and years of service. Businesses initially favored DB plans because they helped reduce worker turnover, as workers understood that their monthly pension amount was based on their income and years of service with their employer.

DB plans provide more retirement security for workers because the businesses that sponsor the plans are required to automatically enroll *all* eligible workers and, with the help of experts, decide how to invest the funds that will be used to make future payments. Businesses must also calculate how much workers will receive each month when they retire and must guarantee and fully fund the plan, even during economic downturns. As a result, the employer (not the employee) bears both the risk of loss if the investment returns are lower than expected *and* the risk that retired workers may live longer than anticipated.[25] Despite the benefits DB plans give workers, businesses started to abandon these plans in the 1980s, and political leaders have refused to require businesses to offer secure retirement plans for their workers. Indeed, rather than require businesses to care about their depreciated workers, Congress implicitly endorsed employers' decisions to abandon their workers when it replaced the defined benefit (DB) plan for federal civilian workers and created what we know as defined contribution (DC) plans.[26]

When the Tax Reform Act (TRA) of 1986 created DC accounts, the federal government started offering market-based accounts to public employees. Almost immediately, private employers started to ditch their DB plans and offer their workers 401ks or 403b DC accounts that essentially shift the responsibility of planning and funding retirement plans from employers to workers. In contrast to DB plans, both employers and employees make contributions to DC accounts, though employers are not required to contribute to their employees' retirement plans even if the businesses offer this workplace retirement option. Not surprisingly, employers overwhelmingly preferred DC plans because they had no duty to automatically enroll all eligible workers, nor were they required to hire professional managers to ensure that workers have saved enough when they retire. Moreover, employers have no duty to ensure their former workers will have adequate retirement savings, as retirement savings in DC accounts are not guaranteed. Instead, contributions to DC accounts typically are invested in mutual funds, whose performance will vary based on the stock market.[27]

By the mid-1990s, the total amount of assets held in DC plans surpassed the amount held in DB plans, and a 2021 Congressional Research Service report found that only 15 percent of private-sector workers had access to a DB plan, down from the roughly 50 percent that could participate in DB plans in the 1980s.[28] Since the early 2000s, and particularly after the 2007–2009 Great Recession, the DC versus DB gap has consistently widened, as shown in figure 8.

Workers whose retirement funds are held in market-based DC accounts must determine on their own how much they need to save to maintain their preretirement standard of living (often called the replacement rate) or how long they likely will live once they retire (the longevity risk). Unlike Social Security or DB plan payments, workers whose retirement savings are held in market-based DC accounts can never predict how the funds they invested will perform and workers often will not know how much they have in retirements savings until it is time to withdraw money from their accounts.

As the Federal Reserve aptly observed, self-directed DC retirement accounts require ordinary workers to have the skills to digest complicated

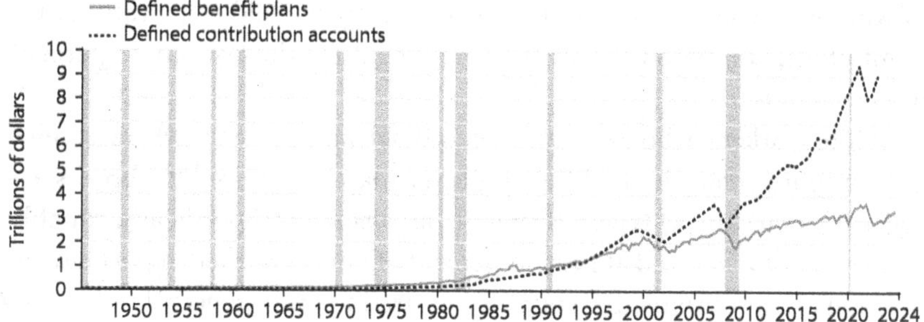

Figure 8. Asset levels for private DB pension plans (total funded) and DC pension accounts (total financial assets), 1945–2024. Shaded areas indicate US recessions.
SOURCE: Board of Governors of the Federal Reserve System (US), retrieved from Federal Reserve Bank of St. Louis, "FRED," accessed June 25, 2025, https://fred.stlouisfed.org/series/BOGZ1FL572000075Q#.

financial language and product features, then decide where (or whether) to invest their retirement savings.[29] Shifting retirement savings hazards from businesses to workers can be catastrophic, particularly if workers retire during an economic downturn, as happened during the 2007–2009 Great Recession (and the early days of the COVID pandemic), when many watched in horror as their retirement savings disappeared. After the Great Recession, the US Commerce Department prepared a report that emphasized the financial struggles middle-class families will continue to face without "a responsible private sector that offers decent jobs and benefits."[30]

Chapter 4 showed how businesses have radically transformed the workforce since the 1980s by replacing secure jobs with part-time or temporary jobs. Although roughly two-thirds of private-sector workers have *access* to a DC retirement account, and half of workers *overall* make regular contributions to retirement savings accounts, the workers least likely to have retirement savings are the ones whose employers do not offer retirement savings plans: LMI, non-White, and noncollege workers.[31] Virtually all rich and lower-rich workers who work for employers who offer DC plans participate in and contribute to those plans. Given the types of jobs LMI workers typically have, they are significantly less likely (35%) to have access to an employer-provided retirement plan than higher-income workers (80%).[32] Just before the COVID-19 pandemic, the top 20 percent of workers owned more than 66 percent of assets held in private retirement plans, compared to less than 8 percent for the bottom 50 percent of households.[33]

White workers, who earn more than Black and Latino workers, receive a disproportionate share of the employer matches in (and tax breaks associated with) 401(k) type retirement savings plans. Specifically, roughly 62 percent of Black and almost 70 percent of Latino workers report having no assets in a retirement account, compared to only 37 percent of White workers, and the average amount of retirement savings of White workers was roughly ten times the amount of Black and Latino workers. Noncollege workers—who are disproportionately LMI and non-White—also are less likely to have access to an employer-provided retirement plan than college graduates. Even lower-income and noncollege workers who have access to an employer-provided DC account typically do not contribute the maximum amount, even if their employers match their contributions.[34]

LMI workers also face retirement savings shortfalls. even if they have a DC account, due to plan features that let them borrow against or prematurely withdraw their retirement savings. Roughly 25 percent of workers prematurely withdraw money from DC accounts to pay for routine expenses or emergencies, like medical expenses or burial costs, and Black and Latino workers withdraw money at rates that exceed rates for White workers. Withdrawing funds from retirement savings accounts to pay current expenses is costly in both the short and long term. Workers are harmed short term because of the hefty tax that is imposed when borrowers prematurely withdraw money from a DC account. The long-term harm early retirement withdrawals cause is even more troubling, as these withdrawals may result in workers having no retirement savings if they stop working before they replenish the withdrawn contributions.[35]

To disguise the fact that they no longer care about their retired workers, businesses contend that what they are doing is giving workers more "choices" about how to save for retirement. Employers argue that DC plans let workers choose whether to contribute to their retirement savings account or use their current wages and invest them in other ways, or use them to pay current expenses. Businesses further contend that eliminating DB plans also gives workers the freedom to choose how much they want to invest and where they want to invest their retirement funds. Then, as they approach retirement, workers can choose how much (or little) to withdraw from their DC accounts, whether to take out a lump sum or convert their account balances to an annuity, and how to manage their savings to make sure they do not run out of money before they die. Predictably, this lifetime of retirement "choices" has increased the risk that workers will not have enough saved, either because they did not invest the right amounts or because their market-based investments have plunged in value when they want to retire.

THE DIRE CONSEQUENCES OF HAVING NO SAVINGS

Before the 1980s, LMI adults (like my parents) saved more. My parents knew they needed savings because of the obstacles they understood they would face in housing and lending markets. More important than *knowing* the importance of savings was their actual ability to amass short- and long-term savings. The last chapter showed how having too much debt can have deadly consequences for LMI families. The consequences are equally dire for LMI families who do not have adequate savings.

As illustrated throughout this book, households who lack savings struggle to pay for a college degree that would help them (or their children) find a higher-wage job. The lack of short-term cash savings also makes it harder for noncollege and LMI workers to make a down payment on a home, to invest in the stock market, to start small businesses that could increase their overall household wealth, or to amass long-term (i.e., retirement) savings. Studies prepared by the Consumer Financial Protection Bureau and private think tanks consistently find that households, particularly if they are non-White or LMI, with emergency savings are less likely to use payday lenders or other AFS providers, overdraw their bank accounts, or deplete their retirement savings by withdrawing funds from DC accounts.[36]

Likewise, surveys conducted after the pandemic showed that workers with as little as $1,000 in emergency savings were better able to protect their retirement savings and generally avoid financial ruin than families with no savings. Indeed, the catastrophic consequences of not having savings were on full display during the 2018–2019 government shutdown and again during the early weeks of the 2020 COVID shutdown. To the bewilderment of Trump and some of his billionaire/millionaire cabinet members, some middle-class furloughed federal workers were forced to borrow from friends or relatives, sell household goods on eBay, run up credit card debt, turn to predatory AFS products, raid their retirement savings, or create GoFundMe accounts just to make ends meet. Then, during the COVID pandemic, middle-class families joined poor families in food lines and found themselves at risk of being evicted or losing their homes, until Congress passed foreclosure moratorium laws.

As shown in the last chapter, many LMI and non-White older workers approach retirement with mortgage and student loan debt, and some are increasing debt faster than they build retirement savings. In addition, income instability and the lack of retirement savings has increased the number of older LMI homeowners who use reverse mortgages or home equity loans to pay their preretirement and retirement expenses.[37] Just as LMI families who are drowning in debt must make painful and potentially life-threatening short- and long-term financial trade-offs , those who lack savings must also make painful choices. They must decide whether to pay current expenses, to divert funds to retirement savings, or to continue working well past their FRA to earn money to pay their bills and save for retirement. In fact, though some older workers retired during the pandemic to avoid going in person to potentially deadly workplaces, many had to "unretire" once they realized they had insufficient retirement savings.[38]

There is another consequence to the retirement savings crisis that LMI older adults are facing, and it affects the financial security of their younger relatives. Congress created the Social Security system to prevent older adults from having to depend on relatives to survive when they stopped working. Unfortunately, the retirement savings crisis has made it harder for some college-educated younger workers to acquire the markers of the middle class because they are providing financial assistance to family and friends. Indeed, many financially successful non-White college graduates understand that it is more likely that they will give financial assistance *to* their older, poorer relatives (and friends) than receive money *from* them.[39]

Black, Latino, and South and East Asian adults are more likely than White households to make child-to-parent transfers. Non-White adult children often make these child-to-parent transfers because of a custom of "filial piety," and a recent Pew Research survey indicates that Latino adults are especially likely to feel pressure to support family members and some adult children who make child-to-parent transfers assume that the "tax" for these child-to-parent transfers will likely increase as their income increases.[40] Some older LMI adults who know they must retire before their FRA and who have no (or little) savings in an employer-provided retirement plan no longer even try to plan for retirement and instead hope that their children will support them when they can no longer work. As an example, older LMI adults (*especially* renters) who lack savings or home equity often depend on their adult children to help pay their living expenses and to help defray (or pay entirely) the soaring costs for senior housing. And as we vividly witnessed during the 2020 COVID shutdown, some adult children stopped working (or they worked multiple jobs) to care for their parents or pay for their home health care or living expenses.[41]

While noble, when young LMI adults choose (or feel dutybound) to make child-to-parent transfers, this choice exacerbates income and wealth inequality gaps, as adult children with wealthy relatives are less likely to make these transfers and, as a result, have more income to pay their bills and amass short- and long-term savings. In the shadows and without widespread public attention is the reality that the retirement savings crisis for *older* adults is now making it harder for *younger* adults to buy homes, start small businesses, pay their *own* children's college expenses (without excessive borrowing), or retire comfortably.

WHY PEOPLE DO NOT SAVE

Before political leaders develop a "New Deal" program to help LMI workers build both emergency and retirement savings, they must first dispel and reject misleading narratives about why LMI families struggle to save. While governmental agencies and private entities have a clear sense of how much people save or should save and why savings are important, there are multiple and competing narratives about *why* America's middle class saves too little. Just as political leaders have allowed businesses to weaponize the concept of "choice" when suggesting that workers desire part-time or contracted jobs, notions of free will and choice are used to explain why LMI families lack short- and long-term savings.

The most popular trope assumes that LMI families save too little because they are too materialistic and choose to spend too much. The "work harder/spend less" narrative gained traction nationally in the 1980s, when conservative politicians like Ronald Reagan conjured up stereotypical tropes, like the "welfare queen" who refused to get a job but who constantly bought Air Jordans and designer handbags.[42] This thinly veiled racialized trope has stubbornly persisted, as evidenced by Trump's first secretary of education, Ben Carson's, stunningly insensitive comments in 2017 that people are poor because they lack "the right mindset" and their parenting habits instill a "poverty of spirit" in their children.[43] Other politicians have advanced slightly less-racialized but equally judgmental tropes by suggesting that LMI families are financially insecure because they spend too much money on women, movies, cellphones, and "booze."[44]

A slightly less judgmental but equally condemning narrative assumes that LMI families save too little because they were never taught the importance of saving. This narrative is somewhat supported by research that shows that lower-income people who participate in educational programs have higher savings rates even if they lacked savings before they started the financial literacy programs. Although few states require K–12 students to take a course on personal finance education, and not all states even require high schools to offer a financial literacy course, the assumption has merit. Research shows that there is a positive association between the amount of financial education low-income participants receive and their personal rates of saving.[45] Because most children and young adults do not take a financial literacy course in K–12 schools or in college, how, whether, or why people save generally is informed by personal values, emotions, early-life experiences, psychological characteristics, and misperceptions.

Most children develop savings habits (both good and bad) and form attitudes about savings in childhood from family and friends. People who are raised in a financially imprudent household are more likely to spend too much and save too little when they are adults. Similarly, adults are less likely to be good money managers if they were financially irresponsible when they were young. Indeed, one reason rich and lower-rich college graduates have greater retirement savings is that their parents are more likely to be college graduates who stressed the importance of savings.[46]

The assumption that greater willpower or financial literacy education are the cure-alls that would increase savings by LMI workers ignores the employment realities facing these workers and also ignores the reality that many LMI workers simply do not have the bandwidth to learn how to save when they are struggling to make ends meet on stagnant income. In fact, while financial illiteracy or bad personal characteristics (including a lack of willpower) can theoretically explain why Americans do not save, this theory does not explain why savings rates have changed dramatically since the 1980s, but the human brain has not. Household savings by LMI workers have plummeted since the 1980s because they simply do not earn enough to save. As long as LMI workers struggle to secure full-time and permanent jobs, they will struggle to save.

HELPING LMI WORKERS ACHIEVE THE MIDDLE-CLASS DREAM OF A STABLE RETIREMENT

The shift to self-funded retirement plans has thrown older and retired LMI workers into a perpetual state of financial instability and uncertainty. Some states offer retirement savings plans for workers whose employers do not provide private retirement savings plans, and Congress tucked provisions into the 2022 appropriations bill that should alleviate part of the retirement savings crisis. That is, the SECURE 2.0 legislation makes it easier for workers who have access to a DC plan to save for emergencies and for retirement by requiring most (but not all) employers to automatically enroll their workers in retirement savings plans. SECURE 2.0 also gives smaller businesses incentives to create a retirement plan and provides ways for student loan borrowers to simultaneously build retirement savings and reduce their educational debt. The legislation also makes it easier for part-time, gig, and contract workers to participate in DC plans.

SECURE 2.0 is welcome relief for workers whose employers offer a retirement plan. But it does not go far enough because Congress did not *require* businesses to offer a retirement savings plan for their workers. Moreover, although workers can make a one-time annual penalty-free withdrawal of $1,000 from their retirement accounts, Congress has done nothing to help LMI workers avoid the need to use their retirement savings to pay current expenses.[47] Rather than relying on faux choices or Band-Aid legislation to help workers save for retirement, federal leaders must take bolder and more concrete actions.

The final chapter of this book provides a sweeping "Middle Class New Deal" that could help restore financial stability to the American middle class. In the interim, political leaders should take smaller steps to help LMI workers amass retirement savings. At a minimum, businesses that offer a DC plan should be required to auto-enroll *all* workers—whether classified as employees or contractors—and require workers to opt *out of* rather than *into* coverage. Employers who offer DC plans and contribute to their employees' accounts also should be required to make significantly higher contributions to retirement accounts for their LMI workers relative to the percentage of income contributions they make for their rich and lower-rich workers. Finally, federal and state leaders should collaboratively find ways to help states create retirement plans that would auto-enroll workers in individual retirement accounts even if the worker's employer does not sponsor a retirement plan.[48]

My parents and other LMI families could accumulate regular and retirement savings because they had full-time permanent jobs that paid them enough to afford the markers of the middle class, including the ability to retire comfortably. As we have seen throughout this book, political leaders have abandoned LMI families and have done little to help them become and remain middle class. If political leaders want to help families become and remain middle class and believe in the American Dream, they must take bold actions. The next and final chapter of this book includes transformative proposals to change how this country educates, employs, and houses LMI families.

PART 4 Restoring the Middle Class

8 The Middle-Class New Deal

America's middle class is in crisis—quick fixes and empty promises will not save it. While fixing the crisis will not be easy, political leaders have shown us that they know how to respond to economic catastrophes quickly and decisively. After the Great Depression and World War II threatened to push the US economy to the brink of collapse, political leaders swiftly sprang into action. They saved the US economy by enacting multipronged and permanent legislation that helped LMI families buy homes, earn bachelor's degrees, and find jobs with wage and nonwage benefits. This bold and comprehensive legislative response saved the US economy and in the process created the American middle class.

More recently, when the country faced the dual existential crises of a health pandemic and a potential economic depression, political leaders at the local, state, and federal levels averted a financial catastrophe by enacting bold and sweeping legislation, including the Coronavirus Aid, Relief, and Economic Security (CARES) Act, the Coronavirus Response and Consolidated Appropriations Act, and the American Rescue Plan. These and other federal, state, and local legislative responses helped businesses remain afloat and ensured that, despite soaring unemployment rates during the early weeks of the COVID lockdowns, American families would not lose their homes or be forced to file for bankruptcy while scientists scrambled to develop the coronavirus vaccine.

Congressional leaders acted with urgency because they understood the severity of the Great Depression and the COVID pandemic, and because they believed they had a duty to help struggling American families. But while New Deal legislation was permanent, most COVID legislation was temporary and, for that reason, failed to fix the challenges LMI families have faced since at least the 1980s. Unlike the political leaders who helped create the middle class after the Depression and World War II, since the 1980s political leaders have not been willing to enact, or even propose, bold and audacious solutions to the economic challenges many Americans are facing.

Since the 1980s, America's political leaders have been too timid and too cautious. Rather than pass comprehensive legislation that could actually help restore the middle class, they instead have opted for milquetoast, piecemeal measures that address specific symptoms of financial instability but largely ignore the deeper systemic forces behind the middle-class crisis. As an example, one reason young LMI parents struggle financially is the childcare unaffordability crisis this country has had for decades. When COVID shuttered childcare facilities, workforces, and schools, we saw the role that affordable and accessible childcare plays in the lives of LMI families. COVID also exposed the role that K–12 schools play in providing crucial nonacademic services for families.

COVID exposed a "secret" that public education advocates and teachers have known for decades: K–12 public schools double as childcare and social services facilities that make it possible for LMI parents (especially mothers) to earn income. Though *all* parents struggled to work and care for their children during the strictest phases of the COVID shutdown, LMI parents were particularly hard hit and struggled the most because they were more likely to be (1) essential workers who could not work remotely or (2) employed in low-wage, temporary, part-time, and contracted jobs that did not provide paid leave. Though essential workers had the greatest need for childcare, when a limited number of childcare facilities started to reopen, LMI parents often could not access those facilities because of long waiting lists and because the facilities were forced to raise their prices to offset the additional expenses caused by

COVID-based health and safety measures. Moreover, these facilities were rarely in locations that allowed LMI parents to leave their children there and still get to work on time.[1]

Fortunately, some state and local leaders allocated funding to ensure essential workers had reliable childcare. But despite the universal recognition of the role accessible and affordable childcare plays in the lives of working LMI parents, and despite the need for a comprehensive plan to resolve the childcare crisis, COVID relief was temporary.[2] Likewise, despite the undisputed need for more accessible and affordable childcare, because childcare did not neatly fit into a narrow infrastructure "box," Congress refused to include permanent funding for childcare in the 2022 Infrastructure Investment and Jobs Act.[3]

The COVID childcare funding responded to a temporary crisis but did nothing to help LMI parents long term. Of course, quick or temporary fixes are better than no fixes at all. But if political leaders truly want to restore the middle class that they created more than a half century ago, they cannot continue to use narrow, semantic, pedantic, and siloed legislative approaches. They must be bold. They must create and enact innovative, comprehensive, nontraditional, and public-private solutions to restore our struggling and shrinking middle class. If they refuse to think and act big, as their predecessors did almost a century ago, this country may never again have a stable and financially secure middle class.

RETHINKING EDUCATION: FAMILY-FRIENDLY SCHOOL POLICIES

One thing federal, state, and local leaders must do before even attempting to reform K–12 systems to help LMI children become and remain middle class is to ensure that the proposals they consider are culturally appropriate and grounded in sound educational theories. To avoid enacting proposals that might appropriately respond to the educational needs of rich and lower-rich children, political leaders must consult with national, state, or local educators who have institutional competence and a proven track record of creating and implementing programs that help LMI students succeed academically.[4] In addition, political leaders must acknowledge that additional funding, alone, will not help restore America's middle class.

The proposals outlined in chapter 2 include additional funding to repair buildings in LMI neighborhoods and improve broadband access in those neighborhoods. More funding is a good start. At a minimum, additional funding would make it more likely that LMI children will be literate when they graduate from high school and that they receive an education that prepares them to succeed in college and be more competitive in job markets. Likewise, additional funding would ensure that LMI neighborhoods will be better maintained so that *no* child is forced to learn in the deplorable conditions described in the Detroit, Michigan, litigation. But while funding can help close some gaps, money alone cannot close the vast K–12 educational chasm between rich and lower-rich children and LMI children because of the shadow education of tutors, college consultants, and coaches that high-income children receive from their parents.

Not every LMI district or school will need or want to implement all the proposals in this and previous chapters, as there is no one-size-fits-all solution to the educational challenges LMI children and young adults are facing. Nonetheless, to ensure that LMI children have an equitable chance of becoming and remaining middle class, state and local educational leaders must adopt a New Deal Educational Plan that will *radically* reenvision and restructure how and when LMI children are educated. Leaders must also consider how to better utilize public-school buildings in LMI neighborhoods in ways that would improve the lives of children and their parents.[5]

To start, state and local educational leaders must revamp the antiquated public-school calendar. As discussed in chapter 2, when my parents were selecting elementary and middle schools for me and my brother in the 1970s, they had to synchronize their educational decisions with my father's work schedule, my mother's college class schedule, and the location of a safe (and free) after-school childcare facility (which ended up being a public library). LMI parents typically balance the need to earn income, care for young children, and remain involved in their children's school lives in private, in silence, and with little help from political leaders. Unlike rich and lower-rich parents, they do not have live-in nannies and often do not have paid child leave. Even assuming they are living with another adult, they rarely have the financial luxury to have one parent forego income and become a stay-at-home parent to take care of their children and LMI parents are less likely to have the option to work fully remotely.

To help LMI parents, state and local political and educational leaders must develop more parent-centric ways to use K–12 buildings before and after school and during the summer months. The New Deal Educational Plan starts from the premise that there is no sound pedagogical reason for the K–12 academic calendar to be based on a Monday–Friday (8:00 a.m. to 4:00 p.m.) schedule that starts around Labor Day and ends around Memorial Day. The New Deal Educational Plan must also acknowledge, as economists consistently report, that family-unfriendly policies that do not allow parents enough time to care for their children disproportionately harm lower-income families.[6]

The K–12 calendar is archaic and was created during an era when schoolchildren needed to work on their families' farms. Given how badly this schedule aligns with parents' typical work schedules, it is the antithesis of a *friendly* school policy. A New Deal Educational Plan would view school buildings in LMI neighborhoods as community-based service centers whose mission includes a commitment to providing both safe and affordable care for young children when K–12 schools are not in session and making it easier for parents to work yet remain involved in their children's learning.

To better align parents' workdays with children's school days, Congress should appropriate funding to give school districts or individual K–12 schools incentives to create or expand before- and after-school programs and full-day enrichment programs when schools are closed for in-service days or parent-teacher conferences. Educational experts should design the specific contours of this New Deal Educational Plan, but the 2019 Family Friendly Schools Act (FFSA)—introduced in Congress by then Senator Kamala Harris—provides a useful framework. The FFSA was designed to establish "family-friendly" school policies and to reenvision schools as "supplemental 21st century community learning centers." To that end, the FFSA proposed funding for grants to help school districts offer programs and activities when schools are closed but workplaces are not.[7]

The primary focus of K–12 schools should always be to educate children ages five to eighteen. Nonetheless, the New Deal Educational Plan should explicitly acknowledge what we all saw during the pandemic—that public buildings provide childcare services for LMI parents and make it possible for them to work or return to school to get training so they can get a better job.[8] Political leaders must ensure that school buildings continue to respond to the needs of the entire community and should recharacterize public schools as community service centers whose mission is to help solve the work-life challenges LMI parents face when they try to earn income, care for their children, and place their children in the best position to become and remain middle class.

Because it is unreasonable to expect overworked public school teachers, staff, and administrators to do everything by themselves, political leaders should find ways to use market mechanisms to increase onsite preschool or childcare services for parents and people who work in those schools. Creating public-private partnerships to provide on-site childcare services would do more than just help LMI parents better synchronize their work and childcare obligations through convenient and affordable childcare. Accessible and affordable childcare could also encourage teachers, counselors, or principals with young children to teach (or remain in) LMI schools rather than abandon those schools to take higher-paying jobs in more highly resourced schools. In addition to helping with teacher retention issues, public-private partnerships could also provide private funding to bolster the budgets of LMI schools.

A Harvard Business School report confirms that up to one-third of employees quit their jobs because of work-childcare imbalances. Similarly, the FFSA acknowledges that roughly 40 percent of workers do not have paid leave and more than half of families make job-related changes during the summer because they lack affordable and accessible childcare.[9] Whether the school operates the childcare facility solely or with a private partner, the childcare facilities should use sliding-scale fees to charge parents or educators and should also give the parents and educators of the children in LMI schools admissions preference. Because LMI schools receive little funding from parent- or booster-controlled organizations, operating auxiliary childcare would give LMI schools money to pay for additional technology or other educational benefits that rich and lower-rich schools routinely offer the children they educate.

In addition to before- or after-school childcare services, political leaders should also provide funding for school districts to provide robust full-day enrichment programs at K–12 schools in LMI neighborhoods when schools are not in session. This programming should be open to all students in the school district and should charge on a sliding-fee scale. The goal of full-day enrichment programs in the New Deal Educational Plan would be to provide academic and vocational programming to help narrow achievement gaps between LMI and rich and lower-rich children. Thus, at a minimum, children who participate in programming on days that schools are closed (e.g., on in-service days) should receive tutoring or homework help. Assuming the schools have stable broadband, programming should also offer students online access to academic or vocational enrichment activities offered at other schools or to test prep services offered by entities like Khan Academy and the College Board.

To further respond to the work-childcare imbalances LMI parents face, local school districts or schools must better utilize the summer months. Admittedly, students and teachers need breaks from school, and this country's educational policies have never assumed that children will attend school year-round. Nonetheless, the archaic eight- to nine-month academic calendar significantly burdens LMI parents who cannot afford long summer "vacation" breaks. Rich and lower-rich families typically use the summer break for vacations or to expose their young children to new extracurricular opportunities. For LMI families, summer break is more likely to be an unwelcome and inconvenient financial burden. While all parents typically scramble each spring to try to piece together safe and affordable supervision for their children during the summer, the summer break is particularly burdensome for LMI parents, as they typically have—at most—two weeks of vacation each year, if their jobs even provide this benefit.

The full-time teachers at LMI schools should not be forced to teach in the before/after, full-day, or summer programs, as many may want a break from teaching. Nonetheless, adding a summer "trimester" can be part of both the New Deal Educational Plan *and* a New Deal Employment Plan for middle-class school teachers. Many K–12 teachers already need to work during the summer, given the low wages teachers are paid, so the summer trimester would help teachers supplement their teaching salaries and work in an educational setting, rather than in the seasonal hospitality and leisure industries.

In addition to the burdens on parents that the long summer break creates, this extended break also often harms LMI students by exacerbating the loss of knowledge during the "summer slide." As discussed in more detail in chapter 2, one reason poor and non-White students have larger educational losses during the summer is that their parents cannot afford to give them an expensive shadow education of academic camps or enrichment activities. While most school districts offer summer classes, programming is typically remedial and designed to help students who failed to progress to the next class year. Not surprisingly, most LMI students who attend summer school view it as a punishment. This view is in sharp contrast to how summer school is viewed by rich and lower-rich families.

Rich and lower-rich parents enroll their older children in academic camps and enrichment activities to help narrow any potential summer educational losses and, rather than use summers to solely remediate, use them as a time for advancement. For example, some rich and lower-rich parents enroll their children in state-mandated nonacademic courses, like health or speech, during the summer to free up space in their children's regular school year schedule. This allows their children either to take *more* rigorous academic classes that will make them more competitive in the college application process or to take *fewer* academic classes to give them more time to study for their remaining classes. Some parents even use the summer to enroll their children in academic courses (online or in another school district) that they will take for credit in the regular school in the next school year. Having their children study course materials in advance gives the students a head start when they take the course for credit during the next academic year, which increases their chances of earning a higher grade.

Although public schools should continue to offer remedial classes during the summer, summer trimester programming should mainly be designed to give LMI students some of the benefits that rich and lower-rich students receive in their shadow education. Using a recent Bloomberg Philanthropies initiative as a model, the summer trimester aspect of the New Deal Educational Plan should offer a mix of college preparatory, career counseling, and vocational training activities. For example, during the summers, LMI students could research suitable colleges, complete college test preparation classes, prepare applications for financial aid, and—for those who do not intend to attend college—learn how to craft an effective résumé. Summer programming could also include teaching LMI students the "soft" work skills that would help them develop interpersonal, communication, and leadership talents that employers assert young workers lack.[10]

It is highly unlikely that programming during summer trimesters can fully replicate the benefits rich and lower-rich students receive from their expensive shadow educations. Moreover, summer trimester instructors are unlikely to have the same level of insider knowledge about college admission trends that expensive independent consultants have, particularly as many of them are former college admissions officers. To help close this information gap and ensure summer instructors provide accurate admissions advice and quality feedback on students' draft college essays or draft résumés, funding to the LMI schools should be enough to allow schools to send summer instructors to training sessions offered by organizations like the Independent Educational Consultants Association or the Higher Education Consultants Organization.

Even if summer trimester instructors cannot replicate the level of instruction expensive college consultants give rich and lower-rich children, LMI students often attend schools that have one (or no) guidance counselor, whereas the schools that rich and lower-rich students attend often have dedicated college and career or dual credit counselors in addition to the private consultants who often help them. Likewise, because elite schools are more likely to admit a rich college applicant even if LMI applicants have comparable test scores, the summer trimester alone cannot eradicate the benefits rich or lower-rich children receive *simply because they are rich.*[11] Still, while summer trimester programming might not fully replicate a parent-provided shadow education, a little is better than nothing for the LMI students who might otherwise receive *no* help with the college application process.

Just as coaches target LMI high school athletes who have the potential to earn an athletic scholarship to be student-athletes in college, teachers should target LMI students whose academic records suggest they would do well in college and explain the benefits of the summer programming. Despite the academic and vocational benefits summer programming can offer, older LMI high school students who need (or want) to earn money during the summer may resist going to school in the summer. To encourage LMI students and their parents to potentially forego summer earnings and go to school instead, school districts should explore private-sector partnerships that could provide LMI students with stipends comparable to the wages they would earn from a part-time job in the low-wage food services industry.

LMI students should not be paid to attend summer programming. Nonetheless, giving LMI students money to engage in an activity that will help them in the future can teach them the benefits of delayed gratification, which, as chapter 7 explained, may have the additional benefit of helping increase their long-term household savings. Although the public-private partnership should determine the criteria and payment period for the stipend program, schools or districts could look to proposals for baby bonds, which are designed to give high school graduates money that they can use to defray postsecondary educational expenses or start small businesses.[12]

Another way to encourage older high school students to attend the summer trimester would be to link their attendance to state-mandated testing graduation requirements. Some states have already started to relax or modify these high-stakes testing requirements, and most waived or delayed state-mandated tests during the COVID pandemic. States that moved away from these testing mandates often replaced the tests with performance assessments that require students to engage in activities or projects that demonstrate their understanding of the materials taught in the course. To give LMI students an additional incentive to participate in the summer trimester, state and federal educational leaders should permanently waive testing requirements for high school students who successfully complete summer programming activities and successfully complete some type of performance assessment.

THE NEW DEAL EMPLOYMENT PLAN

The US Department of Commerce warned in 2010 that American families will not realize their middle-class dreams if there is not a healthy economy and a private sector that offers workers decent jobs and benefits. The collective bargaining agreements organized labor negotiated with large

US businesses after the Depression and World War II forced employers to be accountable for their current workers' health needs and their retired workers' future income needs. Unlike the CEO of the first employer-provided pension plan, who treated the cost of providing a pension for retired workers as a necessary business expense, today's corporate executives no longer believe they have any obligation to help their workers realize their middle-class dreams. And as chapter 4 revealed, political leaders have allowed businesses to destroy decent jobs that offer decent wages.

The proposals outlined at the end of chapter 4, like revising Pell Grant rules to make noncredit skills training more affordable and giving businesses tax incentives to retrain workers rather than replace them with machines, would help LMI workers receive short-term job skills training and at least require businesses to think about the investments they make in their workers. But these proposals cannot force businesses to feel responsible for whether their employees can become or remain middle class. Moreover, things like skills training will not give LMI workers true job security if federal and state elected officials continue to express outright hostility to organized labor and continue to allow businesses to convert permanent and full-time jobs (with benefits) into temporary and part-time jobs.

Conservative politicians and business leaders regularly assert that the financial success of businesses will result in "trickle down" benefits to workers and give workers more "choices" in the workplace. Those assertions simply are not borne out by the realities LMI workers have faced since the 1980s, and trickle down policies are not the best way to protect or respect worker autonomy. Despite these hollow assertions of the importance of worker autonomy and choice, political leaders do not seem to care that the employment laws and policies they have enacted since the 1980s have encouraged businesses to maximize corporate profits at the expense of LMI workers. Likewise, they seem indifferent to the fact that their policies have fueled the financial instability and insecurity of LMI workers and caused their income and wealth to "trickle up" to the top 1 percent. While laws cannot force businesses to care about their workers, a bold New Deal Plan would force political leaders to stop enacting anti-worker legislation that prevents LMI workers from engaging in collective action to help them become and remain middle class.[13]

Making Workplace Choices Meaningful

Without union opposition, businesses have outsourced (either globally or domestically) and eliminated jobs, cut employees' benefits, and kept wages stagnant for all but the highest paid workers. Without a powerful, collective voice, workers cannot pressure businesses to offer job skills training or retraining and, with fewer unions, the apprenticeships that historically helped noncollege workers receive on-the-job training have diminished. Although some political leaders contend that unions repress worker "autonomy" and that giving workers more "choices" in their employment—such as whether to work part time or as an independent contractor—is the best path to financial stability, their actions belie their claims of genuine support for worker autonomy or choice.

A New Deal Employment Plan must consider bold and innovative policies to give workers more autonomy over their preferred mix of wage and nonwage compensation. Surveys conducted before and since the pandemic reveal that workers, particularly gig workers, would forgo cash to have money contributed to a retirement account. Similarly, women and younger workers often prefer nonwage compensation over higher wages, which is not new as mothers have historically elected to have lower-wage jobs (like being a public-school teacher) in exchange for shorter workdays or the ability to have summers off to care for their children. Likewise, some spouses will choose to be paid more as an independent contractor—even if the job does not provide benefits—if their spouse's job provides health insurance or other nonwage benefits for the family.[14]

After the pandemic, some employers (and most federal agencies, starting in 2025) required workers to return to work in person rather than have a partial or fully remote work arrangement. Political leaders who truly believe in choice and worker autonomy should ensure that the New Deal Employment Plan lets workers with caregiving duties for young children or older or disabled family members choose lower wages in exchange for having a permanent remote work arrangement.[15] Similarly, workers with adult or child caregiving responsibilities should have the option to choose between a shorter period of paid (or partially paid) leave. In addition, to help young adults reach the traditional milestones of adulthood (marriage and having children), political leaders should make sure that *all* workers have the right to some period of unpaid leave even if they work for a smaller business that is not required to offer twelve weeks of unpaid leave.[16]

Likewise, the New Deal Employment Plan should give LMI workers better access to nonwage compensation (including health insurance, retirement plans, and student loan forgiveness plans) that will help them avoid drowning themselves in medical and other debt and should also help them save more for retirement. For example, workers with educational debt (but no children) may prefer nonwage compensation like a student loan forgiveness program rather than a paid family leave benefit. Workers with no student loan debt who are struggling to find affordable housing may prefer nonwage compensation in the form of housing down payment assistance rather than a student loan forgiveness benefit. Or workers who are at risk of losing their jobs to automation may prefer lower wages in exchange for employer-provided on-the-job training, personal development courses, or tuition reimbursement benefits for skills training classes.

The laissez-faire labor market approach political leaders have adopted has not resulted in workers having more autonomy or better choices in the workplace. LMI workers are struggling, but it is not because they are choosing to have low-wage, part-time, temporary, or gig jobs. Likewise, workers are not choosing to drown themselves in medical debt by accepting a job that does not provide health insurance any more than older LMI workers are choosing to take jobs that do not help them save for retirement. Political leaders who genuinely believe in worker "choice" and "autonomy" must be willing to back up those hollow words with action. They must implement policies and programs that offer LMI workers meaningful opportunities that will help them become and remain middle class.

Tailoring Relief to the Most Needy

When Federal Reserve Chair Jerome H. Powell testified before the Senate Committee on Banking, Housing, and Urban Affairs in June 2020 about the burdens the pandemic placed on workers, he aptly observed that the burdens did not fall evenly on all workers and that "those least able to withstand the downturn have been affected most."[17] *All* LMI workers are struggling. Nonetheless, skills-based or workforce training programs should target the groups that are struggling the most in today's labor market.

Chapter 4 explained that non-White and noncollege LMI workers struggle more than other workers to find permanent, full-time jobs that pay them enough to become and remain middle class. Given persistently high long-term unemployment and underemployment rates for young Black and Latino men and rising unemployment rates for lower-income noncollege White men, the New Deal Employment Plan should target these groups. Moreover, just as political leaders need to tailor any New Deal Educational Plan to the needs of LMI (not rich or lower-rich) children, they also must ensure that a New Deal Employment Plan is devoid of exclusionary or racial biases.

The Trump administration and Elon Musk slashed the size of the federal workforce, even though these jobs are solidly middle-class jobs. Notwithstanding DOGE's near demolition of the federal workforce and recent Supreme Court decisions that denigrate the importance of having a diverse workforce, the New Deal Employment Plan should ensure that non-White LMI workers have equitable access to jobs that help them become and remain middle class. One way to preserve the middle-class workforce and also provide educational benefits for LMI children would be to create a more diverse K–12 educator pipeline in ways proposed in the Biden administration's *COVID-19 Handbook*.[18]

The handbook stresses the importance of increasing the supply of non-White teachers (particularly those who teach in schools that educate LMI children) and notes the troubling cultural, racial, and income "mismatch" between the income and race of teachers and the students they educate in LMI schools. The handbook documents the benefits that non-White students receive even if they only have one same-race teacher in their early grades. It emphasizes that having a diverse teaching staff increases the likelihood that the teachers who educate LMI students will actually believe that these students have the capacity to succeed academically. While the main goal of diversifying the workforce at schools in LMI neighborhoods would be to increase job opportunities for LMI and non-White educators, having teachers who believe in non-White and LMI students would dovetail with the New Deal Educational Plan's goal of closing K–12 achievement gaps and college attendance and graduation disparities.

Studies clearly and consistently show that "racial matching" (in which students have teachers of their race) and overall teacher diversity increases test scores and attendance and graduation rates for non-White students. For example, a recent study of full-time teachers in Austin, Texas, revealed that White teachers have higher expectations for White and Asian students than for Black or Latino students even when the students' actual academic abilities demonstrate otherwise. In addition to the plague of low expectations, studies repeatedly and clearly show that Black (in particular) and Latino students (particularly males) regardless of their income are disciplined at higher rates than White students. Given this, having a more diverse group of teachers can help narrow educational disparities, decrease K–12 expulsion and suspension rates for non-White males, help more LMI non-White adults have stable and secure jobs, and encourage LMI and non-White children to aspire to become a teacher, a quintessential middle-class profession.[19]

Schools or districts that create summer programming as part of a New Deal Education or Employment Program should recruit non-White and LMI instructors who are adjunct community college professors or guidance counselors, both of whom are chronically underpaid, or teachers who retired from LMI schools.[20] Regardless of their race, educators like these are more likely to have success teaching LMI and non-White students, and they also would be better equipped to provide culturally appropriate instruction. Schools/districts should also recruit LMI student teachers who are seeking certification but are not yet certified to teach full time.

Hiring LMI college students to work in schools in LMI neighborhoods during the regular school year or during the summer session would accomplish several goals. First, the money students earn could help defray college expenses and reduce the amount they need to borrow to attend college. This paid clinical teaching experience would also give them valuable on-the-job training and a professional reference they could use when they seek a permanent and full-time job. A fairly easy way to defray the school/district costs of hiring LMI college students would be for Congress to revise funding requirements for federal work-study rules and allow LMI college students who are majoring in education, English, or STEM fields to be paid with work-study funds if they teach in before- or after-school programs, in full-day enrichment programs, or during the summer trimester.

Policymakers should target LMI adults who face barriers that make it more likely that they will not be hired in jobs that pay them enough to become and remain middle class. For example, political leaders should increase funding for programs that educate or provide job training for currently or formerly incarcerated people. Though the Biden administration relaxed rules starting in the 2023–2024 school year, for over two decades the US Department of Education prevented incarcerated persons from using Pell Grants to pay for their education. Given the Trump administration's draconian cuts to the Department of Education and recently projected shortfalls to the Pell program, it is unclear whether the department will reverse the Biden rules. Even if the Biden changes are not reversed, more needs to be done given the overrepresentation of non-White (particularly Black and Latino) males in incarcerated populations.[21]

Creating and expanding the ways incarcerated (or formerly incarcerated) persons can obtain free (or low-cost) short- or longer-term job training and helping them earn bachelor's degrees should not be perceived as being "soft on crime" because educating current or formerly incarcerated people would provide benefits to more than just LMI households. Specifically, data collected by the Vera Institute repeatedly show that recidivism rates for incarcerated people who participate in postsecondary education programs are roughly 50 percent lower than rates for others and even lower for formerly incarcerated people with a bachelor's degree. Making it easier for formerly incarcerated workers to receive postsecondary training that makes them more employable will create a more diverse workforce and also have positive spillover effects in non-White neighborhoods, for non-White families, and for society overall.[22]

To further help formerly incarcerated young adults find ways to become and remain middle class, local policymakers should enact "ban the box" laws. Currently, businesses are allowed to ask job applicants to disclose arrest or conviction records when they apply for jobs. The New Deal Employment Plan should prohibit businesses from refusing to hire an applicant based on their criminal history *unless* (1) the applicant's arrest or conviction background disqualifies them from the job or (2) the business has conditionally offered the applicant a job. Finally, state political leaders should evaluate state licensing requirements to ensure that potential workers are not unreasonably banned from occupations simply because they served time in prison unless the applicant's background is disqualifying for reasons unrelated to their criminal conviction.

THE NEW DEAL HOUSING PLAN

Political leaders must design and implement a New Deal Housing Plan that broadly reenvisions the role that housing plays in the lives of LMI households. Because federal leaders have refused to build enough public housing for poor renters, and most local leaders are unwilling to eliminate exclusionary zoning laws, LMI families have faced a housing affordability crisis for decades. LMI families will always struggle to find affordable housing unless political leaders are willing to place the *needs* of those families above the *wishes* of rich and lower-rich households.

Political leaders must reject NIMBY demands for exclusionary zoning policies that prevent LMI workers from living in higher-opportunity neighborhoods and having their children attend high-performing public schools. Chapter 2 explained that rich and lower-rich resist attempts to have affordable housing built in their neighborhoods and will ruthlessly fight any change to their children's school attendance boundaries that would allow LMI children to attend their neighborhood school. Chapter 5 likewise showed that homeowners are willing to delegate their rights as property owners to their HOAs, knowing the HOA will enforce property restrictions that exclude LMI renters.

The Federal Reserve reported that in June 2025, homeownership unaffordability levels increased to their *highest level on record*.[23] The political inaction and complacence of political leaders has helped create and maintain economically (and often racially) segregated neighborhoods and communities that let rich and lower-rich people silo themselves in high-priced communities that are far away from LMI families. As for LMI workers, many live in overpriced rental housing that is far from where they work, which exacerbates the logistical challenges working parents with young children already face. Worse yet, because of skyrocketing home prices, "housing" for some LMI workers (including some retirees) in high-cost regions may be an RV or a car.[24]

Housing policies should no longer start from the premise that homeownership is the only desirable form of housing and the only housing form that should be subsidized *particularly* as homeownership is increasingly out of reach for young LMI workers. Instead, political leaders must enact laws and policies that reflect the reality that stable and affordable housing—whether owned or rented, and in whatever form—is now the marker of what it means to be a financially secure member of the middle class. Thus, in addition to implementing the more narrowly tailored proposals in chapter 5 (including repealing homeownership tax subsidies for people who buy large homes and enacting laws that make it easier to build smaller homes), political leaders must reevaluate all policies—even those that do not explicitly involve mortgages—to ensure that those policies are not exacerbating the affordable housing crisis.

Chapter 5 showed that one reason LMI families are pushed out of affordable housing is that political leaders often deem LMI neighborhoods to be blighted, and this causes these neighborhoods to be destroyed in urban renewal programs. One reason LMI neighborhoods are so vulnerable is that political leaders and city planners systematically neglect these neighborhoods, which then decreases the value of the neighborhoods in the politicians' eyes, and in the eyes of potential residents. There is a consistent pattern of public and private disinvestment in LMI communities and, unlike upper-income White neighborhoods, LMI and non-White neighborhoods receive subpar municipal services—like infrequent garbage collection and delayed street or electrical repairs.[25]

Urban renewal programs, inextricably tied to gentrification, mostly harm LMI households because, even if revitalization programs "succeed" in revitalizing a neighborhood and home values increase, property taxes increase as well. Higher home prices benefit existing homeowners but often make it harder for LMI renters to buy homes in gentrifying neighborhoods and increase the risk that LMI homeowners will be displaced from their homes because they cannot afford to pay the higher property taxes. Moreover, gentrification almost always increases the cost of renting properties in the revitalized areas, which increases the risk that existing LMI renters will be displaced and potential LMI renters will be priced out.

Even property owners who may not want to increase their rental prices or evict their renters often feel compelled to do so once their property taxes increase. And even if property owners in gentrifying neighborhoods do not immediately raise rents or sell, LMI renters face housing insecurity because owners resist offering long-term leases out of concern that they might need to impose a sudden rent increase if property taxes suddenly increase. As a result, even renters who are not immediately evicted find themselves pushed into precarious month-to-month agreements, which gives them little stability or protection from being displaced in the future. One way to encourage landlords in gentrifying neighborhoods to continue renting to LMI households despite higher property taxes would be for localities to provide tax abatements if they agree not to increase rental prices and agree to continue renting to LMI renters.[26]

In addition to these proposals and the more narrowly tailored housing proposals in chapter 6, political leaders must broadly reflect and draw on the lessons we learned about place and space during the 2020 COVID pandemic. Rather than assuming places can only be used for their original purposes, city leaders should reimagine how existing structures can be repurposed to create more affordable housing. Some cities had already started to engage in creative housing planning even before the pandemic, when they bought motels and converted them into longer-term housing to address the increase in the unhoused population. During the initial COVID shutdowns, however, virtually every structure in this country was used in ways that were unimaginable before March 2020.

Homes underwent the most dramatic transformation, as they went from being used primarily for shelter to being used as classrooms and workplaces. Commercial properties, convention centers, and hotels were also retrofitted and used as makeshift hospitals, shelters, or housing for essential workers. Other less noticeable shifts in the ways we viewed space involved changes to how restaurants, K–12 schools, and universities were used. For example, before we learned the meaning of *social distancing*, people went to restaurants to stay and eat a meal. COVID transformed restaurants from being places where people came to eat to places where people briefly gathered before they took prepared meals home. Additionally, public school buildings did not just educate children from 8:00 to 4:00 during the pandemic; they were transformed into food distribution centers or COVID testing and vaccination sites.

Even before the pandemic, dwindling college enrollments caused smaller four-year colleges to close, and this pattern continued during and after the pandemic. Rather than reopen shuttered colleges as educational institutions, many campuses are now being sold to private developers, and buildings that were dorms have been converted to apartments or other housing units. Likewise, cities like Austin, Texas, are turning schools that were shuttered because of declining enrollments into childcare centers, often using market mechanisms like public-private partnerships or partnerships with nonprofit organizations like the United Way. The "adaptive reuse" of real property continues to turn empty office towers in cities into apartment buildings or converts empty or abandoned buildings into satellite campuses for universities. Finally, religious organizations that owned large facilities but realized they were rarely used by their congregants due to dwindling church attendance formed "Yes, in God's Back Yard" (YIGBY) movements and placed affordable housing on religious properties.[27]

Local leaders should not simply view vacant or publicly owned lands as opportunities to sell land to the highest commercial purchaser. Instead, they should agree to sell the land only if the buyer agrees to include affordable housing in its development project.[28] To encourage larger-scale attempts to build affordable housing on vacant or underutilized public or private land, the Department of Housing and Urban Development and states should allocate additional funding to localities that partner with developers who agree to buy deteriorating housing, church properties, vacant malls, hotels, and dormitories and convert those structures into affordable housing. Cities should also explore the possibility of creating more affordable housing for sale through a community land trust (CLT).

CLTs or land banks are nonprofit private organizations or local government authorities that buy or use vacant land or delinquent properties and create permanent affordable single- or multifamily housing. CLTs typically retain ownership of the land, then sign long-term (often ninety-nine-year-year) leases with an LMI family, who purchases the house but not the land. A split ownership model that excludes the price of the land from the home purchase price makes homeownership affordable, particularly in areas that are experiencing rising prices or gentrifying, as the trust permanently owns the land. This joint ownership model also helps increase

LMI household wealth, as buyers receive their equity and a percentage of the home's appreciated value when they sell the house.[29]

Finally, the New Deal Housing Plan should encourage residents who live in neighborhoods with unkempt property to repair or revitalize those properties themselves. For example, the Memphis Mow to Own Program encourages existing residents (whether renters or homeowners) to invest in their own communities by letting them purchase vacant city- or county-owned lots at nominal prices as long as they agree to maintain the lot over a specified period. If residents can purchase the dilapidated properties in a program like Mow to Own and they have the ability to restore the properties, they could resell or rent the properties, both of which would increase their household savings/wealth.[30] To facilitate this, the New Deal Housing Plan also should give states or localities incentives to partner with local residents and community colleges to help existing residents rehabilitate abandoned or dilapidated housing in LMI neighborhoods.

For example, community colleges should receive incentives to create short-term and lower-cost certificates to teach LMI workers how to renovate their own homes or dilapidated properties that could be transferred to CLTs. Giving workers skills to rehabilitate or restore housing would accomplish several goals that are beneficial to LMI households. First, restoring rather than demolishing housing could increase the supply of affordable housing in LMI neighborhoods. Second, giving residents skills to renovate their own homes would help increase their household wealth.

THE NEW DEAL DEBT AND SAVINGS PLAN

During the pandemic, the US Department of Education paused student loan payments for borrowers who were struggling to repay those loans, and the Biden administration used executive orders after the pandemic to discharge student loan debt for certain borrowers.[31] Educational debt forgiveness programs are a good start, particularly for borrowers who attended for-profits, but this narrowly tailored form of debt relief will not help most LMI workers because most noncollege workers never attended college. Similarly, while some states created college savings programs for newborns to help LMI parents save for college, modest college savings accounts will not come close to leveling the playing field for LMI children, who must compete against rich and lower-rich children and the expansive and expensive shadow education those children have had since birth.[32]

While the New Deal Savings Plan should support programs that help LMI workers save, it should also help LMI children learn more about savings. For example, local schools that create a summer trimester can include programming that explains why it is important to have emergency and retirement savings and why it is risky to use high-cost AFS lenders. Summer programming should likewise stress that students should not drown themselves in educational debt to attend a for-profit institution and should, instead, attend a lower-cost public or nonprofit private institution. Summer financial literacy programming (or even full-day enrichment programming) in schools with stable broadband should (1) show students online Ted Talks that discuss basic financial information; (2) have students participate in activities like stock market games; (3) have students use educational video games like Financial Football; and (4) use online (or in-person) role-playing activities to help young people learn how to build credit, establish relationships with banks, or use online or mobile financial services.

The New Deal Savings Plan should also help K–12 children see the importance of savings and the risks of using AFS lenders. One way to do this would involve public-private partnerships with banks or community development financial institutions (CDFIs). For example, political leaders should give CDFIs or other lenders incentives to open bank branches in LMI high schools, as lenders like Capital One, Windsor Federal Savings, and A+ Federal Credit Union have already done in predominantly non-White high schools. If schools opt to give older students summer trimester stipends, they should require the students to deposit those funds in person in the high school bank branch (if there is one), as this could help normalize using banks and increase the students' trust in traditional banking.

A recent FDIC report that examined school bank branches shows the benefits of having convenient banking locations in lower-income neighborhoods. The report indicates that school bank branches yield benefits for K–12 students by increasing students' financial literacy, self-esteem, and school attendance rates. School bank branches typically offer accounts with no (or low) maintenance fees and allow customers to open accounts with low (often $1) balances. This type of banking service can help close credit gaps and meet the banking needs of historically neglected individuals and communities.[33]

Research shows that children who grow up in a neighborhood with banks are more likely to trust traditional financial institutions, be more financially literate, and build and manage credit better when they are adults. Thus, in addition to exposing LMI students to the importance of savings, having bank locations in LMI neighborhoods would reduce the number of banking deserts—communities that lack an independent bank or a branch of a larger bank—and give non-White families access to low-cost financial institutions that can offer small loans to cover emergency or unexpected expenses.[34]

The last two chapters of this book explain that one reason non-White LMI families have more debt, but less savings, is the existence of banking deserts. Banking deserts are disproportionately found in urban and rural areas, whose residents are almost always lower income. Although almost twenty-five thousand banks have closed in the last century throughout the United States, the National Community Reinvestment Coalition found that almost 25 percent of the bank branches that closed just before the pandemic were in LMI neighborhoods. For example, almost 10 percent of the Wells Fargo branches that existed in LMI communities in 2017 had closed by 2020, and more than 90 percent of the bank branches that shut down immediately after the Great Recession were located in LMI neighborhoods. Although Black-owned banks approve a higher percentage of loans to Black borrowers than other banks, they closed at twice the rate of the total number of banks in the 1980s, and there are now fewer than twenty-five Black-owned banks in this country.[35]

Because K–12 schools should be viewed as community-based service centers, high school bank branches should be staffed by lenders who have a proven track record of helping LMI and non-White customers navigate the mortgage, car, small business, and small dollar loan application process. Indeed, just as school districts should strive to hire summer trimester instructors who share the demographic characteristics (race and class) of the students at the LMI school, the bank branch should employ full-time adult workers who are (or were) LMI, as this would facilitate trust-building relationships with LMI customers. Banking employees who are (or were) LMI are more likely to understand their customers' savings behavior and can help improve their financial literacy.

Just as FinTech lenders may be more appealing to entrepreneurs because of their convenience and flexibility relative to traditional lenders, high school branch banking hours should have more convenient banking hours. At a minimum, bank branches should be open when the high schools are open and should include hours before and after the typical workday. Finally, in addition to providing safe and convenient traditional banking for residents in LMI neighborhoods, high school bank branches can also provide part-time jobs for older LMI students.[36] In addition to earning money, LMI students would receive on-the-job training that would make them more competitive for full-time jobs. Likewise, working in a professional setting could provide a job reference for students who do not intend to go to college.

DATA COLLECTION AND THE MIDDLE-CLASS NEW DEAL

Peter Drucker, a management theorist, is commonly attributed with saying what gets measured gets done. Political leaders will never be able to enact laws and policies that help LMI Americans become and remain middle class if they make decisions based on the unsubstantiated assertions of people who have no genuine interest in helping LMI families become financially stable. To ensure we preserve the American middle class, federal, state, and local policymakers must chronicle with legitimate data how existing laws and policies make it easier (or harder) for families to obtain the markers of the middle class and must design ways to help LMI families.

For example, if NIMBYs oppose a proposed affordable housing project and contend that the project will reduce their property values or increase density or parking problems, local planning or zoning boards should demand that the NIMBYs provide legitimate data to substantiate those assertions. A recent policy brief produced by the Center for Housing Policy for the John D. and Catherine T. MacArthur Foundation concluded that "the vast majority of studies" reached the conclusion that affordable housing does not depress neighboring property values in high-opportunity neighborhoods and may actually raise values. Because data likely would show that the NIMBY claims are specious, placing the burden on NIMBY neighbors to prove that the proposed housing will harm them should increase the approval rate for affordable housing proposals.[37]

Political leaders should also implement additional policies to detect when REIC actors are engaging in acts that make it harder for LMI families to become and remain middle class. The Biden administration adopted this approach in a day 1 executive order (since rescinded by the Trump administration) that created an equitable data working group. The rescinded EO declared that "for too many, the American Dream remains out of reach. Entrenched disparities in our laws and public policies, and in our public and private institutions, have often denied that equal opportunity to individuals and communities." Acknowledging that "assessments will better equip agencies to develop policies and programs that deliver resources and benefits equitably to all," the order required all federal agencies to "assess whether, and to what extent, its programs and policies perpetuate systemic barriers to opportunities and benefits for people of color and other underserved groups."[38]

One assessment that has historically detected racism in housing markets is matched-pair discrimination testing. To ensure that non-White renters have equitable access to housing and that REIC actors do not steer non-Whites away from White neighborhoods, political leaders must increase funding for these assessments and consider funding them using penalties assessed against entities that have engaged in discriminatory housing practices. Policymakers should also allocate funding to create a database of federal appraisal reports to better study, understand, and address real estate appraisal bias. The Biden administration created a task force (now disbanded) to examine and propose solutions to eliminate racial and ethnic biases in home valuations, and the task force forced the Federal Housing Finance Agency to release forty-seven million appraisal reports that disclosed that appraisers *continue* to place higher values on White-occupied homes and to devalue homes occupied by non-Whites.[39]

Congress should also include enhanced data collection requirements in the Community Reinvestment Act (CRA). The CRA, passed in 1977 to respond to redlining and other forms of mortgage lending discrimination, authorizes federal regulatory agencies to evaluate whether banks are meeting the needs of traditionally underserved LMI communities. While the CRA encourages banks to approve loans and gives them points for engaging in certain activities that serve LMI communities, it does not *require* banks to open branches in non-White neighborhoods. Although redlining remains illegal, reverse redlining and NIMBYism continue to make it harder for LMI families to buy homes and increase their household wealth. Given this, the CRA should be required to collect and report data on (1) banks' efforts to participate in programs that increase the supply of affordable housing, (2), which traditional banks have closed branches in non-White neighborhoods, and (3) banks' efforts to provide lower-cost banking services in LMI neighborhoods.[40]

While financial literacy programs can help LMI children and adults learn how to balance a budget, no conclusive data confirm that financial illiteracy is the primary reason LMI (particularly non-White) families disproportionately use high-cost AFS providers. To determine whether lending decisions push LMI and non-White families toward high-cost financial products that increase their debt and destroy their ability to save, Congress should require credit card companies and AFS providers to collect and disclose (1) data on the race and income of their customers and (2) credit approval and denial rates by race and income. Armed with better data, academic and governmental researchers, task forces, and entities like the Consumer Financial Protection Bureau can then determine whether those entities (or the algorithms they use) are targeting non-White borrowers and whether they are still engaging in discriminatory lending practices.

SAVING THE AMERICAN DREAM

The middle class, as we knew it, is gone. Until recently, most Americans called themselves middle class. They hoped and believed they would be okay if they just worked hard and played by the rules. They hoped and believed their children would have better lives than theirs. After decades of neglect by local, state, and federal leaders, many Americans have lost hope.

America's middle class is in crisis, and the crisis is having a particularly devastating effect on young LMI adults. They are struggling to become financially independent or to reach the traditional "milestones" of adulthood like having a permanent full-time job that pays them enough to pay their bills and save. They cannot find affordable homes to buy or even to rent. They are not getting married or starting families because they do not think they can afford to do so. Many know that if they are not born rich or lower rich, their only mobility may be downward.

America's leaders must help LMI families believe that the American Dream of upward mobility is still possible for them and their children. These leaders must give America's middle class reason to hope, and they must act now.

Notes

PROLOGUE: THE STRUGGLING MIDDLE CLASS

1. US Department of Commerce, *Middle Class in America.*

2. Pew Research Center, "Americans More Upbeat on the Economy; Biden's Job Rating Remains Very Low."

CHAPTER 1. THE BIRTH OF AMERICA'S MIDDLE CLASS

1. Some historians suggest that "middle-class" colonists instigated the American Revolution, and that we had a thriving middle class of small merchants and clerks in the mid-1800s or when White settlers were allowed to become landowners when the country seized Indian land. Putnam, *Our Kids: The American Dream in Crisis*, 32. Most social scientists conclude that we did not have a meaningful middle class in this country until the Great Depression. McNamee and Miller, *The Meritocracy Myth.*

2. I recounted aspects of my parents' path to the middle class and how they became homeowners in an earlier work. Dickerson, "Millennials, Affordable Housing and the Future of Homeownership."

3. My parents never cared whether we attended school with poor children. But because both attended racially segregated K–12 schools, and my father was

a public school teacher in Memphis, they knew that local and state political and educational leaders have always devalued and neglected the schools that primarily educate non-White and lower-income students. Throughout this chapter, I use the words *high* or *low* wealth, income, or poverty to refer to schools and neighborhoods. While I recognize that only parents earn income, the wealth or income of the students' parents largely determines how public schools are funded and how they are viewed by local and state educational leaders.

4. US Department of the Treasury, "The State of Labor Market Competition"; Chetty et al., "The Fading American Dream: Trends in Absolute Income Mobility Since 1940." Ironically, Black and Latino parents are generally more optimistic that their children will experience upward mobility than comparable White parents. Chetty et al., "Race and Economic Opportunity in the United States: An Intergenerational Perspective."

5. Suddath, "The Middle Class."

6. In his first televised presidential debate, Bill Clinton was asked whether his proposed tax increase would hurt the middle class. He responded that his plan would only tax families with incomes over $200,000. In vowing to protect the middle class, he labeled that group as people who earned no more than $52,000 (just over $100,000 in today's dollars). He also signaled that he understood the political significance and clout of the middle class during his 1992 acceptance speech for the nomination to be the Democratic candidate for president when he declared:

> [I]n the name of all those who do the work, pay the taxes, raise the kids and play by the rules—in the name of the hard-working Americans who make up our forgotten middle class, I proudly accept your nomination for Presidency of the United States.
>
> I am a product of that middle class. And when I am President you will be forgotten no more.

"Transcript of First TV Debate Among Bush, Clinton and Perot," *New York Times*; "Transcript of Speech by Clinton Accepting Democratic Nomination," *New York Times*.

7. US Department of Commerce, *Middle Class in America*, 25.

8. Paul Taylor et al., "Inside the Middle Class: Bad Times Hit the Good Life"; Pew Research Center, "Despite Recovery, Fewer Americans Identify as Middle Class."

9. Cashell, *Who Are the "Middle Class"?*

10. Wolfe, *One Nation, After All*, 2; Reeves et al., "Defining the Middle Class: Cash, Credentials, or Culture? " What it means to be middle class has changed since the 1980s. More than 70 percent of respondents polled in the 1990s felt that being a homeowner signified middle-class status, but only 41 percent of respondents believed that by 2016. Roper Center, "The Meaning of Middle Class."

11. US Department of Commerce, *Middle Class in America*, 25.

12. US Department of the Treasury, "State of Labor Market Competition."

13. Gabler, "The Secret Shame of Middle-Class Americans."

14. Reeves, "The Dangerous Separation of the American Upper Middle Class"; Reeves, *Dream Hoarders: How the American Upper Middle Class Is Leaving Everyone Else in the Dust, Why That Is a Problem, and What to Do About It.*

15. Treisman, "University of Texas, MIT and Others Announce Free Tuition for Some Undergraduates." Any numerical cutoff will exclude people who self-identify as middle class. Nonetheless, an underinclusive definition is preferable to a vague values-based definition that allows people who "feel" middle class to bemoan their inability to pay for their children to attend NYU or the University of Chicago rather than more moderately priced colleges like Virginia State or Middle Tennessee State University. Likewise, a rigid cutoff makes clear that renters who cannot afford to buy a home in places like Manhattan or San Diego or who cannot afford to vacation in Aspen are not middle class.

16. Homans, "Is the U.S. Ready for Post-Middle-Class Politics?"

17. Harkin, *Opening Statement, the Endangered Middle Class: Is the American Dream Slipping Out of Reach for American Families?*

18. Gonzalez, "What the Comfort Class Doesn't Get: People with Generational Wealth Control a Society That They Don't Understand." During legislative efforts to repeal the Affordable Care Act, Trump stated that young adults could get health insurance for $12 a year despite estimates that the actual cost was more than ten times that amount per month. Then, during the 2018–2019 government shutdown, neither he nor his cabinet officials understood why furloughed middle-class workers needed to visit food banks, sell personal items on eBay, or use crowdfunding web pages to pay their bills. Bloom, "President Trump Says Young People Pay $12 for Health Insurance." Likewise, during his colossally incompetent handling of the COVID-19 pandemic, Trump extolled the strength of the stock market, without realizing that few poor or middle-class Americans own stock. He also seemed unaware of the potentially catastrophic financial losses unemployed workers faced, including being sued for not making student loan payments or being evicted from their homes. Kochhar and Sechopoulos, "COVID-19 Pandemic Pinches Finances of America's Lower-and Middle-Income Families"; "Excerpts from the Times's Interview with Trump," *New York Times*; Parker and Fry, "More Than Half of U.S. Households Have Some Investment in the Stock Market."

19. Some of the angry (White) middle-class voters who support Trump are anxious because of financial insecurity. But it has been clear since 2016 that a significant portion of these voters also embrace a virulently racist and anti-Semitic ideology, the great replacement theory, that posits that Western "elites" (who purportedly are being manipulated by Jews) want to replace and disempower White Americans. Because race is often a part of their anxiety, they blame Democrats for letting companies send their jobs to China or Mexico and for letting undocumented or unqualified "DEI" workers take "their" jobs, and they

attack affirmative action and DEI initiatives on college campuses because they believe those programs make it harder for *them* to succeed. They support Trump because of his promise to turn back the clock and "Make America Great Again"—for them.

20. Muro and Kulkarni, "Voter Anger Explained—in One Chart."

CHAPTER 2. EDUCATING LOWER- AND MIDDLE-INCOME CHILDREN

1. Like most of Memphis, the neighborhood we lived in (Parkway Village) is now overwhelmingly Black. The junior high school we attended, which was high performing throughout the 1980s, was taken over by the State of Tennessee because of low student academic performance.

2. *Brown v. Board of Education of Topeka*, 347 U.S. 483, 493 (1954).

3. The Court explicitly ruled that education is not among the fundamental rights protected by the US Constitution. *San Antonio Indep. Sch. Dist. v. Rodriguez*, 411 U.S. 1, 35 (1973). The Court's later decision in *Students for Fair Admissions v. Harvard*, 600 U.S. 181 (2023), striking down affirmative action in the college admissions process, virtually guarantees that existing K–12 and college educational disparities will remain for the foreseeable future.

4. Even after *Brown*, some White parents tried to keep Black children from attending school with their children. Some removed their children from public schools and enrolled them in segregationist private academies. Communities like Emporia, Virginia, created smaller and less racially diverse public school districts, which state legislators condoned when they passed laws that authorized or even mandated that localities let White parents use vouchers to enroll their children in schools outside their home district. *Wright v. Council of City of Emporia*, 407 U.S. 451 (1972); Commission to Examine Racial Inequity in Virginia Law, *Interim Report*; Hankerson, "Decades After Brown Decision, Virginia Is Still Grappling with School Segregation."

5. Cahalan et al., *Indicators of Higher Education Equity in the United States: 2022 Historical Trend Report*, 29.

6. The federal government provides limited and targeted public school funding that typically is earmarked for specific students (like English-language learners, at-risk students, and students who receive special education services) or specific activities (like school lunches or technical or skills training). While conservative political leaders routinely target free school breakfast and lunch programs, the US Department of Agriculture's National School Lunch Program plays a critical role in the lives of LMI schoolchildren and their parents, as we saw during the COVID pandemic when Congress expanded the program to respond to food insecurity in LMI households.

7. Youngman, *A Good Tax: Legal and Policy Issues for the Property Tax in the United States*, 61–63; Griffith, "Who Pays the Tab for K–12 Education? How States Allocate Their Share of Education Costs."

8. Monarrez, "School Attendance Boundaries and the Segregation of Public Schools in the United States."

9. Wilson, "White Cities, White Schools."

10. Aiko and Gazley, "The Rise of School-Supporting Nonprofits"; Markovits, *The Meritocracy Trap: How America's Foundational Myth Feeds Inequality*, 127.

11. US Government Accountability Office, *Student Population Has Significantly Diversified, But Many Schools Remain Divided Along Racial, Ethnic, and Economic Lines*, 14–15, 19; Owens et al., "Trends in Racial/Ethnic and Economic School Segregation, 1991–2020."

12. 418 U.S. 717 (1974).

13. *Gary B. v. Snyder*, 329 F. Supp. 3d 344, 365, 366 (E.D. Mich. 2018).

14. *Gary B. v. Whitmer*, 957 F.3d 616, 646 (6th Cir. 2020).

15. *Gary B. v. Whitmer*, 957 F.3d at 646.

16. Chambers and LeBlanc, "Settlement for Detroit Literacy Lawsuit Eyes Nearly $100M in Funding."

17. Students who attend high-poverty schools also have higher incarceration rates and are more likely to live in racially and economically segregated neighborhoods when they are adults, which then consigns their children to the same type of educational experiences they had as children. Johnson, "Long-Run Impacts of School Desegregation & School Quality on Adult Attainments."

18. Keri Mitchell, "How Suburbanites Cheat Their Way Into Booker T. Washington." LMI parents who cannot find affordable housing in neighborhoods with high-performing schools sometimes use fake addresses for their children, though that places them at risk of being fined or jailed if their deception is detected.

19. Markovits, *The Meritocracy Trap*, 124–133 Putnam, *Our Kids: The American Dream in Crisis*, 178–179.

20. CLASP, *Course, Counselor, and Teacher Gaps: Addressing the College Readiness Challenge in High-Poverty High Schools*; Wolff and Carlson, "Who Chooses Donors? Submission and Funding Patterns on the Nation's Largest Education Crowdfunding Platform."

21. Chronically low wages, school shootings, and escalating attacks on public education have been driving teachers out of classrooms for decades. The fear of returning to potentially unsafe classrooms during COVID, combined with vitriolic right-wing attacks against teachers and librarians (who were cast as groomers who are indoctrinating students), increased the volume of educators who left the teaching profession. At the National Education Association's annual meeting in 2023, Biden's Secretary of Education Miquel Cardona lamented the onslaught of the intentional, toxic disrespect public schoolteachers are facing and quipped

that teachers went straight from "the pandemic to persecution." Cardona, "Time to End Toxic Disrespect."

22. Putnam, *Our Kids*, 165–166, 172–173; Garcia and Weiss, *The Teacher Shortage Is Real, Large, and Growing, and Worse Than We Thought.*

23. Avery et al., *A Review of the Role of College Counseling, Coaching, and Mentoring on Students' Postsecondary Outcomes*; CLASP, *Course, Counselor, and Teacher Gaps*, 9–10; Boushey, *Unbound: How Inequality Constricts Our Economy and What We Can Do About It*, 52.

24. Haberle and Tegeler, "Coordinated Action on School and Housing Integration: The Role of State Government"; Hasan and Kumar, "Digitization and Divergence: Online School Ratings and Segregation in America."

25. US Government Accountability Office, *Student Population Has Significantly Diversified.*

26. Rojas, "Louisiana Will Get a New City After a Yearslong Court Battle"; US Government Accountability Office, *Student Population Has Significantly Diversified*, 27.

27. Cooperstock, "The Demographics of School District Secession." Residents of communities that seek to secede from cities, like wealthy Buckhead residents seek to do in Atlanta, try to conceal what are often racist and elitist views by arguing that their desire to secede from school districts (or cities) is because they want to maintain the quality or character of their neighborhoods. Amy, "Georgia Senators Reject Buckhead Efforts to Leave Atlanta"; Rosen, "Atlanta's Controversial 'Cityhood' Movement."

28. Hailey, "Racial Preferences for Schools: Evidence from an Experiment with White, Black, Latinx, and Asian Parents and Students." Despite research showing that children who attend schools with students who are not poor and whose parents have college degrees perform better, rich, lower rich, and White parents often claim that they are concerned that having lower-income students attend their children's schools will hinder their children's academic performance. Empirical research does not support these claims. Students who transfer from high- to low-poverty schools receive significantly positive educational benefits with no resulting harm to the students who were already attending the low-poverty schools. Schwartz, *Housing Policy Is School Policy: Economically Integrative Housing Promotes Academic Success in Montgomery County, Maryland*; Putnam, *Our Kids*, 164–165.

29. Grigsby, "How Dallas ISD Plans to Stop the Suburban Cheaters Stealing Admission Slots at Prestigious Booker T."

30. The word *parenting* itself is a relatively new concept. Before the 1980s, parents simply raised (or reared) their children.

31. The shadow education that starts when children are young exacerbates income inequality and intergenerational mobility. Boushey, *Unbound*, 42–45. Research indicates that rich and lower-rich parents in states with wide income inequality gaps

spend more on "parenting" than in states where income inequality gaps are smaller. Schneider et al., "Income Inequality and Class Divides in Parental Investments."

32. Markovits, *The Meritocracy Trap*, 120; Putnam, *Our Kids*, 166–168.

33. Markovits, *Meritocracy Trap*, 130.

34. Park et al., "Inequality Beyond Standardized Tests: Trends in Extracurricular Activity Reporting in College Applications Across Race and Class"; Koller, *More Than Play: How Law, Policy, and Politics Shape American Youth Sports*.

35. Heise, "The Distribution of In-Person Public K-12 Education in the Time of COVID: An Empirical Perspective." LMI and non-White adults were more likely to be frontline essential workers, which is why LMI and non-White children were also disproportionately more likely to have parents or caregivers die from COVID. Pandemic-related disruptions, like the loss of a loved one, caused students who attended high-poverty schools to have alarming learning losses.

36. Mervosh et al., "What the Data Says About Pandemic School Closures, Four Years Later"; Kane and Reardon, "Parents Don't Understand How Far Behind Their Kids Are in School."

37. Tedeneke, "What Are 'Pandemic Pods,' and Why Are They a Problem for Diversity?"

38. Quinn and Polikoff, "Summer Learning Loss: What Is It, and What Can We Do About it?"

39. Markovits, *Meritocracy Trap*, 128–131.

40. These well-known disparities caused some universities to eliminate the early decision process. Giancola and Kahlenberg, *True Merit: Ensuring Our Brightest Students Have Access to Our Best Colleges and Universities*.

41. Golden and Purohit, "The Newest College Admissions Ploy: Paying to Make Your Teen a "Peer-Reviewed' Author."

42. Kasakove, "The College Admissions Scandal: Where Some of the Defendants Are Now."

43. Markovits, *Meritocracy Trap*, 124–133; Bivens et al., "It's Time for an Ambitious National Investment in America's Children: Investments in Early Childhood Care and Education Would Have Enormous Benefits for Children, Families, Society, and the Economy," 8.

44. US Department of Education, "U.S. Department of Education Releases *COVID-19 Handbook*, vol. 2, *Roadmap to Reopening Safely and Meeting All Students' Needs*."

45. As we saw during the initial COVID shutdowns, the digital divide combined with occupationally segregated workforces made it more likely that higher-income college graduates could safely work from home, while lower-wage, noncollege workers typically returned to face-to-face jobs or stopped working, particularly if they did not have stable broadband in their homes. Bergson-Shilcock and Taylor, *Closing the Digital Skill Divide*.

46. The White House, "The American Jobs Plan."

CHAPTER 3. EDUCATING LOWER- AND MIDDLE-INCOME ADULTS

1. Cahalan et al., *Indicators of Higher Education Equity*, 9.

2. Bound and Turner, "Going to War and Going to College: Did World War II and the G.I. Bill Increase Educational Attainment for Returning Veterans?," 1, 6–7; Draut, "The Growing College Gap," 91.

3. Turner and Bound, "Closing the Gap or Widening the Divide: The Effects of the G.I. Bill and World War II on the Educational Outcomes of Black Americans," 145, 151–152; Onkst, "'First a Negro . . . Incidentally a Veteran': Black World War Two Veterans and the G. I. Bill of Rights in the Deep South, 1944–1948." Now, roughly 25 percent of Black graduates with STEM degrees graduate from HBCUs. UNCF, "The Impact of HBCUs on Diversity in STEM Fields."

4. Like my father and most young Black adults until the 1970s, she also attended and graduated from an HBCU (Lane College) in Tennessee.

5. Until Congress enacted the Higher Education Act of 1965, student loan options were also limited. The early federal student loan program (created as part of the National Defense Education Act of 1958) primarily focused on graduate students in STEM fields.

6. Cahalan et al., *Indicators of Higher Education Equity*, 29; Saul, "College Enrollment Drops, Even as the Pandemic's Effects Ebb."

7. Aspen Institute Financial Security Program, "The State of Financial Security 2020: A Framework for Recovery and Resilience."

8. Mitchell et al., "State Higher Education Funding Cuts Have Pushed Costs to Students, Worsened Inequality"; Taylor et al., "Partisanship, White Racial Resentment, and State Support for Higher Education."

9. Engler, "Enrollment Algorithms Are Contributing to the Crises of Higher Education."

10. Similarly, one reason political leaders who claim to support middle class families often have no idea how little LMI workers are paid or how hard it is for these workers to make ends meet. For example, after former Speaker of the US House of Representatives Newt Gingrich was fined $300,000 in 1997 (roughly half a million dollars today) for violating House ethics rules, he bemoaned that he was a person "of limited means" who had to borrow money from then Senator Bob Dole to pay the fine. Gingrich proclaimed that he hoped his decision to pay the fine would not set a precedent that could destroy other "middle-class members" of the House. While Gingrich certainly lacked the wealth of his uberrich fellow congressmen like John Davison "Jay" Rockefeller IV or John (Forbes) Kerry, his $175,000 (roughly $297,000 in today's dollars) Speaker's salary was well above median household income in 1997 (roughly $37,000 at the time) and is more than double median household income now.

11. Dēmos, *When Congress Went to College: Comparing Tuition Then and Now at Our Elected Officials' Alma Maters.*

12. Ma et al., "Trends in College Pricing 2018," 4; Hanson, *Average Cost of Community College*; Hanson, *Average Cost of College by Year*.

13. Sullivan et al., "Stalling Dreams: How Student Debt Is Disrupting Life Chances and Widening the Racial Wealth Gap"; Carnevale and Smith, *Balancing Work and Learning: Implications for Low-Income Students*. The lower-paid service-sector jobs LMI students obtain to pay their college expenses are rarely career enhancing. In contrast, rich and lower-rich students are more likely to work in career-enhancing internships (even if unpaid) that align with their college major or field of study.

14. To use simple numbers: students who work thirty hours a week (far more than college advisers recommend) during a forty-week school year could earn up to $18,000 if they were paid $15/hour, or as little as $8,700 if they earned the federal minimum wage. This would be enough to pay for tuition costs for a certificate at a community college (and might be enough to pay for an associate's degree) and maybe a bachelor's degree at a regional public college. They would not earn enough, however, to pay for housing or childcare while they attended college. Under no reasonable economic model could students "work their way" through other colleges. That is, students would need to work more than forty hours a week (for more than fifty-three weeks) to pay tuition for a bachelor's degree at most four-year public universities. As they would need to work more than fifty hours each week to pay tuition at relatively inexpensive private universities, it would be impossible for students to work their way through the most expensive private universities in this country, where tuition and costs easily exceed $70,000.

15. Charron-Chénier et al., "A Pathway to Racial Equity: Student Debt Cancellation Policy Designs"; Houle and Addo, "Racial Disparities in Student Debt and the Reproduction of the Fragile Black Middle Class." A damning 2015 report coauthored by Dēmos and the Institute on Assets and Social Policy reveals that slightly more than half of Black households with outstanding student loan debt have *zero or negative* net worth, compared to only 32 percent of non-Black households with outstanding student loan debt. Huelsman, et al., "Less Debt, More Equity: Lowering Student Debt While Closing the Black-White Wealth Gap."

16. Fawcett and Fortin, "They Have Debt but No Degree: Could Loan Forgiveness Send Them Back to School?"; Sullivan et al., "Stalling Dreams," 9–10.

17. Sallie Mae, *How America Pays for College*, 30.

18. Sjoquist and Winters, "The Effects of State Merit Aid Programs on Attendance at Elite Colleges"; Cornwell et al., "The Enrollment Effects of Merit-Based Financial Aid: Evidence from Georgia's HOPE Program."

19. Woo and Choy, "Merit Aid for Undergraduates: Trends from 1995–96 to 2007–08," 6, 9; Kelly and Adam, "Trends in Undergraduate Nonfederal Grant and Scholarship Aid: Selected Years, 2003–04 to 2015–16," 40.

20. Draut, "Growing College Gap," 93–94.

21. Markovits, *Meritocracy Trap*, 27.

22. Lieber, "Colleges Know How Much You're Willing to Pay." Ironically, when state flagship colleges and universities admitted more out-of-state students, legislators in some of those states further decreased support and funding for those institutions. Klein, *The Great Student Swap.*

23. Burd, *Undermining Pell*, vol. 2, *How Colleges' Pursuit of Prestige and Revenue Is Hurting Low-Income* Students, 4, 10; Lowry, "The Effects of State Higher Education Policies and Institutions on Access by Economically Disadvantaged Students."

24. Harris, "How Popular Merit College Scholarships Have Perpetuated Racial Inequalities"; Sjoquist and Winters, "Effects of State Merit Aid Programs," 529–530.

25. Carville and Greenberg, *It's the Middle Class, Stupid!*; Lieber, "Another Admissions Advantage for the Affluent: Just Pay Full Price"; Rosalsky. "Affirmative Action for Rich Kids: It's More Than Just Legacy Admissions."

26. Jaschik, "Feeling the Heat: The 2013 Survey of College and University Admissions Directors."

27. Douglas-Gabriel, "More Elite Universities Settle Suit over Alleged 'Price-Fixing' Aid Policies: Lawsuit Claims Schools Formed a Cartel That Limited Financial Aid."

28. These "middle-class" financial aid initiatives still leave some LMI students with funding gaps because the aid package often does not cover the full cost of housing or their living expenses. Holpuch, "Which Colleges Offer Free Tuition?"

29. Sallie Mae, *How America Pays for College*, 26.

30. Calahan et al., *Indicators of Higher Education Equity*; Irwin et al., *Report on the Condition of Education 2024*; Saul, "College Enrollment Drops."

31. Lippman et al., *Parent Expectations and Planning for College*, iii; Baum and Steele, *Who Goes to Graduate School and Who Succeeds?*

32. The University of Pennsylvania's Pell Institute prepared a study in 2022 that also showed a significant gap in college enrollment rates based on income and race. Roughly 30 percent of White students belonged to households in the highest income quartile, compared to Latino (12%) and Black (11%) young adults. College enrollment rates for low-income high school graduates were lower across all racial groups—58 percent for White students, 49 percent for Black students, and 63 percent for Latino students—when compared to their peers in the highest income quartile, where enrollment rates were 80 percent for White students, 79 percent for Black students, and 69 percent for Latino students. Cahalan et al., *Indicators of Higher Education Equity*, 57, 67.

33. Roksa and Kinsley, "The Role of Family Support in Facilitating Academic Success of Low-Income Students"; Horowitz and Graf, "Most U.S. Teens See Anxiety and Depression as a Major Problem Among Their Peers."

34. LoGerfo, *The High School Longitudinal Study: A First Look at Fall 2009 Ninth-Graders*, 12; Lippman et al., *Parent Expectations*, 10; Kuh et al., *What Matters to Student Success: A Review of the Literature*, 22–25.

35. "Current Term Enrollment Estimates" reports prepared by the National Student Clearinghouse Research Center (NSCRC) show that while enrollments have returned to pre-COVID levels for almost all groups, the pandemic declines exacerbated the enrollment and attendance gaps between non-White and poor students (particularly males) compared to White, rich, or lower-rich students (particularly females). National Student Clearinghouse Research Center, "Current Term Enrollment Estimates." Enrollment rates at public flagship and elite private colleges quickly increased postpandemic, much faster than rates at regional four-year colleges and community colleges, who struggled to entice their students to return to their campuses.

36. Katznelson, *When Affirmative Action Was White: An Untold History of Racial Inequality in Twentieth-Century America*, 138–141; *Students for Fair Admissions v. Harvard*, 600 U.S. 181 (2023); US President, "Executive Order 14099: Ending Illegal Discrimination and Restoring Merit-Based Opportunity."

37. Hanson, "College Enrollment & Student Demographic Statistics."

38. For example, 70 percent of adults with at least one parent with a bachelor's degree also have a bachelor's degree, compared to 26 percent of their first-generation peers. Fry, "First-Generation College Graduates Lag Behind Their Peers on Key Economic Outcomes"; Board of Governors of the Federal Reserve System, *Economic Well-Being of US Households in 2023*"; Boushey, *Unbound*, 52.

39. Carnevale, et al., *Born to Win, Schooled to Lose: Why Equally Talented Students Don't Get Equal Chances to Be All They Can Be*, 5, 25.

40. Hanson, "College Graduation Statistics." Students from the top quartile of family income account for 41 percent of bachelor's degree recipients, while students from the bottom income quartile make up just 11 percent of the students who earn a bachelor's degree. Chetty et al., "Mobility Report Cards: The Role of Colleges in Intergenerational Mobility."

41. Neumann and Fitzpayne, "Building a Lifelong Learning System: A Roadmap for Cities," 13; Ma and Baum, "Trends in Community Colleges: Enrollment, Prices, Student Debt, and Completion," 7–8.

42 Carnevale et al., *Born to Win, Schooled to Lose*; Carnevale et al., *Our Separate & Unequal Public Colleges: How Public Colleges Reinforce White Racial Privilege and Marginalize Black and Latino Students*, 1–3.

43. Nathenson, et al., "Moving Upward and Onward: Income Mobility at Historically Black Colleges and Universities"; Bevins et al., "How HBCUs Can Accelerate Black Economic Mobility."

44. Rothwell, "Black Students at Top Colleges: Exceptions, Not the Rule."

45. Cottom, *Lower Ed: The Troubling Rise of For-Profit Colleges in the New Economy*.

46. Cottom, *Lower Ed*, 31–36. After the Great Recession, a new crop of (unaccredited) private companies—including StraighterLine, Sophia, and Saylor Academy—entered the for-profit space and allowed students to "complete"

academic classes in a few days. Despite these promises, students found they could not transfer their credits or could only transfer them to another for-profit. Eaton and Swaak, "Thousands of Students Take Courses Through Unaccredited Private Companies: Here's a Look into One of Them."

47. Holland and DeLuca, "'Why Wait Years to Become Something?': Low-Income Youth and the Costly Career Search in For-Profit Trade Schools"; Cellini and Turner, "Gainfully Employed?," 1, 6, 16, 26.

48. Enrollments increased by roughly 33 percent at private nonprofits but only 24 percent at public colleges from roughly 2000 to 2018. In 2010, students at for-profits reached a high of 10 percent of total college enrollments. National Center for Education Statistics, "Table 303.25, Total Fall Enrollment in Degree-Granting Postsecondary Institutions, by Control and Level of Institution: 1970 through 2018"; Cahalan, *Indicators of Higher Education Equity*, 18.

49. Smith et al., "Promising or Predatory? Online Education in Non-Profit and For-Profit Universities."

50. Cottom, *Lower Ed*, 99.

51. Marto, "Who Applies to and Enrolls at Selective Colleges?"

52. For example, of students who attend elite private and public colleges and universities, roughly 70 percent are from families in the top earnings quintile, 15 percent are from the richest 1 percent of families. but less than 2 percent are from the bottom quartile. The percentage of Black (5%) and Latino (7%) college students who attend the most selective colleges is smaller combined than the percentage of White (17%) students who attend selective colleges. Lawyers for Civil Rights: Boston, "Federal Civil Rights Complaint Challenges Harvard's Legacy Admissions."

53. Cahalan, *Indicators of Higher Education Equity*, 76, 113; Hanson, "College Enrollment & Student Demographic Statistics."

54 Addo, "At the Intersection of Race, Occupational Status, and Middle-Class Attainment in Young Adulthood."

55. Bleemer and Quincy, *Changes in the College Mobility Pipeline Since 1900*. College graduates from poor families earn more than their noncollege peers. Still, the college premium that workers who are born poor receive relative to their noncollege peers is smaller than the college premium rich college workers receive relative to rich noncollege workers. Hershbein, "A College Degree Is Worth Less If You Are Raised Poor."

56. Bergson-Shilcock and Taylor, *Closing the Digital Skill Divide*. Reports from the Georgetown University Center on Education and the Workforce emphasize that LMI young adults struggle to find full-time and permanent jobs that pay them enough to become and remain middle class because of their K–12 and postsecondary educational deficits, lack of access to work-based learning like apprenticeships or paid internships, and little to no career counseling. Carnevale et al., *How Limits to Educational Affordability, Work-Based Learning, and Career Counseling Impede Progress Toward Good Jobs*.

57. Hoachlander et al., *Vocational Education in the United States: 1969–1990*, 24; Liu et al., *Public High School Students' Career and Technical Education Coursetaking: 1992–2013*, 3, 5-6; US Department of Education, *National Assessment of Career and Technical Education: Final Report to Congress*.

58. Holzer and Baum, "Overcoming the Stigma of Voc Ed in Today's CTE."

59. University of Northern Iowa, "Materials Science and Engineering"; Tennessee College of Applied Technology Northwest, "TCAT Northwest and UT Martin Articulation Agreement."

60. Irwin et al., *Report on the Condition of Education 2024*, at 3.

CHAPTER 4. FINDING A (GOOD) JOB

1. Stiglitz, *The Price of Inequality: How Today's Divided Society Endangers Our Future*, xiv.

2. When my father realized my parents would need more money to pay their bills, like today's young entrepreneurs, he saw that he could create a side business from his part-time job. That is, each day he watched as the plant discarded eggs and giblets that Campbell's Soup did not use to make soup. He saw value in those discarded items, so he collected the discards, took some home for my mother to cook, and sold the rest to families in the Black Nashville community.

3. Goldin and Margo, "The Great Compression: The Wage Structure in the United States at Mid-Century." Because of the social connotations associated with the middle class, manual laborers like plumbers or construction workers have never been viewed as middle class, though many earn more than teachers do now.

4. Howell and Kalleberg, "Declining Job Quality in the United States: Explanations and Evidence."

5. Ruckelshaus and Leberstein, "Manufacturing Low Pay: Declining Wages in the Jobs That Built America's Middle Class."

6. Even when employment rates have increased for noncollege workers, STEM jobs have proliferated and, since the 1980s, have at times accounted for 75 percent of job growth. US Government Accountability Office, "Which Workers Are the Most Affected by Automation."

7. US Department of the Treasury, "The State of Labor Market Competition"; Greenhouse, *Beaten Down, Worked Up: The Past, Present, and Future of American Labor*," 39–40. The United Automobile Workers, the most powerful union in the United States during the Great Compression, went on an almost four-month strike at General Motors, which at that time was one of the largest US businesses. The strike itself yielded no major gains for workers, but General Motors ultimately agreed to increase wage and nonwage compensation for its employees to avoid future walkouts.

8. A strong labor voice in the Department of Labor was largely absent until 2021, when President Biden nominated the former leader of a building and construction trades organization in Boston (Marty Walsh) as his labor secretary.

9. For example, some southern politicians used racist scare tactics to discourage workers from joining unions, suggesting that "White women and White men will be forced into organizations with Black African apes who they will have to call brother or lose their jobs." Mirer, "Right-to-Work Laws: History and Fightback," 30, 32.

10. *Janus v. American Federation of State, County, and Municipal Employees, Council 31*, 138 S. Ct. 2448 (2018).

11. US Department of the Treasury, "Labor Unions and the Middle Class."

12. Since the 1980s, political leaders have routinely pitted public unionized workers against private nonunionized workers and insinuated that union workers (*particularly* labor leaders) weaponize collective bargaining to force taxpayers to pay public workers more than private nonunionized workers receive.

13. DeSilver and Schaeffer, "The State of the U.S. Postal Service in 8 Charts."

14. Mishel, "The Enormous Impact of Eroded Collective Bargaining on Wages"; Shierholz, "Strengthening Labor Standards and Institutions to Promote Wage Growth." While noncompetes have long been the norm in the high-wage, high-tech industry, businesses now force low-wage fast-food workers, yoga instructors, construction workers, and hair stylists to agree to these clauses. Rosenfeld, *You're Paid What You're Worth: And Other Myths of the Modern Economy*, 74–79.

15. Lowrey, "Where Did the Government Jobs Go?"; Kiersz, "The Percentage of Workers in Government Is at a 54-Year Low." Public K–12 school districts had not recovered from worker shortages even after the pandemic. Unions could not convince local leaders to increase pay for teachers even though teachers were being demonized and cast as groomers by local and state officials.

16. US Department of the Treasury, "State of Labor Market Competition"; Van Green, "Majorities of Adults See Decline of Union Membership as Bad for the U.S. and Working People"; McCarthy, "U.S. Approval of Labor Unions at Highest Point Since 1965."

17. Airlines asked unionized airline workers to accept wage and nonwage concessions after 9/11, and workers (wrongly) assumed that they would receive their fair share of the companies' profits in exchange for sacrificing out of a sense of patriotic duty. Once the airlines rebounded, however, corporate leaders used their cash reserves to increase shareholder earnings by buying back corporate stock rather than restoring wages and benefits for workers.

18. Emanuel, "Some Health Care Workers Say They Are 'Forgotten' in COVID-19 Vaccination Plans"; Dean et al., "Mortality Rates from COVID-19 Are Lower in Unionized Nursing Homes."

19. US Department of the Treasury, "State of Labor Market Competition"; Farber et al., "Unions and Inequality over the Twentieth Century: New Evidence from Survey Data."

20. Howell, "From Decent to Lousy Jobs: New Evidence on the Decline in American Job Quality, 1979–2017"; Ravikumar and Shao, "Labor Compensation and Labor Productivity: Recent Recoveries and the Long-Term Trend."

21. Once income for corporate executives was indexed to stock prices, and businesses used excess profits for stock buybacks, corporate leaders had even more incentives to reduce labor costs and maximize corporate profits. Rosenfeld, *You're Paid What You're Worth*; Mishel and Kandra, "CEO Pay Has Skyrocked 1,322% Since 1978."

22. Gould and Kandra, "Inequality in Annual Earnings Worsens in 2021: Top 1% of Earners Get a Larger Share of the Earnings Pie While the Bottom 90% Lose Ground"; Mather and Jarosz, "The Demography of Inequality in the United States,"5.

23. Rosenfeld, et al., "Union Decline Lowers Wages of Nonunion Workers: The Overlooked Reason Why Wages are Stuck and Inequality Is Growing"; Charles, Hurst, and Schwartz, "The Transformation of Manufacturing," 1–2, 10; Carnevale et al., *America's Divided Recovery: College Haves and Have Nots*, 2, 4, 15, 33.

24. US Department of the Treasury, "State of Labor Market Competition"; Schmitt and Zipperer, "The Decline in African-American Representation in Unions and Manufacturing, 1979–2007." The overall share of Black manufacturing workers dropped from 23.9 percent in 1979 to 9.8 percent just before the start of the 2007–2009 Recession, while declines for White manufacturing workers were smaller (dropping from 23.5 percent to 11.7 percent). Charles et al., "Transformation of Manufacturing." From 2010 to 2016, wages for Black union members were 41.5 percent larger than wages for their nonunion member counterparts, whereas the gap for White union versus nonunion workers was only 26.3 percent. Weller and Madland, "Union Membership Narrows the Racial Wealth Gap for Families of Color.

25. Bucknor, *Black Workers, Unions, and Inequality*, 3; Congressional Budget Office, "Comparing the Compensation of Federal and Private-Sector Employees, 2011 to 2015"; Landry, *The New Black Middle Class*, 70, 119, 121, 212; Cooper and Wolfe, "Cuts to the State and Local Public Sector Will Disproportionately Harm Women and Black Workers."

26. Rosenfeld and Kleykamp, "Organized Labor and Racial Wage Inequality in the United States," 2, 4–5; Greenhouse, *Beaten Down*; Frymer and Grumbach, "Labor Unions and White Racial Politics."

27. National Employment Law Project, "Big Business, Corporate Profits, and the Minimum Wage Data Brief." As an example, "personal services" is a worker-driven sector that largely did not exist before the 1980s and includes jobs like in-home chefs, dog walkers, massage therapists, and personal trainers. These jobs

offer workers *flexibility* and often high hourly rates, but as we saw during the COVID recession, these jobs provide little job *stability* when the people who use these services typically are higher-income families who reduce their discretionary spending during recessionary periods.

28. Federal Reserve Bank of St. Louis, *Employment Level—Part-Time for Economic Reasons, All Industries*; Auray, et al., "Multiple Jobholders," 1–2; Bureau of Labor Statistics, "Multiple Jobholders by Selected Characteristics 2018–2019."

29. Katz and Krueger, "The Rise and Nature of Alternative-Work Arrangements in the United States," 1; Weber, "Some of the World's Largest Employers No Longer Sell Things, They Rent Workers."

30. Zipperer et al, "National Survey of Gig Workers Paints a Picture of Poor Working Conditions, Low Pay"; Pew Research Center, "The State of Gig Work in 2021."

31. The domestic outsourcing practices that companies like Google and Nissan used before the pandemic illustrate just how dramatically businesses have transformed labor markets. A 2019 report disclosed that more than half of Google's global workforce *and nearly 70 percent* of the workforce at Nissan's factory in Smyrna, Tennessee, were lower-wage temporary or contracted workers who were paid less than permanent workers who performed the same tasks. These workers received virtually no nonwage compensation. Wakabayashi, "Google's Shadow Work Force: Temps Who Outnumber Full-Time Employees."

32. During the initial COVID shutdown, some contingent faculty reported that they were expected to absorb the costs to move their courses online or buy computers and web cameras, pay for technical support, and even pay for their own Zoom accounts. Ross, "A Snapshot of Pandemic Life for Adjunct Faculty Members."

33. Autor et al., "The Unexpected Compression: Competition at Work in the Low Wage Labor Market"; US Department of Labor, Bureau of Labor Statistics, *Occupational Outlook Handbook*.

34. Peetz et al., "The Role of Income Volatility and Perceived Locus of Control in Financial Planning Decisions"; Kelly and Holian, "Education, Employment, and Earnings: Expectations of 2009 Ninth-Graders in 2016," 7.

35. US Department of Labor, Bureau of Labor Statistics, "Employment Projections: Earnings and Unemployment Rates by Educational Attainment, 2024"; National Center for Education Statistics, "Employment and Unemployment Rates by Educational Attainment."

36. Noncollege Black and Latino mothers had the highest job losses during the pandemic and, relative to men, it took them longer to recover from the pandemic. Institute for Women's Policy Research, "Women at Work: Five Years Since the Start of the COVID-19 Pandemic."

37. Federal Reserve Bank of St. Louis, *Unemployment Rate—Bachelor's Degree and Higher, 25 Yrs. & Over and High School Graduates, No College, 25 Yrs. & Over.*

38. Truesdale, "Better Jobs, Longer Working Lives: Proposals to Improve the Low-Wage Labor Market for Older Workers"; Weil, *The Fissured Workplace.*

39. Shierholz, "Strengthening Labor Standards and Institutions"; Manyika et al., *Independent Work: Choice, Necessity, and the Gig Economy.* COVID was one of the first times gig workers and independent contractors received benefits typically reserved for statutory workers, as the Pandemic Unemployment Assistance (PUA) program made them eligible for unemployment compensation. National Employment Law Project, "Unemployment Insurance Provisions in the Coronavirus Aid, Relief, and Economic Security (CARES) Act."

40. The Obama administration's Trade Adjustment Assistance Community College and Career Training grant program and the Biden administration's Inflation Reduction Act and bipartisan infrastructure law tried to increase the number and range of apprenticeship options and workforce development training, particularly in areas like clean energy and wind turbine repair and assembly. US Department of Labor, "Trade Adjustment Assistance Community College and Career Training"; Camardelle, "Five Charts to Understand Black Registered Apprentices in the United States."

41. Hegewisch, "Breaking Down Occupational Segregation Key to Women's Economic Success."

42. Zessoules and Ajilore, "Wage Gaps and Outcomes in Apprenticeship Programs."

43. US Department of the Treasury, "State of Labor Market Competition." Some employers insist on noncompete clauses even for fast-food workers or seasonal part-time workers, like summer camp counselors. Greenhouse, *Beaten Down*, 8.

44. US Department of Labor, Wage and Hour Division, "Fact Sheet #71: Internship Programs Under the Fair Labor Standards Act"; Agrawal, "College Internships Matter More Than Ever—but Not Everyone Can Get One"; Laurison and Friedman, *The Class Ceiling: Why It Pays to Be Privileged*; Hora, "Unpaid Internships and Inequality: A Review of the Data and Recommendations for Research, Policy, and Practice."

45. The trade school my mother attended in the 1950s trained her to be a secretary in less than one year.

46. Eaton et al., "The Financialization of US Higher Education"; Looney and Yannelis, "A Crisis in Student Loans? How Changes in the Characteristics of Borrowers and in the Institutions They Attended Contributed to Rising Loan Defaults."

47. Strohl et al., *The Great Misalignment: Addressing the Mismatch Between the Supply of Certificates and Associate's Degrees and the Future Demand for Workers in 565 US Labor Markets.*

48. York, "Tax Treatment of Worker Training"; Powell, "Getting Back to a Strong Labor Market"; Fife et al., "Supporting Employer-Provided Training," 5.

CHAPTER 5. FINDING AFFORDABLE HOUSING

1. Martinez, *Statement, Increasing Minority Homeownership, and Expanding Homeownership to All Who Wish to Attain It.*

2. Dickerson, *Homeownership and America's Financial Underclass*, 39; Getter, *Introduction to Financial Services: The Housing Finance System.*

3. FHA policies required lenders and appraisers to confirm the borrower's "characteristics" (including race) and disclose whether the borrower intended to buy a home in a racially mixed neighborhood or an all-White neighborhood that was at risk of being "infiltrated" or "invaded" by Blacks or immigrants. Michney and Winling, "New Perspectives on New Deal Housing Policy: Explicating and Mapping HOLC Loans to African Americans," 155; Dickerson, *Homeownership*, 146.

4. Estimates are that only 2 percent of FHA-insured mortgage loans went to non-White homebuyers during the first thirty-five years of the program. Taylor, *Race for Profit: How Banks and the Real Estate Industry Undermined Black Homeownership*, 34–35. While having Black homeowners would deem a neighborhood unsafe, if a Black domestic servant lived in the home, White neighborhoods would continue to be deemed safe. White homeowners "would accept black servants living in their homes or in building in the alleys behind their homes but not African Americans who could afford to live on the main streets of their neighborhoods." Herbin-Triant, *Threatening Property: Race, Class, and Campaigns to Legislate Jim Crow Neighborhoods*, 119.

5. As Professor Abbye Atkinson has noted in her work on debt and social subordination, Black borrowers were often "relegated to borrow in the loan grey market where they paid exorbitant interest on loans that did not carry many of the safety precautions enjoyed by the FHA-subsidized conventional loans." Atkinson, "Borrowing Equality," 1418.

6. Tucker, *Trial and Error: The Education of a Courtroom Lawyer*; Taylor, *Race for Profit*, 48–49.

7. *Buchanan v. Warley*, 245 U.S. 60, 82 (1917).

8. Groner and Helfeld, "Race Discrimination in Housing." The Supreme Court invalidated a racial covenant in *Hansberry v. Lee*, 311 U.S. 32 (1940), but these covenants were not deemed unconstitutional until *Shelly v. Kraemer*, 334 U.S. 1 (1948). Roughly half of all homes built in the 1950s and 1960s were constructed using FHA-insured loans, and many of those homes included racist deed covenants. Dickerson, *Homeownership*, 152.

9. My Aunt Eva was a maid her entire working life, was never rich or lower rich, and never earned enough to lend my father money to buy a home. She was able to lend my father money for a down payment only because her husband had recently died, and she could give my father part of the proceeds she received from my Uncle David's life insurance policy.

10. Rusk, "The 'Segregation Tax': The Cost of Racial Segregation to Black Homeowners."

11. My father was determined to never again be the victim of real estate agent steering. By the time they went home shopping the second time, he had become involved with the Memphis Branch-NAACP and ultimately became the longest serving president of that branch in its almost one-hundred-year history.

12. One of our next-door neighbors prominently placed a "For Sale" sign in his front yard the day after we moved in. He removed the sign about a week later, but by then there was no way to thaw what would become my father's glacial relationship with that neighbor. This odious act was a common tactic that White owners used to "welcome" their new Black neighbors. Brooks and Rose, *Saving the Neighborhood: Racially Restrictive Covenants, Law, and Social Norms.*

13. The actions of REIC actors and political leaders exacerbated the racial wealth gap that was created more than a century ago when federal leaders refused to offer reparations to the descendants of enslaved persons. The gap narrowed between the 1960s and 1980s, but the gains were short-lived and the gap has expanded almost continuously since the 1980s. A recent study attributes the "large and lasting" racial wealth gap to "the enormous difference in initial wealth between Black and White Americans on the eve of the Civil War." Derenoncourt et al., "Wealth of Two Nations: The U.S. Racial Wealth Gap, 1860–2020."

In addition to not closing the gap after the Civil War, political leaders allowed the gap to expand after World War II through the 1960s by helping White families buy homes using low-cost federally insured mortgage products but making it almost impossible for Black families to buy homes. As a result, White families amassed housing equity wealth during a time when home prices were rising. This wealth then helped White families become and remain middle class and gave them an asset they could bequeath to their children but deprived non-White families and their heirs of decades of housing wealth. Dickerson, *Homeownership*, 65–66.

14. Housing Act of 1937, Pub. L. 93-383, 88 Stat. 653; Housing Act of 1949, Pub. L. 81-171, 63 Stat. 413.

15. McCarty, *Introduction to Public Housing*; Faircloth, "From Jim Crow to Gentrification: Race, Urban Renewal, Architecture, and Tourism in the Urban South, Memphis Tennessee, 1954–1991."

16. Taylor, *Race for Profit*, 41, 143; Turner and Green, "Causes and Consequences of Separate and Unequal Neighborhoods."

17. Bell et al., "*Prohibiting Discrimination Against Renters Using Housing Vouchers Improves Results*"; Center on Budget Policy and Priorities, "77% of Low-Income Renters Needing Federal Renters Assistance Don't Receive It."

18. Tseng et al., *Opportunity, Race, and Low Income Housing Tax Credit Projects.*

19. *Village of Euclid, Ohio v. Ambler Realty Co.*, 272 U.S. 365, 394, 47 S. Ct. 114, 120–121, 71 L. Ed. 303 (1926).

20. *Village of Euclid*, at 388.

21. Trump and Carson, "We'll Protect America's Suburbs: We Reject the Ultraliberal View That the Federal Bureaucracy Should Dictate Where and How People Live."

22. Dickerson, "Systemic Racism and Housing," 1552; Badger and Bui, "Cities Start to Question an American Ideal: A House with a Yard on Every Lot."

23. "The Zoning Law and Its Benefits," *New York Times*; Kusito, "As Land Use Rules Rise, Economic Mobility Slows, Research Says."

24. Shaver, "Single-Family Zoning Preserves Century-Old Segregation, Planners Say: A Proposal to Add Density Is Dividing Neighborhoods."

25. While these restrictions are ostensibly race neutral, they disproportionately harm non-White families (who are more likely to live in multigenerational households) and LMI occupants (who may need roommates to help pay the housing costs). Schuetz, "Under US Housing Policies, Homeowners Mostly Win, While Renters Mostly Lose"; Kusito, "As Land Use Rules Rise."

26. Dickerson, "Systemic Racism and Housing," 1560–1562; Cheung and Meltzer, "Why and Where Do Homeowners Associations Form?" Written accounts of HOA meetings involving affordable housing protests quote existing homeowners referring to renters as "those people" or suggesting that allowing low-income children, renters, or homeless children to attend their neighborhood schools will harm the school's academic rating. Taylor, *Race for Profit*, 116–117, 121–122.

27. The proposed housing development remains in limbo, and affordable housing cannot be built in most of Marin County because of zoning laws and HOA objections. Not surprisingly, the county remains predominantly White (less than 3% of Marin County residents are Black), and the only affordable housing is in a predominantly non-White neighborhood. Dillon, "Marin County Has Long Resisted Growth in the Name of Environmentalism: But High-Housing Costs and Segregation Persist."

28. Kirk, "The NIMBY Fight That Rocked an Iowa City."

29. Faircloth, "From Jim Crow to Gentrification"; Kellam and Hansen, "The Last Houses of Shoe Lane: How a Virginia College Expanded by Uprooting a Black Neighborhood."

30. Archer, "White Men's Roads Through Black Men's Homes: Advancing Racial Equity Through Highway Reconstruction"; Susaneck, "Mr. Biden, Tear Down This Highway"; Cohen and Ricketts, "Arrival of Interstate Highway System Brought Housing Wealth, but to Whom?"

31. Faircloth, "From Jim Crow to Gentrification"; Taylor, *Race for Profit*, 76–88; Groner and Helfeld, "Race Discrimination in Housing", 438–440; Capeci, "From Different Liberal Perspectives: Fiorello H. La Guardia, Adam Clayton Powell, Jr., and Civil Rights in New York City, 1941–1943."

32. Boushey, *Unbound*, 184.

33. The White House, "President Clinton and Vice President Gore, Bringing Homeownership Rates to Historic Levels"; The White House: "President George W.

Bush, Expanding Homeownership"; The White House, "President George W. Bush, A Home of Your Own: Expanding Opportunities for All Americans."

34. Kochhar et al., "Through Boom and Bust: Minorities, Immigrants and Homeownership."

35. For example, a somewhat obscure mortgage fee called "loan-level pricing adjustments" increases the amount of a loan's interest and is assessed based on the borrower's credit score and the amount of the down payment. Lenders disproportionately impose this fee on non-White (particularly Black) borrowers who often have lower credit scores and less wealth to make a down payment compared to White borrowers. Lenders imposed this fee, though, even when the borrower's income and wealth indicated that they could repay a less expensive mortgage loan. Aronowitz et al., *The Unequal Costs of Black Homeownership*; Levitin, "How to Start Closing the Racial Wealth Gap."

36. Gillis, "The Input Fallacy"; Bartlett et al., "Consumer-Lending Discrimination in the FinTech Era." Paired testing studies of White/Black or White/Latino teams who posed as applicants for mortgage loans showed that non-White borrowers were steered to higher-cost subprime mortgages even when assigned slightly more favorable financial qualifications (higher credit scores, slightly higher incomes, a larger down payment, and better work histories) than White testers. During the application process, lenders were less likely to help non-White testers find ways to lower their home-buying costs, and throughout the housing boom lenders flooded Black neighborhoods with higher-cost subprime mortgage products. National Fair Housing Alliance, *The Crisis of Housing Segregation: 2007 Fair Housing Trends Report*. Some lenders displayed overtly racist behavior. Some referred to Black neighborhoods as slums or "the hood," called non-White neighborhoods ghettoes, and called the subprime loans they pushed on borrowers in Black neighborhoods "ghetto loans." Jacobson, Affidavit, *Mayor & City Council of Baltimore v. Wells Fargo*.

37. Joint Center for Housing Studies, "High-Income Black Homeowners Receive Higher Interest Rates than Low-Income White Homeowners"; US Department of Housing and Urban Development, "Unequal Burden: Income and Racial Disparities in Subprime Lending in America."

38. Paul Taylor et al., "Wealth Gaps Rise to Record Highs Between Whites, Blacks, and Hispanics"; Bocian et al., *Foreclosures by Race and Ethnicity: The Demography of a Crisis*.

39. Schindler and Zale, "The Harms of Liminal Housing Tenure: Installment Land Contracts and Tenancies in Common"; Roche, "The Time Has Come to Help America's Forgotten Homebuyers."

40. Flitter, "Berkshire Hathaway-Owned Lender to Pay $20 Million in Redlining Case: Trident Mortgage Discouraged Minorities in Philadelphia from Applying for Home Loans, the Authorities Say." One survey found that 45 percent of Black potential homebuyers reported discriminatory treatment, compared to

25 percent for Asian and 31 percent for Hispanic potential homebuyers. NPR, "Discrimination in America: Final Summary."

41. *In re: Navy Federal Mortgage Discrimination Litigation*; Carr and Zonta, *2022 State of Housing in Black America: The Elusive Dream of Black Homeownership.*

42. Dickerson, "Systemic Racism and Housing," 1567–1568; Dickerson, *Homeownership,* 150–151, 170–171; Choi et al., "Long Island Divided." A 2024 article in the *New York Times* revealed that a White buyer attempted to rescind an agreement to sell a condo to a buyer when she discovered that the buyer, a molecular biologist and science communicator whose online moniker is "Dr. Raven the Science Maven," is Black. Kamin, "She Made an Offer on a Condo. Then the Seller Learned She was Black."

43. Howell, "2022 Appraised Update"; Frame et al., "Impact of Minority Representation at Mortgage Lenders."

44. The White House, "Biden-Harris Administration Announces New Actions to Build Black Wealth and Narrow the Racial Wealth Gap"; Ali, "Black Appraisers Call Out Industry's Racial Bias and Need for Systemic Change."

45. Gross, "Bank of America Tests No-Down-Payment Mortgages in Black and Hispanic Neighborhoods"; US Census Bureau, *Quarterly Residential Vacancies and Homeownership, Second Quarter 2020.*

46. Adams, "Putting Race Explicitly into the CRA"; Deo et al., "Association Between Historical Neighborhood Redlining and Cardiovascular Outcomes Among US Veterans With Atherosclerotic Cardiovascular Diseases."

47. Jackson, "Briefing for the Council of Urban Professionals and the Network Professionals Association."

48. McClelland et al., "New Evidence on the Effect of the TCJA on the Housing Market."

49. Meschede et al., *Misdirected Housing Supports: Why the Mortgage Interest Deduction Unjustly Subsidizes High-Income Households and Expands Racial Disparities*; Drukker et al., *The Mortgage Interest Deduction: Revenue and Distributional Effects*; Fischer and Barbara Sard, *Federal Housing Spending Is Poorly Matched to Need.*

50. Other homeownership subsidies include the ability to deduct state and local property taxes, interest they pay on home equity loans or lines of credit, and capital gains tax (up to $500,000 for married taxpayers or $250,000 for an individual taxpayer), which gives some owners tax-free profits when they sell their houses.

51. Mondragon and Wieland, "Housing Demand and Remote Work"; Sommer and Sullivan, "Implications of US Tax Policy for House Prices, Rents, and Homeownership."

52. Fry, "Young Adults in the U.S. Are Reaching Key Life Milestones Later Than in the Past."

53. US Census Bureau, "Historical Households Tables, Table HH-4, HH-6"; Perry, "New US Homes Today Are 1,000 Square Feet Larger Than in 1973 and Living Space per Person Has Nearly Doubled."

54. Neighborhood Homes Investment Act of 2021. While the Low-Income Housing Tax Credit has helped increase the amount of low-income, multifamily rental housing, the supply of one-to-four-family housing units has dried up, in large part because of the "value gap" that occurs when building costs exceed the postconstruction value of the housing.

55. Schindler and Zale, "Harms of Liminal Housing Tenure."

56. Freddie Mac, "Family Budget Burdens Squeezing Housing: Child Care Costs."

CHAPTER 6. DROWNING IN DEBT

1. Senator Elizabeth Warren—a former bankruptcy law professor—has written extensively about the struggles LMI workers and middle-class families face to make ends meet. Warren and Warren Tyagi, *The Two-Income Trap: Why Middle-Class Mothers and Fathers Are Going Broke*; Warren, *This Fight Is Our Fight: The Battle to Save America's Middle Class*. Similarly, scholars like Professor Sara Sternberg Greene have shown how credit has become a lifeline for families who find themselves buried in unmanageable debt. Greene, "The Bootstrap Trap."

2. Foohey et al., *Debt's Grip: Risk and Consumer Bankruptcy*.

3. Draut, *Strapped: Why America's 20- and 30-Somethings Can't get Ahead*, 31.

4. Board of Governors of the Federal Reserve System, *Economic Well-Being of U.S. Households in 2022*; Gravier, "More Than Half of Federal Student Loan Borrowers Owe Less Than $20,000—Here's Where Everyone Else Stands"; Looney and Yannelis, "Borrowers with Large Balances: Rising Student Debt and Falling Repayment Rates."

5. Woo et al., "Repayment of Student Loans as of 2015 Among 1995–96 and 2003–04 First-Time Beginning Students: First Look"; Baum and Looney, "Who Owes the Most in Student Loans: New Data from the Fed."

6. Eaton, *Bankers in the Ivory Tower: The Troubling Rise of Financiers in US Higher Education*. Students who attend for-profits borrow more and are three times as likely to pay for their college expenses using higher cost private loans than students who attend public or private nonprofit colleges. Hanson, "Student Loan Debt Statistics."

7. Levine et al. "Borrowers with Certain Educational Experiences Appear More Likely to Default"; Atkinson, "Marginalized Debt."

8. Darolia et al., "Do Employers Prefer Workers Who Attend For-Profit Colleges? Evidence from a Field Experiment."

9. Hanson, "Student Loan Debt by Race"; Di et al., "A Rescue or a Trap?—An Analysis of Parent Plus Student Loans," 3; Looney and Yannelis, "Borrowers with Large Balances"; Scott-Clayton, *The Looming Student Loan Default Crisis Id Worse than WE Thought.*

10. Foohey et al., *Debt's Grip.*

11. Charron-Chénier et al. "Pathway to Racial Equity"; Fawcett and Fortin, "They Have Debt but No Degree"; Scott-Clayton, *Looming Student Loan Default Crisis*; Carnevale et al., *The College Payoff: Education, Occupations, Lifetime Earnings.*

12. Student Borrower Protection Center, "Educational Redlining"; Granville, "Parent Plus Borrowers: The Hidden Casualties of the Student Debt Crisis."

13. PLUS loans originally were designed for parents to help pay their children's undergraduate education expenses; the acronym stands for parent loans for undergraduate students. Parents can now use PLUS loans to pay for graduate school expenses as well.

14. Board of Governors of the Federal Reserve System, *Economic Well-Being of US Households in 2022*, 65; Gallagher and Rendon, "CFI in Focus: Understanding Older Student Loan Borrowers"; Di et al., "Rescue or a Trap?."

15. Brito et al. "Racial Capitalism in the Civil Courts."

16. Federal Reserve Bank of New York Research and Statistics Group, *Quarterly Report on Household Debt and Credit.*

17. United States Senate, *Nomination of Alan Greenspan: Hearing Before the Committee on Banking, Housing, and Urban Affairs.*

18. Board of Governors of the Federal Reserve System, *Economic Well-Being of US Households in 2020*; Andriotis, "Credit-Card Debt Returns to Levels Before Covid-19 Pandemic."

19. Foohey et al., *Debt's Grip*; Stavins, "Credit Card Debt and Consumer Payment Choice: What Can We Learn from Credit Bureau Data?"

20. Reutschlin and Asante-Muhammad, "The Challenge of Credit Card Debt for the African American Middle Class." Lower-income users effectively subsidize the perks credit card companies give their higher-income credit card holders as they pay for these rewards by increasing the merchant interchange fees. Merchants typically pass along those fees to all buyers, which increases the costs of goods and services. Thus, while LMI credit card customers do not receive perks, they pay higher prices so that credit card issuers can give those perks to higher-income customers. Agarwal et al. *Who Pays for Your Rewards? Redistribution in the Credit Card Market*; Freeman, "Payback: A Structural Analysis of the Credit Card Problem," 154, 185–186.

21. Foohey, "Bursting the Auto Loan Bubble in the Wake of COVID-19"; Eisen and Roberts, "The Seven-Year Auto Loan: America's Middle Class Can't Afford Its Cars"; Singletary, "Many Americans are Car Poor from Their Auto Loans: Here's Why."

22. Phippen, "How Toyota May Have Started Overcharging Minority Customers"; Foohey et al., *Debt's Grip*; Carmona, "Understanding Latino Wealth to Address Disparities and Design Better Policies"; Angwin et al. "Minority Neighborhoods Pay Higher Car Insurance Premiums Than White Areas with the Same Risk."

23. Foohey and Martin, "Fintech's Role in Exacerbating or Reducing the Wealth Gap," 483; Baradaran, *How the Other Half Banks: Exclusion, Exploitation, and the Threat to Democracy.*

24. Leslie, "Banking Deserts, Structural Racism, and Merger Law."

25. Board of Governors of the Federal Reserve System, *Economic Well-Being of US Households in 2022*, 39–40.

26. Faber, "Segregation and the Cost of Money: Race, Poverty, and the Prevalence of Alternative Financial Institutions;" Koren, "Former Wells Fargo Workers Say They Targeted Immigrants and Native Americans"; Broady et al., "Seven Economic Facts About the U.S. Racial Wealth Gap"; Faber and Friedline, *The Racialized Costs of Banking.*

27. Butrica and Mudrazija, "Financial Security at Older Ages," 7; Macey, "Fair Credit Markets: Using Household Balance Sheets to Promote Consumer Welfare." In 2023 the Consumer Financial Protection Bureau found that Black and Latino consumers who earned between $20,001 and $50,000 were significantly more likely to borrow using buy-now-pay-later (BNPL) than White consumers who earned less than $20,000. In addition, high school graduates were less likely than consumers with at least a bachelor's degree to use BNPL Shupe et al., "Consumer Use of Buy Now, Pay Later: Insights from the CFPB Making Ends Meet Survey."

28. David U. Himmelstein et al., "Medical Bankruptcy: Still Common Despite the Affordable Care Act"; Consumer Financial Protection Bureau, *Medical Debt Burden in the United States*; Levey, "100 Million People in America Are Saddled with Medical Debt."

29. Aspen ETIC, "Lifting the Weight: Consumer Debt Solutions Framework"; Foohey et al., *Debt's Grip*; Consumer Financial Protection Bureau, *Medical Credit Cards and Financial Plans.*

30. Board of Governors of the Federal Reserve System, *Economic Well-Being of US Households in 2022*, 34; Federal Reserve Bank of New York Research and Statistics Group, *Quarterly Report on Household Debt and Credit*; Levey, "100 Million in America Saddled with Medical Debt."

31. As economists Anne Case and Angus Deaton have thoroughly documented in *Deaths of Despair and the Future of Capitalism*, medical debt and the high costs of health care have especially been brutal for noncollege Americans, particularly White men, and rising mortality rates for middle-class whites due to self-harm and the opioid crisis have been characterized as "flatly astonishing—actually unprecedented." Markovits, *Meritocracy Trap*, 31.

32. Bach, "New Data Shows Long Covid Is Keeping as Many as 4 Million People Out of Work"; Brenan, "Record High in U.S. Put Off Medical Care Due to Cost in 2022."

33. Lopes et al., *Health Care Debt In the U.S.: The Broad Consequences Of Medical And Dental Bills*; Dixon and Traub, *Desegregating Opportunity: Why Uprooting Occupational Segregation Is Critical to Building a GoodJobs Economy*. Black Americans also are less likely to have health insurance because they disproportionately live in southern states that have refused to expand Medicaid. Hill et al., *Health Coverage by Race and Ethnicity, 2010–2023*.

34. Foohey, "Fines, Fees, and Filing Bankruptcy."

35. Kaiser-Schatzlein, "Alabama Takes from the Poor and Gives to the Rich"; Aspen ETIC, "Lifting the Weight"; Aspen Institute Financial Security Program, "Fines, Fees, and Financial Security in the US South"; US Commission on Civil Rights, "Targeted Fines and Fees Against Communities of Color"; US Department of Justice, Civil Rights Division, *Investigation of the Ferguson Police Department*.

36. Consumer Financial Protection Bureau, "CFPB Survey Finds One-in-Four Consumers Contacted by Debt Collectors Feel Threatened"; Foohey, "Fines, Fees, and Filing Bankruptcy"; Hasan et al., *Disparities in Debt: Why Debt is a Driver in the Racial Wealth Gap*; Pew Research Center, "How Debt Collectors Are Transforming the Business of State Courts."

37. Hasan et al., *Disparities in Debt: Why Debt Is a Driver in the Racial Wealth Gap*, 7–8; Silver-Greenberg et al., "When Unpaid Student Loan Bills Mean You Can No Longer Work."

38. Just as the stereotypical image of the beleaguered middle-class American is a White noncollege male in the Midwest, Black women are often racialized as unemployed mothers with multiple children (with different fathers) who live in large urban cities and depend on welfare. In addition to the blatantly racist overtones, this "individual behavior" narrative ignores the systematic barriers that make it harder for non-White adults to graduate from college and be hired in high-wage jobs. Moreover, this contention is not empirically sound and conflicts with survey data that show that Black households, regardless of household income or educational attainment, spend less and save more than comparable White households. Charron-Chénier et al., "Race and Consumption: Black and White Disparities in Household Spending"; Wolff, "The Asset Price Meltdown and the Wealth of the Middle Class."

39. Atkinson, "Borrowing Equality."

40. The view that home equity is a good form of credit or that it can help homeowners build wealth caused homeowners to view their homes as ATMs—not shelters. This, ultimately, placed their long-term housing at risk, and many lost everything during the 2007–2009 Great Recession.

41. President George W. Bush, "At O'Hare, President Says 'Get on Board.'"

42. Foohey et al., *Debt's Grip* (chronicling stories of bankruptcy debtors feeling shame, guilt, depression, fear, and hopelessness because they could not pay their bills).

43. Fry, "Young Adults in U.S. Are Much More Likely Than 50 Years Ago to Be Living in a Multigenerational Household"; Chien and Morris, "Accounting for Age: The Financial Health of Millennials." Educational debt appears to account for about 20 percent of the decline in homeownership among young adults, and the average age for first-time homebuyers has increased from twenty-nine in the early 1980s to thirty-six. Mezza et al., "Can Student Loan Debt Explain Low Homeownership Rates for Young Adults"; National Association of Realtors, "The Impact of Student Loan Debt."

44. Faber and Rich, "Financially Overextended: College Attendance as a Contributor to Foreclosures During the Great Recession"; Van Dam, "Sending Your Kids to College Increases Chances You'll Lose Your House"; Silvestrini, "Borrowers Over 50 with Student Loan Debt."

45. US Government Accountability Office, "Retirement Security: Debt Increased for Older Americans over Time, but the Implications Vary by Debt Type,"10, 14; Butrica and Mudrazija, "Financial Security at Older Ages"; Herbert et al., *Health Spending Among Older Adults Before and After Mortgage Payoff*; Consumer Financial Protection Bureau, *Snapshot of Older Consumers and Student Loan Debt.*

CHAPTER 7. TRYING TO SAVE

1. Saez and Zucman, "Wealth Inequality in the United States Since 1913: Evidence from Capitalized Income Tax Data"; Aspen ETIC, "Lifting the Weight," 13.

2. Board of Governors of the Federal Reserve System, *Economic Well-Being of US Households in 2022*, 33; Chetty et al., "The Economic Impacts of COVID-19: Evidence from a New Public Database Built Using Private Sector Data."

3. Board of Governors of the Federal Reserve System, *Economic Well-Being of US Households in 2022*; Parker et al., "Economic Fallout from Covid-19 Continues to Hit Lower-Income Americans the Hardest."

4. Jones, "What Percentage of Americans Own Stock?"; Saad and Jones, "What Percentage of Americans Own Stock?"; Derenoncourt et al., "Wealth of Two Nations"; Frank, "The Wealthiest 10% of Americans Own a Record 89% of All U.S. Stocks."

5. DeSilver, "A Booming U.S. Stock Market Doesn't Benefit All Racial and Ethnic Groups Equally."

6. Bennett and Chien, "The Large Gap in Stock Market Participation Between Black and White Households"; Natella et al., "Wealth Patterns Among the Top 5% of African-Americans." The racial wealth gap expanded after the Great

Recession and the COVID pandemic in part because White household savings were concentrated in the stock market (which rebounded faster), while Black and Latino household wealth was concentrated in homes, which took longer to regain value. Kochhar and Cillufo, "How Wealth Inequality Has Changed in the U.S. Since the Great Recession, by Race, Ethnicity and Income."

7. Ray et al., "Homeownership, Racial Segregation, and Policy Solutions to Racial Wealth Equity."

8. Munnell et al., "Wills, Wealth, and Race."

9. Hannon, "Saving for College and Section 529 Plans"; US Government Accountability Office, "A Small Percentage of Families Save in 529 Plans." Former President Obama quickly learned how popular 529 plans are with rich and lower-rich households when he proposed a slight tax increase on these plans. Although he (rightly) concluded that his proposal would not harm most middle-class households, it caused an uproar among Republican and Democratic congressional leaders and their lower-rich constituents, They accused him of engaging in "middle-class" warfare, and their vitriolic and bipartisan opposition forced Obama to almost immediately abandon the proposal. Douglas-Gabriel, "Obama Drops Proposal to Cut Tax Benefits of 529 College Savings Plans."

10. Rothwell et al., "The Devaluation of Assets in Black Neighborhoods: The Case of Commercial Property"; Macey, "Fair Credit Markets"; Sanghi et.al., "What Can be Done to Promote Black Entrepreneurship?"; Kroeger and Wright, "Entrepreneurship and the Racial Wealth Gap: The Impact of Entrepreneurial Success or Failure on the Wealth Mobility of Black and White Families"; de Zeeuw and Barkley, "Mind the Gap: Minority-Owned Small Businesses' Financing Experiences in 2018."

11 Addo, "At the Intersection of Race"; Fairlie et al., "Black and White: Access to Capital Among Minority-Owned Startups."

12. Bone et al., "Shaping Small Business Lending Policy Through Matched-Paired Mystery Shopping."

13. Meyer and Schweitzer, "The Impact of the Pandemic on US Businesses: New Results from the Annual Business Survey"; Mills and Battisto, "Double Jeopardy: COVID-19's Concentrated Health and Wealth Effects in Black Communities."

14. Orozco et al., "The Ongoing Impact of COVID-19 on Latino-Owned Businesses"; Kim et al., "Black Entrepreneurs, Job Creation, and Financial Constraints"; Lederer and Oros, "Lending Discrimination Within the Paycheck Protection Program"; Perlmeter, "How PPP Loans Eluded Small Businesses of Color." Ironically, although non-White entrepreneurs struggled to receive PPP assistance, more than a dozen organizations designated as hate groups by the Anti-Defamation League or the Southern Poverty Law Center appear to have received this pandemic relief. Glaser and Solon, "Accused Hate Groups Receive Pandemic Aid."

15. Lee et al., *Disinvestment, Discouragement and Inequity in Small Business Lending*. Relying on housing equity to fund a small business is also harder for Black and Latino entrepreneurs who are homeowners as they typically have less housing equity relative to White entrepreneurs given historical discrimination in housing markets and because appraisers continue to devalue their homes.

16. Perry et al., "Black Wealth Is Increasing, but So Is the Racial Wealth Gap."

17. Employee Benefit Research Institute and Greenwald Research, *34th Annual Retirement Confidence Survey*.

18. Federal leaders initially excluded agricultural workers and domestic servants (who were primarily non-White) from the program. DeWitt, "The Decision to Exclude Agricultural and Domestic Workers from the 1935 Social Security Act."

19. US Government Accountability Office, "The Nation's Retirement System."

20. Caplan and Rabe, "The Older Population: 2020"; Fry and Braga. "Older Workers Are Growing in Number and Earning Higher Wages."

21. US Government Accountability Office, "Shorter Life Expectancy Reduces Projected Lifetime Benefits for Lower Earners."

22. Social Security payments constitute more than half of retirement income for most (86%) lower-income retirees and 44 percent of income for many middle-income retirees. US Government Accountability Office, "Most Households Approaching Retirement Have Low Savings," 3–4; Biggs, "Social Security and the Poverty Line."

23. Shu and Payne, "Social Security Claiming Intentions: Psychological Ownership, Loss Aversion, and Information Displays"; Social Security Administration, *A Summary of the 2024 Annual Social Security and Medicare Trust Fund Reports*.

24. Atkinson, "Marginalized Debt"; Social Security Administration, "Historical Background and Development of Social Security"; US Government Accountability Office, "Nation's Retirement System."

25. Schumann, "Compensation from World War II through the Great Society."

26. Gould and Shierholz, "The Compensation Penalty of 'Right-to-Work' Laws." Businesses may have abandoned DB plans for rank-and-file workers, but they have continued to include deferred (and largely tax-free) guaranteed pension benefits in compensation packages for CEOs and other top corporate executives. Hacker and Pierson, *Winner-Take-All Politics: How Washington Made the Rich Richer—And Turned Its Back on the Middle Class*, 63–64.

27. Atkinson, "Marginalized Debt," 808–809.

28. Myers and Topoleski, "A Visual Depiction of the Shift from Defined Benefit (DB) to Defined Contribution (DC) Pension Plans in the Private Sector." Workers who only have access to a DC plan are more likely to save for retirement if the plan automatically enrolls them in the retirement savings account. Pew Research Center, "Employer-Sponsored Retirement Plan Access, Uptake, and Savings."

29. Myers and Topoleski, "A Visual Depiction of the Shift from Defined Benefit (DB) to Defined Contribution (DC) Pension Plans in the Private Sector."

30. US Department of Commerce, *Middle Class in America*. DB plans are not totally risk free, as employers can freeze or terminate them. If businesses terminate a DB plan, the Pension Benefit Guaranty Corporation (PBGC) provides limited insurance, but the benefits retirees will receive are capped. Pension Benefit Guaranty Corporation, "Maximum Monthly Guarantee Tables."

31. Unfortunately, even middle-class workers with retirement savings do not have fifteen years' worth of savings, which is the median lifespan postretirement. Board of Governors of the Federal Reserve System, *Economic Well-Being of US Households in 2022*, 3, 11; US Government Accountability Office, "Most Households Approaching Retirement Have Low Savings."

32. Choukhmane et al., "Who Benefits from Retirement Saving Incentives in the U.S.? Evidence on Gaps in Retirement Wealth Accumulation by Race and Parental Income."

33. Tamborini and Kim, "Education and Contributory Pensions at Work: Disadvantages of the Less Educated."

34. Lewis and Messy, "Financial Education, Savings and Investments: An Overview," 18, 30; Brown et al., "Retirement in America: Out of Reach for Working Americans?"; US Government Accountability Office, "Low Defined Contribution Savings May Pose Challenges"; Aspen Institute Financial Security Program, "The State of Financial Security 2020: A Framework for Recovery and Resilience"; Pew Research Center, "Employer-Sponsored Retirement Plan"; Merrill Lynch, *Finances in Retirement: New Challenges, New Solutions*, 21, 29; US Government Accountability Office, "Most Households Approaching Retirement," 16, 30–31.

35. Choukhmane et al., "Who Benefits from Retirement Saving Incentives in the U.S.?"; Carrns, "Hardship 401(k) Withdrawals, Explained"; Siegel, "Workers Tap Retirement Savings as a Last Resort." While workers who start accepting social security benefits before their FRA also face an early withdrawal penalty, they nonetheless still receive monthly benefits, though smaller, for life.

36. Fulford et al., *Making Ends Meet in 2022: Insights from the CFPB Making Ends Meet Survey*; Rademacher et al., "Rise and Shine: Improving Retirement and Enhancing Savings"; Bhutta et al., "Disparities in Wealth by Race and Ethnicity in the 2019 Survey of Consumer Finances"; Biggs et al., "Why Are 401(K)/IRA Balances Substantially Below Potential?"; Rhee, "Race and Retirement Insecurity in the United States," 1, 4.

37. Collison and Cho, "Life in Retirement: Pre-Retiree Expectations and Retiree Realities"; Morrissey et al., "The Older Workers and Retirement Chartbook."

38. Butrica and Mudrazija, "Financial Security at Older Ages."

39. Meschede et al., "Family Achievements?: How a College Degree Accumulates Wealth for Whites and Not for Blacks"; Smythe, "The Impact of Social

Security Eligibility on Transfers to Elderly Parents and Wealth-Building among Adult Children."

40. NPR, "Personal Experiences of U.S. Racial/Ethnic Minorities"; O'Brien, "Depleting Capital? Race, Wealth and Informal Financial Assistance"; McKernan et al., "Do Financial Support and Inheritance Contribute to the Racial Wealth Gap?"; Noe-Bustamante et al., "A Majority of Latinas Feel Pressure to Support Their Families or to Succeed at Work"; Smythe, "Child-to-Parent Intergenerational Transfers, Social Security, and Child Wealth Building."

41. Belbase et al., "What Resources Do Retirees Have for Long-term Services & Supports?"; US Government Accountability Office, "Income and Wealth Disparities Continue through Old Age."

42. Brown, *The Whiteness of Wealth*, 19; Fung, "The Luxury of Telling Poor People That iPhones Are a Luxury."

43. DelReal, "Ben Carson Calls Poverty 'a State of Mind' During Interview."

44. Griffiths, "Grassley Derides Those Who Spend All Their Money 'on Booze or Women or Movies.'" While political leaders routinely castigate and demonize non-White LMI households who struggle to become and remain middle class, with the possible exception of former senator (now Vice President) J. D. Vance's best-selling book, *Hillbilly Elegy*, conservative political leaders prefer to assume that structural (not individual) factors are the reasons White LMI adults struggle to make ends meet. For example, Vivek Ramaswamy, who briefly co-led (with Elon Musk) the "Department of Government Efficiency" (DOGE), publicly stated that American culture values mediocrity over excellence. Because his statement was perceived to blame White middle-class workers for making unwise individual choices, he was ousted from DOGE and essentially banished from the inner circles of the Republican Party.

45. Turnham, "Attitudes to Savings and Financial Education Among Low-Income Populations: Findings from the Financial Literacy Focus Groups"; Council for Economic Education, *2022 Economic and Personal Finance Education in our Nation's Schools*; Kim and Chatterjee, "Childhood Financial Socialization and Young Adults' Financial Management," 62; Hibbert et al., "Financial Prudence and Next Generation Financial Strain."

46. Most American adults are loathe to discuss their personal finances publicly and often resist improving their financial competency even though, as social media demonstrates, people will share excruciatingly intimate details about politics; religion; and their weight, sex lives, or medical conditions with random strangers. Pinsker, "Why So Many Americans Don't Talk About Money." Even if they are not financially literate, rich or lower-rich adults can afford to hire financial advisers to help them plan for retirement.

47. O'Brien, "Secure 2.0 Clears Congress as Part of Omnibus Appropriations Bill, Will Bring More Changes to U.S. Retirement System."

48. US Government Accountability Office, "Low Defined Contribution Savings."

CHAPTER 8. THE MIDDLE-CLASS NEW DEAL

1. More than half of Americans (particularly LMI, Latino, or rural parents) live in "childcare deserts" that lack a sufficient number of licensed and affordable childcare facilities. Because some LMI workers have jobs that require them to start working before dawn, or they work past 6:00 p.m., and on the weekends, they have always struggled to find childcare outside of normal working hours. Becker, "Middle-Income and Rural Families Disproportionately Grapple with Child-Care Deserts, New Analysis Shows."

2. When the country needed women to work in manufacturing plants to fill in for male workers who were fighting in World War II, Congress allocated funds to expand childcare facilities in communities with defense industries to help mothers find safe and convenient childcare. Like the COVID relief, though, these wartime childcare facilities were temporary. National Historic Landmarks Program, *World War II & The American Home Front* 27, 67–69.

3. For example, in legislative funding debates during the COVID pandemic, Congress obsessed over whether a particular congressional employee had the authority to approve a quirky Senate special legislative process ("reconciliation") that would allow Congress to avoid an anticipated filibuster and pass funding relief. Federal leaders also argued over minute details about the specific type of rent and mortgage moratoria to adopt and quibbled over the precise number of weeks unemployment payments should last. They endlessly debated whether a bill denominated "infrastructure" could include funding for child and elder care. Whether deemed to be critical "infrastructure" or not, federal and state leaders must find ways to provide greater childcare subsidies for LMI working parents and revise tax laws to give employers tax incentives to offer additional and more robust childcare employee benefits (like backup emergency childcare or pretax flexible spending accounts).

4. For example, political leaders should rely on the expertise of principals or teachers at LMI schools, education professors at HBCUs or HSIs, community college professors, or professors from education departments at public and private nonprofit universities whose student enrollments are more than 50 percent non-White or LMI. An additional benefit of awarding curriculum grants to HBCU professors is that doing so could help close the funding disparities between public HBCUs and public PWIs that political leaders created by systematically underfunding HBCUs. Perry et al., "The Supreme Court's Decision to Strike Down Affirmative Action Means That HBCU Investment Is More Important Than Ever"; Smith, "Achieving Financial Equity and Justice for HBCUs."

5. A collateral benefit of making infrastructure improvements to schools in LMI neighborhoods and placing enhanced educational programs in those schools is that more parents would be encouraged to keep their children in neighborhood public schools rather than enroll them in one of the lightly regulated (and often privately operated) charter schools that are cropping up around the country. Likewise, increasing the desirability of schools in LMI neighborhoods would make it less likely that local school officials would target those schools for closure, as leaders frequently do because lower-income schools often have shrinking enrollments and lower academic performance. Unlike traditional high-poverty schools in K–12 districts, buildings that house magnet schools in lower-income neighborhoods are less likely to be targeted for school closures because those schools typically educate rich and lower-rich children, whose parents will fight efforts to close their children's schools.

6. Boushey, *Unbound*, 45–46.

7. Family Friendly Schools Act of 2019, S. 2784, 116th Cong. (2019).

8. Parents with young children, particularly if they are LMI, who want to return to college or get additional skills training to help them find better jobs often cannot overcome the logistical challenges of synchronizing childcare, work, and college classes.

9. Fuller and Raman, *The Caring Company: How Employers Can Help Employees Manage Their Caregiving Responsibilities—While Reducing Costs and Increasing Productivity.*

10. COVID increased the number of hybrid or fully remote jobs. Because many workers may not regularly see each other (or their supervisors), summer programming could include in-person or online activities that simulate a work environment to help high school students learn how to work in teams or with people they may rarely see in person.

11. Chetty et al., "Diversifying Society's Leaders? The Determinants and Causal Effects of Admission to Highly Selective Private Colleges."

12. Baby Bonds were proposed in the American Opportunity Accounts Act of 2019, S. 2231, 116th Cong. (2019).

13. Blake, "Trump Just Admitted the GOP's Tax Cuts Were Deceptively Sold"; Hendricks and Hanlon, "The TCJA 2 Years Later: Corporations, Not Workers, Are the Big Winners." Economists find little evidence that lowering taxes for the rich leads to sustained economic growth that trickles down to other households. Boushey, *Unbound*, 93.

14. Curtin, "Nearly 80 Percent of Employees Would Prefer One of These 3 Things to a Pay Raise, According to Glassdoor"; Gruber, "How Should We Provide Benefits to Gig Workers?"

15. Political leaders should also encourage employers incentives to subsidize telework expenses (like faster internet) for employees who work remotely, just as they routinely subsidize parking expenses for in-person workers. Likewise,

political leaders should also encourage businesses to subsidize public transportation expenses in ways that are comparable to the parking subsidies for workers who drive to work.

16. Enacting more family-friendly work policies could help reverse or at least stall declining US birthrates. While birthrates have declined for multiple reasons, including better access to contraception and the increase in the number of women with advanced degrees or who are having children at older ages, young adults consistently cite the high cost of housing, childcare, and health care and struggles with work-life balance as reasons they are not having children. Tavernise, "The U.S. Birthrate Has Dropped Again: The Pandemic May Be Accelerating the Decline."

17. Jerome H. Powell, *Semiannual Monetary Policy Report to the Congress, Before the Committee on Banking, Housing, and Urban Affairs, United States Senate.*

18. US Department of Education, "U.S. Department of Education Releases *COVID-19 Handbook.*"

19. Gershenson and Papageorge, "Through Peer Learning, the Benefits of Teacher Diversity Extend Beyond Classroom Walls"; Gershenson et al., *Teacher Diversity and Student Success: Why Racial Representation Matters in the Classroom*; Austin City Mayor's Task Force, *Final Report*, 7.

20. Adjunct professors often earn less than full-time public schoolteachers, rarely participate in university retirement plans, and often rely on public assistance to make ends meet. Flaherty, "Barely Getting By: New Report on Adjuncts Says Many Make Less Than $3,500 per Course and Live in Poverty."

21. People with felony convictions, particularly if they are Black males, have consistently had higher overall unemployment rates. Larson et al., "Felon History and Change in U.S. Employment Rates."

22. Economic Policy Institute, "Racial and Ethnic Disparities in the United States"; US Department of Education, "Education Department Releases Proposed Regulations to Protect Veterans and Service Members, Increase College Oversight, and Increase College Access for Incarcerated Individuals."

23. Federal Reserve Bank of Atlanta, *Home Ownership Affordability Monitor.*

24. Kasakove and Gebeloff, "The Shrinking of the Middle-Class Neighborhood"; Callimachi and Schaff, "In a Snow Paradise, They Live in This Parking Lot."

25. Turner and Green, "Separate and Unequal Neighborhoods."

26. Committee on Financial Services. *Memorandum, Where Have All the Houses Gone? Private Equity, Single Family Rentals, and America's Neighborhoods: Virtual Hearing before the Subcommittee on Oversight and Investigations of the Committee on Financial Services, US House of Representatives.*

27. Horowitz et al., "Most U.S. Teens See Anxiety and Depression as a Major Problem Among Their Peers"; Kimmelman, "Downtowns Are Full of Empty Buildings: Universities Are Moving In"; Bowen, "'Yes in God's Backyard' Seeks Affordable Housing on Religious Land"; Reidy, "Churching NIMBYs: Creating Affordable Housing on Church Property."

28. As an example, Mueller is a public-private partnership between the City of Austin and a private corporation that redeveloped seven hundred acres of land that had been used as a former municipal airport. The project is described as an "interactive mixed-use community, including residential neighborhoods, retail shops and services, offices and employment centers." Mueller promotes energy efficiency but also offers "a wide range of housing choices in order to create a new community of ethnically and economically diverse residents," thus proving that a housing project can be green, Black, and Brown at the same time. Mueller. "Frequently Asked Questions."

29. To ensure homes remain affordable, CLTs impose resale restrictions that require owners to sell their homes to another LMI household. Some CLTs also finance home purchases for qualified buyers, help buyers qualify for mortgage loans, loan money to borrowers who are facing foreclosure, and help buyers sell homes to avoid a foreclosure. Wang et al., "Tracking Growth and Evaluating Performance of Shared Equity Homeownership Programs During Housing Market Fluctuations," 35; Palmer, "Strategies for Sustainable Growth in Community Land Trusts."

30. Klopp, "'Mow to Own' Program Allows Man to Possess Vacant Lot."

31. Green and Cowley, "Broken Promises and Debt Pile Up as Loan Forgiveness Goes Astray"; The White House, "Fact Sheet: President Biden Announces Student Loan Relief for Borrowers Who Need It Most."

32. California legislators recognized the relationship between the ability to pay for college and college enrollment rates by creating a program (CalKIDS) that helps low-income California children save for college (or career training). CalKIDS creates a college savings account with an initial deposit of $25, and while parents are not required to contribute to the account, lower-income parents who open a ScholarShare 529 college savings account can link that account to their child's CalKIDS account.

33. FDIC, "Creating a Youth Savings Program in Your Community: A Road Map for Banks, Schools, and Nonprofits." To further help CDFIs serve LMI communities, Congress should increase funding to ensure CDFIs can grant additional micro-loans to help LMI entrepreneurs start and maintain their own businesses.

34. Leslie, "Banking Deserts, Structural Racism, and Merger Law."

35. Broady et al. "An Analysis of Financial Institutions in Black-Majority Communities: Black Borrowers and Depositors Face Considerable Challenges in Accessing Banking Services"; Edlebi,"Research Brief: Bank Branch Closure Update (2017–2020)"; Leslie, "Banking Deserts."

36. Banking deserts often turn workers, particularly undocumented workers, into "walking ATMs" who are targeted by thieves. Carmona, "Understanding Latino Wealth."

37. Center for Housing Policy, "Don't Put it Here! Does Affordable Housing Cause Nearby Property Values to Decline?" Given the increased use of Uber, Lyft,

Waymo, and other ride-hailing services in dense neighborhoods, local leaders should require existing residents to provide data that prove that car ownership rates for residents of multifamily housing will cause congestion if affordable housing is built. Moreover, to encourage entrepreneurialism, local governments should relax zoning laws and allow residents to operate small businesses in their homes (particularly small-scale, in-home day-care facilities that could alleviate the childcare crisis LMI parents face) *unless* data show that the presence of these businesses would detrimentally effect home prices or increase traffic congestion.

38. Exec. Order No. 13,985, 86 Fed. Reg. 7009 (January 25, 2021).

39. Sinnock, "HUD Approves Pact Resolving Appraisal Bias Charges at JPMorgan Chase"; Kamin, "Black Homeowners Face Discrimination in Appraisals"; Howell and Korver-Glenn, "Neighborhoods, Race, and the Twenty-first-century Housing Appraisal Industry." A March 2021 complaint filed by a fair housing group revealed that appraisers assessed a Black-owned home for $125,000 and $110,000 but increased the value to $259,000 when the Black owner had a White friend pose as her brother while the home was being appraised. Planas, "After She Concealed Her Race, Black Indianapolis Owner's Home Value More Than Doubled."

40. The penalties for banks who fail to meet the banking needs of LMI households are limited to the potential inability to acquire a new bank, open a new bank branch, or merge certain banking operations.

Bibliography

Adams, Stella J. "Putting Race Explicitly into the CRA." In Federal Reserve Bank of San Francisco, *Community Development Innovation Review*. 2009. https://www.frbsf.org/community-development/wp-content/uploads/sites/3/putting_race_explicitly_cra.pdf.

Addo, Fenaba R. "At the Intersection of Race, Occupational Status, and Middle-Class Attainment in Young Adulthood." *AEA Papers and Proceedings* 112 (2022): 48–52.

Agarwal, Sumit, Andrea Presbitero, André F. Silva, and Carlo Wix. *Who Pays for Your Rewards? Redistribution in the Credit Card Market*. Finance and Economics Discussion Series 2023-007. Board of Governors of the Federal Reserve System, 2023.

Agrawal, Nina. "College Internships Matter More Than Ever—but Not Everyone Can Get One." *Washington Post*, March 30, 2024. https://www.washingtonpost.com/education/2024/03/30/college-internships-programs-expand-access/.

Aiko, Ashlyn A., and Beth Gazley. "The Rise of School-Supporting Nonprofits." *Education Finance and Policy* 9, no. 4 (Fall 2014): 541–566.

Ali, Safia Samee. "Black Appraisers Call Out Industry's Racial Bias and Need for Systemic Change." *NBC News*, June 7, 2021. https://www.nbcnews.com/news/us-news/black-appraisers-call-out-industry-s-racial-bias-need-systemic-n1269452.

Amy, Jeff. "Georgia Senators Reject Buckhead Efforts to Leave Atlanta." AP, March 2, 2023. https://apnews.com/article/buckhead-city-secession-vote-fa2922b5d611512bfd6eocc6f38eoo2c.

Andriotis, AnnaMaria. "Credit-Card Debt Returns to Levels Before Covid-19 Pandemic." *Wall Street Journal*, October 28, 2022.

Angwin, Julia, Jeff Larson, Lauren Kirchner, and Surya Mattu. "Minority Neighborhoods Pay Higher Car Insurance Premiums Than White Areas with the Same Risk." *ProPublica*, April 5, 2017. https://www.propublica.org/article/minority-neighborhoods-higher-car-insurance-premiums-white-areas-same-risk.

Archer, Deborah N. "White Men's Roads Through Black Men's Homes' Homes: Advancing Racial Equity Through Highway Reconstruction." *Vanderbilt Law Journal* 73 (2020): 1259–1330.

Aronowitz, Michelle, Edward L. Golding, and Jung Hyun Choi. *The Unequal Costs of Black Homeownership*. MIT Golub Center for Finance and Policy, 2020. https://gcfp.mit.edu/wp-content/uploads/2020/10/Mortgage-Cost-for-Black-Homeowners-10.1.pdf.

Aspen ETIC. "Lifting the Weight: Consumer Debt Solutions Framework." The Aspen Institute, November 14, 2018. https://www.aspeninstitute.org/publications/lifting-the-weight-consumer-debt-solutions-framework/.

Aspen Institute Financial Security Program. "Fines, Fees, and Financial Security in the US South." Aspen Institute, January 2020. https://www.aspeninstitute.org/blog-posts/fines-fees-and-financial-security-in-the-us-south/.

Aspen Institute Financial Security Program. "The State of Financial Security 2020: A Framework for Recovery and Resilience." Aspen Institute, 2020. https://www.aspeninstitute.org/events/financial-security-2020/.

Atkinson, Abbye. "Borrowing Equality." *Columbia Law Review* 120 (2020): 1403–1469.

Atkinson, Abbye. "Marginalized Debt." *Duke Law Journal* 71 (2022): 773–846.

Auray, Stéphane, David Fuller, and Guillaume Vandenbroucke. "Multiple Jobholders." *Economic Synopses* 32 (2018): 1–2.

Austin City Mayor's Task Force on Institutional Racism and Systemic Inequities. *Final Report*. March 31, 2017. http://www.austintexas.gov/edims/document.cfm?id=274706.

Autor, David, Arindrajit Dube, and Annie McGrew. "The Unexpected Compression: Competition at Work in the Low Wage Labor Market." National Bureau of Economic Research Working Paper Series 31010. May 2024. https://www.nber.org/papers/w31010.

Avery, Christopher, Jessica Howell, and Lindsay Page. *A Review of the Role of College Counseling, Coaching, and Mentoring on Students' Postsecondary Outcomes*. College Board Research, 2014. https://files.eric.ed.gov/fulltext/ED556468.pdf.

Bach, Katie. "New Data Shows Long Covid Is Keeping as Many as 4 Million People Out of Work." The Brookings Institution, August 24, 2022. https://www.brookings.edu/articles/new-data-shows-long-covid-is-keeping-as-many-as-4-million-people-out-of-work/.

Badger, Emily, and Quoctrung Bui. "Cities Start to Question an American Ideal: A House with a Yard on Every Lot." *New York Times*, June 18, 2019.

Baradaran, Mehrsa. *How the Other Half Banks: Exclusion, Exploitation, and the Threat to Democracy*. Harvard University Press, 2015.

Bartlett, Robert, Adair Morse, Richard Stanton, and Nancy Wallace. "Consumer-Lending Discrimination in the FinTech Era." *Journal of Financial Economics* 143 (2022): 30–56.

Baum, Sandy, and Adam Looney. "Who Owes the Most in Student Loans: New Data from the Fed." The Brookings Institution, October 9, 2020. https://www.brookings.edu/blog/up-front/2020/10/09/who-owes-the-most-in-student-loans-new-data-from-the-fed/.

Baum, Sandy, and Patricia Steele. *Who Goes to Graduate School and Who Succeeds?* Access Group, 2017. https://www.urban.org/sites/default/files/publication/86981/who_goes_to_graduate_school_and_who_succeeds_1.pdf.

Becker, Amanda. "Middle-Income and Rural Families Disproportionately Grapple with Child-Care Deserts, New Analysis Shows." *Washington Post*, June 22, 2020.

Belbase, Anek, Anqi Chen, and Alicia H. Munnell. "What Resources Do Retirees Have for Long-Term Services & Supports?" Center for Retirement Research at Boston College, *Issue in Brief*, no. 21-16 (September 2021). https://crr.bc.edu/wp-content/uploads/2021/09/IB_21-16-2.pdf.

Bell, Allison, Barbara Sard, and Becky Kopenick. *Prohibiting Discrimination Against Renters Using Housing Vouchers Improves Results*. Center on Budget and Policy Priorities, 2018. https://www.cbpp.org/research/housing/prohibiting-discrimination-against-renters-using-housing-vouchers-improves-results.

Bennett, Julie, and YiLi Chien. "The Large Gap in Stock Market Participation Between Black and White Households." Federal Reserve of St. Louis, *Economic Synopses*, no. 7 (2022). https://doi.org/10.20955/es.2022.7.

Bergson-Shilcock, Amanda, and Roderick Taylor. *Closing the Digital Skill Divide*. National Skills Coalition, February 2023. https://nationalskillscoalition.org/wp-content/uploads/2023/02/NSC-DigitalDivide_report_Feb2023.pdf.

Bevins, Frankki, Kathryn Fox, Duwain Pinder, Jimmy Sarakatsannis, and Shelley Stewart III. "How HBCUs Can Accelerate Black Economic Mobility." McKinsey Institute for Black Economic Mobility, 2021. https://www.mckinsey.com/industries/education/our-insights/how-hbcus-can-accelerate-black-economic-mobility.

Bhutta, Neil, Andrew C. Chang, Lisa J. Dettling, and Joanne W. Hsu. "Disparities in Wealth by Race and Ethnicity in the 2019 Survey of Consumer Finances." Board of Governors of the Federal Reserve System, 2020. https://www.federalreserve.gov/econres/notes/feds-notes/disparities-in-wealth-by-race-and-ethnicity-in-the-2019-survey-of-consumer-finances-20200928.html.

Biggs, Andrew G. "Social Security and the Poverty Line." *AE Ideas*, September 26, 2022. https://www.aei.org/economics/social-security-and-the-poverty-line/.

Biggs, Andrew G., Alicia H. Munnell, and Anqi Chen. "Why Are 401(K)/IRA Balances Substantially Below Potential?" Center for Retirement Research, 2019. https://crr.bc.edu/why-are-401k-ira-balances-substantially-below-potential/.

Bivens, Josh, Emma Garcia, Elise Gould, Elaine Weiss, and Valerie Wilson. "It's Time for an Ambitious National Investment in America's Children: Investments in Early Childhood Care and Education Would Have Enormous Benefits for Children, Families, Society, and the Economy." Economic Policy Institute, April 6, 2016. https://www.epi.org/publication/its-time-for-an-ambitious-national-investment-in-americas-children/.

Blake, Aaron. "Trump Just Admitted the GOP's Tax Cuts Were Deceptively Sold." *Washington Post*, December 20, 2017.

Bloom, Ester. "President Trump Says Young People Pay $12 for Health Insurance—Here's How Much It Actually Costs." *CNBC*, July 20, 2017. https://www.cnbc.com/2017/07/20/trump-thinks-young-people-pay-12-for-health-insurance.html.

Board of Governors of the Federal Reserve System. *Distribution of Wealth in the U.S. Since 1989*. Federal Reserve, 2024.

Board of Governors of the Federal Reserve System. *Economic Well-Being of U.S. Households in 2020*. Federal Reserve, 2021.

Board of Governors of the Federal Reserve System. *Economic Well-Being of U.S. Households in 2022*. Federal Reserve, 2023.

Board of Governors of the Federal Reserve System. *Economic Well-Being of U.S. Households in 2023*. Federal Reserve, 2024.

Board of Governors of the Federal Reserve System. *Private Defined Benefit Pension Funds: Total Funded Assets, Level* (BOGZ1FL572000075Q). Federal Reserve Bank of St. Louis FRED. Accessed June 25, 2025. https://fred.stlouisfed.org/series/BOGZ1FL572000075Q.

Bocian, Debbie Gruenstein, Wei Li, and Keith S. Ernst. *Foreclosures by Race and Ethnicity: The Demography of a Crisis*. Center for Responsible Lending, 2010. https://www.mvfairhousing.com/ai2015/2010-06-18_Foreclosures_by_Race_and_Ethnicity.PDF.

Bone, Sterling A., Glenn L. Christensen, Jerome D. Williams, Stella Adams, Anneliese Lederer, and Paul C. Lubin. "Shaping Small Business Lending

Policy Through Matched-Paired Mystery Shopping." *Journal of Public Policy & Marketing* 38, no. 3 (2019): 391–399.

Boushey, Heather. *Unbound: How Inequality Constricts Our Economy and What We Can Do About It.* Harvard University Press 2019.

Bound, John, and Sarah Turner. "Going to War and Going to College: Did World War II and the G.I. Bill Increase Educational Attainment for Returning Veterans?" National Bureau of Economic Research, Working Paper No. 7452. December 1999. https://www.nber.org/papers/w7452.

Bowen, Andrew. "'Yes in God's Backyard' Seeks Affordable Housing on Religious Land," KPBS, June 5, 2019. https://www.kpbs.org/news/2019/jun/05/yigby-affordable-housing-church-parking-lots/.

Brenan, Megan. "Record High in U.S. Put Off Medical Care Due to Cost in 2022." Gallup, January 17, 2023. https://news.gallup.com/poll/468053/record-high-put-off-medical-care-due-cost-2022.aspx.

Brito, Tonya L., Kathryn A. Sabbeth, Jessica K. Steinberg, and Lauren Sudeall. "Racial Capitalism in the Civil Courts." *Columbia Law Review* 122 (2022): 1243–1286.

Broady, Kristen, Darlene Booth-Bell, and Taylor Griffin. "Seven Economic Facts About the U.S. Racial Wealth Gap." Federal Reserve Bank of Chicago, 2022.

Broady, Kristen, Mac McComas, and Amine Ouazad. "An Analysis of Financial Institutions in Black-Majority Communities: Black Borrowers and Depositors Face Considerable Challenges in Accessing Banking Services." The Brookings Institution, November 2, 2021. https://www.brookings.edu/articles/an-analysis-of-financial-institutions-in-black-majority-communities-black-borrowers-and-depositors-face-considerable-challenges-in-accessing-banking-services/.

Brooks, Richard R., and Carol M. Rose. *Saving the Neighborhood: Racially Restrictive Covenants, Law, and Social Norms.* Harvard University Press, 2014.

Brown, Dorothy. *The Whiteness of Wealth.* Crown Publishing Group, 2021.

Brown, Jennifer Erin, Joelle Saad-Lessler, and Diane Oakley. *Retirement in America: Out of Reach for Working Americans?* National Institute on Retirement Security, 2018. https://www.nirsonline.org/wp-content/uploads/2018/09/FINAL-Report-.pdf.

Bucknor, Cherrie. *Black Workers, Unions, and Inequality.* Center for Economic and Policy Research, August 2016. https://cepr.net/images/stories/reports/black-workers-unions-2016-08.pdf.

Burd, Stephen. *Undermining Pell.* Vol. 2, *How Colleges' Pursuit of Prestige and Revenue Is Hurting Low-Income Students.* New America, 2014.

Bush, President George W. "At O'Hare, President Says 'Get on Board.'" Office of the Press Secretary, September 27, 2001. https://georgewbush-whitehouse.archives.gov/news/releases/2001/09/20010927-1.html.

Butrica, Barbara A., and Stipica Mudrazija. "Financial Security at Older Ages." Center for Retirement Research at Boston College, CRR WP 2020-19, December 2020.

Cahalan, Margaret W., Marisha Addison, Nicole Brunt, et al. *Indicators of Higher Education Equity in the United States: 2022 Historical Trend Report.* Pell Institute for the Study of Opportunity in Higher Education, 2022.

Callimachi, Rukmini, and Erin Schaff. "In a Snow Paradise, They Live in This Parking Lot." *New York Times*, April 11, 2025.

Camardelle, Alex. "Five Charts to Understand Black Registered Apprentices in the United States." Joint Center for Political and Economic Studies, March 20, 2023. https://jointcenter.org/five-charts-to-understand-black-registered-apprentices-in-the-united-states/.

Capeci, Dominic J. "From Different Liberal Perspectives: Fiorello H. La Guardia, Adam Clayton Powell, Jr., and Civil Rights in New York City, 1941–1943." *Journal of Negro History* 62, no. 2 (1977): 160–173.

Caplan, Zoe, and Megan Rabe. "The Older Population: 2020." United States Census Bureau, May 25, 2023. https://www.census.gov/library/publications/2023/decennial/c2020br-07.html.

Cardona, Miguel. "Time to End Toxic Disrespect." *NEA News*, July 2023. https://www.nea.org/professional-excellence/conferences-events/annual-meeting-and-representative-assembly/about-ra/ra-news/secretary-education-miguel-cardona-time-end-toxic-disrespect.

Carmona, Tonatzin. "Understanding Latino Wealth to Address Disparities and Design Better Policies." The Brookings Institution, July 13, 2023. https://www.brookings.edu/articles/understanding-latino-wealth/.

Carnevale, Anthony P., Kathryn Peltier Campbell, Ban Cheah, Artem Gulish, Michael C. Quinn, and Jeff Strohl. *How Limits to Educational Affordability, Work-Based Learning, and Career Counseling Impede Progress Toward Good Jobs.* Georgetown University Center on Education and the Workforce, 2022. https://cew.georgetown.edu/cew-reports/pathway/.

Carnevale, Anthony P., Megan L. Fasules, Michael C. Quinn, and Kathryn Peltier Campbell. *Born to Win, Schooled to Lose: Why Equally Talented Students Don't Get Equal Chances to Be All They Can Be.* Georgetown University Center on Education and the Workforce, 2019. https://cew.georgetown.edu/cew-reports/schooled2lose/.

Carnevale, Anthony P., Tamra Jayasundera, and Artem Gulish. *America's Divided Recovery: College Haves and Have Nots.* Georgetown University Center on Education and the Workforce, 2016. https://cew.georgetown.edu/wp-content/uploads/Americas-Divided-Recovery-web.pdf.

Carnevale, Anthony P., Neil Ridley, Ban Cheah, Jeff Strohl, and Kathryn Peltier Campbell. *Upskilling and Downsizing in American Manufacturing.* Georgetown University Center on Education and the Workforce, 2019.

Carnevale, Anthony P., Stephen J. Rose, and Ban Cheah. *The College Payoff: Education, Occupations, Lifetime Earnings*. Georgetown University Center on Education and the Workforce, 2013. https://repository.library.georgetown.edu/bitstream/handle/10822/559300/collegepayoff-complete.pdf?sequence=1&isAllowed=y.

Carnevale, Anthony P., and Nicole Smith. *Balancing Work and Learning: Implications for Low-Income Students*. Georgetown University Center on Education and the Workforce, 2018.

Carnevale, Anthony P., Martin Van Der Werf, Michael C. Quinn, Jeff Strohl, and Dmitri Repnikov. *Our Separate & Unequal Public Colleges: How Public Colleges Reinforce White Racial Privilege and Marginalize Black and Latino Students*. Georgetown University Center on Education and the Workforce, 2018.

Carr, James H., and Michela Zonta. *2022 State of Housing in Black America: The Elusive Dream of Black Homeownership*. National Association of Real Estate Brokers, 2022.

Carrns, Ann. "Hardship 401(k) Withdrawals, Explained." *New York Times*, December 16, 2022.

Carville, James, and Stan Greenberg. *It's the Middle Class, Stupid!* Penguin Group, 2012.

Case, Anne, and Angus Deaton. *Deaths of Despair and the Future of Capitalism*. Princeton University Press, 2020.

Cashell, Brian W. *Who Are the "Middle Class"?* CRS Report No. RS22627. Congressional Research Service, 2008. https://ecommons.cornell.edu/handle/1813/78986.

Cellini, Stephanie Riegg, and Nicholas Turner. "Gainfully Employed?" National Bureau of Economic Research, Working Paper No. 22287. 2018.

Center for Housing Policy. "Don't Put It Here! Does Affordable Housing Cause Nearby Property Values to Decline?" Insights from Housing Policy Research, 2009. https://furmancenter.org/files/media/Dont_Put_It_Here.pdf.

Center on Budget Policy and Priorities. "77% of Low-Income Renters Needing Federal Renters Assistance Don't Receive It." Accessed June 10, 2025. https://www.cbpp.org/research/housing/three-out-of-four-low-income-at-risk-renters-do-not-receive-federal-rental-assistance.

Chambers, Jennifer, and Beth LeBlanc. "Settlement for Detroit Literacy Lawsuit Eyes Nearly $100M in Funding." *Detroit News*, May 14, 2020. https://www.detroitnews.com/story/news/local/michigan/2020/05/14/whitmer-announces-late-night-settlement-detroit-right-literacy-case/5189089002/.

Charles, Kerwin Kofi, Erik Hurst, and Mariel Schwartz. "The Transformation of Manufacturing." National Bureau of Economic Research Working Paper, March 2018.

Charron-Chénier, Raphael, Joshua J. Fink, and Lisa A. Keister. "Race and Consumption: Black and White Disparities in Household Spending." *Sociology of Race and Ethnicity* 3 (2017): 50–67.

Charron-Chénier, Raphaël, Louise Seamster, Thomas M. Shapiro, and Laura Sullivan. "A Pathway to Racial Equity: Student Debt Cancellation Policy Designs." *Social Currents* 9 (2022): 1–21.

Chetty, Raj, John N. Friedman, Emmanuel Saez, Nicholas Turner, and Danny Yagan. "Mobility Report Cards: The Role of Colleges in Intergenerational Mobility." National Bureau of Economic Research Working Paper No. 23618. July 2017. https://www.nber.org/papers/w23618.pdf.

Chetty, Raj, John N. Friedman, and Michael Stepner. "The Economic Impacts of COVID-19: Evidence from a New Public Database Built Using Private Sector Data." Opportunity Insights Working Paper No. 27431. October 2022. https://opportunityinsights.org/wp-content/uploads/2020/05/tracker_paper.pdf.

Chetty, Raj, David J. Deming, and John N. Friedman. "Diversifying Society's Leaders? The Determinants and Causal Effects of Admission to Highly Selective Private Colleges." Opportunity Insights, July 2023. https://opportunityinsights.org/wp-content/uploads/2023/07/CollegeAdmissions_Nontech.pdf.

Chetty, Raj, David Grusky, Maximilian Hell, Nathaniel Hendren, Robert Manduca, and Jimmy Narang. "The Fading American Dream: Trends in Absolute Income Mobility Since 1940." Equality for Opportunity Project, December 2016. http://www.equality-of-opportunity.org/assets/documents/abs_mobility_summary.pdf.

Chetty, Raj, Nathaniel Hendren, Maggie R. Jones, and Sonya R. Porter. "Race and Economic Opportunity in the United States: An Intergenerational Perspective." *Quarterly Journal of Economics* 153 (2020): 711–783.

Cheung, Ron, and Rachel Meltzer. "Why and Where Do Homeowners Associations Form?" *Cityscape* 16 (2014): 69–92.

Chien, YiLi, and Paul Morris. "Accounting for Age: The Financial Health of Millennials." Federal Reserve Bank of St. Louis, 2018. https://www.stlouisfed.org/publications/regional-economist/second-quarter-2018/accounting-age-financial-health-millennials.

Choi, Ann, Bill Dedman, Keith Herbert, and Olivia Winslow. "Long Island Divided." *Newsday*, November 17, 2019. https://projects.newsday.com/long-island/real-estate-agents-investigation/.

Choukhmane, Taha, Jorge Colmenares, Cormac O'Dea, Jonathan Rothbaum, and Lawrence D. W. Schmidt. "Who Benefits from Retirement Saving Incentives in the U.S.? Evidence on Gaps in Retirement Wealth Accumulation by Race and Parental Income." National Bureau of Economic Research Working Paper Series 32843. August 2024. https://mrdrc.isr.umich.edu/project/who-benefits-from-retirement-saving-incentives-in-the-u-s-evidence-on-racial-gaps-in-retirement-wealth-accumulation/.

CLASP. *Course, Counselor, and Teacher Gaps: Addressing the College Readiness Challenge in High-Poverty High Schools*. June 2015. https://www.clasp.org/sites/default/files/public/resources-and-publications/publication-1/College ReadinessPaperFINALJune.pdf.

Cohen, Jeffrey P., and Lowell R. Ricketts. "Arrival of Interstate Highway System Brought Housing Wealth, but to Whom?" Federal Reserve Bank of St. Louis, 2022. https://www.stlouisfed.org/publications/economic-equity-insights/interstate-highway-system-housing-wealth.

Collison, Catherine, and Heidi Cho. "Life in Retirement: Pre-Retiree Expectations and Retiree Realities." Transamerica Center for Retirement Studies. September 2023. https://www.transamericainstitute.org/docs/library/research/life-in-retirement-preretirees-expectations-retiree-realities-report-september-2023.pdf.

Commission to Examine Racial Inequity in Virginia Law. *Interim Report*. 2019. https://www.virginiamercury.com/wp-content/uploads/2019/12/Interim-Report-From-the-Commission-to-Examine-Racial-Inequity-in-Virginia-Law-1.pdf.

Committee on Financial Services. *Memorandum, Where Have All the Houses Gone? Private Equity, Single Family Rentals, and America's Neighborhoods: Virtual Hearing Before the Subcommittee on Oversight and Investigations of the Committee on Financial Services, US House of Representatives*. 107th Cong. (June 28, 2022).

Congressional Budget Office. "Comparing the Compensation of Federal and Private-Sector Employees, 2011 to 2015." April 2017. https://www.cbo.gov/system/files/115th-congress-2017-2018/reports/52637-federalprivatepay.pdf.

Consumer Financial Protection Bureau. "CFPB Survey Finds One-in-Four Consumers Contacted by Debt Collectors Feel Threatened." January 12, 2017. https://www.consumerfinance.gov/about-us/newsroom/cfpb-survey-finds-over-one-four-consumers-contacted-debt-collectors-feel-threatened/.

Consumer Financial Protection Bureau. *Medical Credit Cards and Financial Plans*. May 2023. https://www.consumerfinance.gov/data-research/research-reports/medical-credit-cards-and-financing-plans/.

Consumer Financial Protection Bureau. *Medical Debt Burden in the United States*. February 2022. https://www.consumerfinance.gov/data-research/research-reports/medical-debt-burden-in-the-united-states/.

Consumer Financial Protection Bureau. *Snapshot of Older Consumers and Student Loan Debt*. January 2017. https://www.consumerfinance.gov/data-research/research-reports/snapshot-older-consumers-and-student-loan-debt/.

Cooper, David, and Julia Wolfe. "Cuts to the State and Local Public Sector Will Disproportionately Harm Women and Black Workers." Economic Policy Institute, *Working Economics Blog*, July 9, 2020. https://www.epi.org/blog/cuts-to-the-state-and-local-public-sector-will-disproportionately-harm-women-and-black-workers/.

Cooperstock, Alexandra. "The Demographics of School District Secession." *Social Forces*, July 30, 2022, 1–37.

Cornwell, Christopher, David B. Mustard, and Deepa J. Sridhar. "The Enrollment Effects of Merit-Based Financial Aid: Evidence from Georgia's HOPE Program." *Journal of Labor Economics* 24 (2006): 761–763.

Cottom, Tressie McMillan. *Lower Ed: The Troubling Rise of For-Profit Colleges in the New Economy*. New Press, 2017.

Council for Economic Education. *2022 Economic and Personal Finance Education in our Nation's Schools*. 2022. https://www.councilforeconed.org/wp-content/uploads/2022/03/2022-SURVEY-OF-THE-STATES.pdf.

Curtin, Melanie. "Nearly 80 Percent of Employees Would Prefer One of These 3 Things to a Pay Raise, According to Glassdoor." *Inc.*, July 6, 2019. https://www.inc.com/melanie-curtin/nearly-80-percent-of-employees-would-prefer-one-of-these-3-things-to-a-pay-raise-according-to-glassdoor.html.

Darolia, Rajeev, Cory Koedel, Paco Martorell, Katie Wilson, and Francisco Perez-Arce. "Do Employers Prefer Workers Who Attend For-Profit Colleges? Evidence from a Field Experiment." *Journal of Policy Analysis and Management* 34, no. 4 (2015): 881–903. https://doi.org/10.1002/pam.21863.

de Zeeuw, Mels, and Brett Barkley. "Mind the Gap: Minority-Owned Small Businesses' Financing Experiences in 2018." *Consumer & Community Context*, 1 (2019): 13–21.

Dean, Adam, Atheendar Venkataramani, and Simeon Kimmel. "Mortality Rates from COVID-19 Are Lower in Unionized Nursing Homes." *Health Affairs* 39 (2020): 1993–2001.

DelReal, Jose A. "Ben Carson Calls Poverty 'a State of Mind' During Interview." *Washington Post*, May 24, 2017.

Dēmos. *When Congress Went to College: Comparing Tuition Then and Now at Our Elected Officials' Alma Maters*. Dēmos, 2016. https://www.demos.org/sites/default/files/publications/DEMOS_DFC_Yearbook_FA_Optimized_0.pdf.

Deo, Salil V., Issam Motairek, Khurram Nasir, et al. "Association Between Historical Neighborhood Redlining and Cardiovascular Outcomes Among US Veterans with Atherosclerotic Cardiovascular Diseases." *JAMA Network Open*, July 11, 2023. https://jamanetwork.com/journals/jamanetworkopen/fullarticle/2807137#google_vignette.

Derenoncourt, Ellora, Chi Hyun Kim, Moritz Kuhn, and Moritz Schularick. "Wealth of Two Nations: The U.S. Racial Wealth Gap, 1860–2020." National Bureau of Economic Research Working Paper 30101. 2022. http://www.nber.org/papers/w30101.

DeSilver, Drew. "A Booming U.S. Stock Market Doesn't Benefit All Racial and Ethnic Groups Equally." Pew Research Center, March 6, 2024. https://www.pewresearch.org/short-reads/2024/03/06/a-booming-us-stock-market-doesnt-benefit-all-racial-and-ethnic-groups-equally/.

DeSilver, Drew, and Katherine Schaeffer. "The State of the U.S. Postal Service in 8 Charts." Pew Research Center, May 14, 2020. https://www.pewresearch.org/fact-tank/2020/05/14/the-state-of-the-u-s-postal-service-in-8-charts/.

DeWitt, Larry. "The Decision to Exclude Agricultural and Domestic Workers from the 1935 Social Security Act." *Social Security Bulletin* 70 (2010). https://www.ssa.gov/policy/docs/ssb/v70n4/v70n4p49.html.

Di, Wenhua, Carla Fletcher, and Jeff Webster. "A Rescue or a Trap?—An Analysis of Parent Plus Student Loans." FRB of Dallas Working Paper No. 2217. September 1, 2022.

Dickerson, A. Mechele. *Homeownership and America's Financial Underclass.* Cambridge University Press, 2014.

Dickerson, A. Mechele. "Millennials, Affordable Housing and the Future of Homeownership." *Journal of Affordable Housing & Community Development Law* 24, no. 3 (2016): 435-465.

Dickerson, A. Mechele. "Systemic Racism and Housing." *Emory Law Journal* 70(7) (2021): 1535–1576.

Dillon, Liam. "Marin County Has Long Resisted Growth in the Name of Environmentalism: But High-Housing Costs and Segregation Persist." *L.A. Times*, January 7, 2018. https://www.latimes.com/politics/la-pol-ca-marin-county-affordable-housing-20170107-story.html.

Dixon, Rebecca, and Amy Traub. *Desegregating Opportunity: Why Uprooting Occupational Segregation Is Critical to Building a GoodJobs Economy.* National Employment Law Project, May 13, 2024. https://www.nelp.org/insights-research/desegregating-opportunity-why-uprooting-occupational-segregation-is-critical-to-building-a-good-jobs-economy/.

Douglas-Gabriel, Danielle. "Obama Drops Proposal to Cut Tax Benefits of 529 College Savings Plans." *Washington Post*, January 27, 2015.

Douglas-Gabriel, Danielle, and Susan Svrluga. "More Elite Universities Settle Suit over Alleged 'Price-Fixing' Aid Policies: Lawsuit Claims Schools Formed a Cartel That Limited Financial Aid." *Washington Post*, January 24, 2024.

Draut, Tamara. "The Growing College Gap." In *Inequality Matters*, edited by James Lardner and David A. Smith. New Press, 2005.

Draut, Tamara. *Strapped: Why America's 20- and 30-Somethings Can't Get Ahead.* Doubleday, 2005.

Drukker, Austin J., Ted Gayer, and Harvey S. Rosen. *The Mortgage Interest Deduction: Revenue and Distributional Effects.* Tax Policy Center of Urban Institute & The Brookings Institution 2018.

Eaton, Charlie. *Bankers in the Ivory Tower: The Troubling Rise of Financiers in US Higher Education.* University of Chicago Press, 2022.

Eaton, Charlie, Jacob Habinek, Adam Goldstein, Cyrus Dioun, Daniela Gs Godoy, and Robert Osley-Thomas. "The Financialization of US Higher Education." *Socio-Economic Review* 14 (2016): 1–29.

Eaton, Charlie, and Taylor Swaak. "Thousands of Students Take Courses Through Unaccredited Private Companies: Here's a Look into One of Them." *Chronicle of Higher Education*, September 27, 2022.

Economic Policy Institute. "Racial and Ethnic Disparities in the United States." Economic Policy Institute Interactive Chartbook. June 2022. https://www.epi.org/publication/disparities-chartbook/.

Edlebi, Jad. "Research Brief: Bank Branch Closure Update (2017–2020)." National Community Reinvestment Coalition Report. December 2020. https://ncrc.org/research-brief-bank-branch-closure-update-2017-2020/.

Eisen, Ben, and Adrienne Roberts. "The Seven-Year Auto Loan: America's Middle Class Can't Afford Its Cars." *Wall Street Journal*, October 1, 2019.

Emanuel, Gabrielle. "Some Health Care Workers Say They Are 'Forgotten' in COVID-19 Vaccination Plans." *NPR*, January 5, 2021.

Employee Benefit Research Institute and Greenwald Research. *34th Annual Retirement Confidence Survey.* Employee Benefit Research Institute and Greenwald Research, April 2024. https://www.ebri.org/docs/default-source/webinars/rcswebinar_062524.pdf.

Engler, Alex. "Enrollment Algorithms Are Contributing to the Crises of Higher Education." The Brookings Institution, September 14, 2021. https://www.brookings.edu/articles/enrollment-algorithms-are-contributing-to-the-crises-of-higher-education/.

Faber, Jacob W. "Segregation and the Cost of Money: Race, Poverty, and the Prevalence of Alternative Financial Institutions." *Social Forces* (2019): 1–30. https://ipums.org/sites/www.ipums.org/files/faber.pdf.

Faber, Jacob W., and Terri Friedline. *The Racialized Costs of Banking.* New America, 2018. https://d1y8sb8igg2f8e.cloudfront.net/documents/The_Racialized_Costs_of_Banking_2018-06-20_205129.pdf.

Faber, Jacob W., and Peter M. Rich. "Financially Overextended: College Attendance as a Contributor to Foreclosures During the Great Recession." *Demography* 55 (2018): 1727–1748.

Faircloth, Justin Micah. "From Jim Crow to Gentrification: Race, Urban Renewal, Architecture, and Tourism in the Urban South, Memphis Tennessee, 1954–1991." PhD diss., University of Virginia, 2013.

Fairlie, Robert W., Alicia Robb, and David T. Robinson. "Black and White: Access to Capital Among Minority-Owned Startups." National Bureau of Economic Research Working Paper 28154. November 2020. http://www.nber.org/papers/w28154.

Farber, Henry S., Daniel Herbst, Ilyana Kuziemko, and Suresh Naidu. "Unions and Inequality over the Twentieth Century: New Evidence from Survey Data." National Bureau of Economic Research Working Paper Series 24587. April 2021. https://www.nber.org/papers/w24587.pdf.

Fawcett, Eliza, and Jacey Fortin. "They Have Debt but No Degree: Could Loan Forgiveness Send Them Back to School?" *New York Times*, September 3, 2022.

FDIC. "Creating a Youth Savings Program in Your Community: A Road Map for Banks, Schools, and Nonprofits." February 2017. https://archive.fdic.gov/view/fdic/6680.

Federal Reserve Bank of Atlanta. *Home Ownership Affordability Monitor.* Accessed June 23, 2025. https://www.atlantafed.org/research/data-and-tools/home-ownership-affordability-monitor.

Federal Reserve Bank of New York Research and Statistics Group. *Quarterly Report on Household Debt and Credit.* Federal Reserve Bank of New York, 2020. https://www.newyorkfed.org/medialibrary/interactives/householdcredit/data/pdf/HHDC_2020Q3.pdf.

Federal Reserve Bank of St. Louis. *All Employees, Manufacturing (MANEP).* Accessed June 25, 2025. https://fred.stlouisfed.org/series/MANEMP.

Federal Reserve Bank of St. Louis. *Employment Level—Part-Time for Economic Reasons, All Industries.* Accessed January 31, 2025. https://fred.stlouisfed.org/series/LNS12032194.

Federal Reserve Bank of St. Louis. "FRED Graph." Accessed January 31, 2025. https://fred.stlouisfed.org/graph/?g=Vkr1.

Federal Reserve Bank of St. Louis. *Unemployment Rate—Bachelor's Degree and Higher, 25 Yrs. & Over and High School Graduates, No College, 25 Yrs. & Over.* Accessed June, 25, 2025. https://fred.stlouisfed.org/series/LNS14027662.

Federal Reserve Bank of St. Louis. *Unemployment Rate—Black or African American.* Accessed June 25, 2025. https://fred.stlouisfed.org/series/LNS14000006.

Federal Reserve Bank of St. Louis. *Unemployment Rate—Black or African American, White, and Hispanic or Latino.* Accessed June 25, 2025. https://fred.stlouisfed.org/series/LNS14000006.

Fellowes, Matt, and Jake Spiegel. *Debt Savers in Defined Contribution Plans: Size, Causes, and Solutions.* HelloWallet, October 2013.

Fife, Anna, Hilary Greenberg, and Alastair Fitzpayne. "Supporting Employer-Provided Training in the COVID-19 Recovery." Aspen Institute, 2020.

FINRA Investor Education Foundation. *Financial Capability in the United States.* FINRA, 2016. https://www.finrafoundation.org/sites/finrafoundation/files/NFCS_2015_Report_Natl_Findings_0_0_0_0.pdf.

Fischer, Will, and Barbara Sard. *Federal Housing Spending Is Poorly Matched to Need.* Center on Budget and Policy Priorities, 2017. https://www.cbpp.org/sites/default/files/atoms/files/12-18-13hous.pdf.

Flaherty, Colleen. "Barely Getting By: New Report on Adjuncts Says Many Make Less Than $3,500 per Course and Live in Poverty." *Inside HigherEd,* April 20, 2020. https://www.insidehighered.com/news/2020/04/20/new-report-says-many-adjuncts-make-less-3500-course-and-25000-year.

Flitter, Emily. "Berkshire Hathaway–Owned Lender to Pay $20 Million in Redlining Case: Trident Mortgage Discouraged Minorities in Philadelphia from Applying for Home Loans, the Authorities Say." *New York Times*, July 27, 2022.

Foohey, Pamela. "Bursting the Auto Loan Bubble in the Wake of COVID-19." *Iowa Law Review* 106 (2021): 2215–2239.

Foohey, Pamela. "Fines, Fees, and Filing Bankruptcy." *North Carolina Law Review* 98 (2020): 419–426.

Foohey, Pamela, Robert M. Lawless, and Deborah Thorne. *Debt's Grip: Risk and Consumer Bankruptcy.* University of California Press, 2025.

Foohey, Pamela, and Nathalie Martin. "Fintech's Role in Exacerbating or Reducing the Wealth Gap." *Illinois Law Review* 2021 (2021): 459–505.

Frame, W. Scott, Ruidi Huang, Erik J. Mayer, and Adi Sunderam. "Impact of Minority Representation at Mortgage Lenders." National Bureau of Economic Research Working Paper No. 30125. June 2022.

Frank, Rober. "The Wealthiest 10% of Americans Own a Record 89% of All U.S. Stocks." *CNBC*, October 18, 2021. https://www.cnbc.com/2021/10/18/the-wealthiest-10percent-of-americans-own-a-record-89percent-of-all-us-stocks.html.

Freddie Mac. "Family Budget Burdens Squeezing Housing: Child Care Costs." Accessed June 14, 2025. http://www.freddiemac.com/research/insight/20200107_family_budget_burdens.page.

Freeman, Andrea. "Payback: A Structural Analysis of the Credit Card Problem." *Arizona Law Review* 55 (2013): 151–199.

Fry, Richard. "First-Generation College Graduates Lag Behind Their Peers on Key Economic Outcomes." Pew Research Center, May 18, 2021. https://www.pewresearch.org/social-trends/2021/05/18/first-generation-college-graduates-lag-behind-their-peers-on-key-economic-outcomes.

Fry, Richard. "A Record One-in-Five Households Now Owe Student Loan Debt." Pew Research Center's Social and Demographic Trends, 2012. https://www.pewresearch.org/social-trends/2012/09/26/a-record-one-in-five-households-now-owe-student-loan-debt/.

Fry, Richard. "Young Adults in the U.S. Are Reaching Key Life Milestones Later Than in the Past." Pew Research Center, May 23, 2023. https://www.pewresearch.org/short-reads/2023/05/23/young-adults-in-the-u-s-are-reaching-key-life-milestones-later-than-in-the-past/.

Fry, Richard. "Young Adults in U.S. Are Much More Likely Than 50 Years Ago to Be Living in a Multigenerational Household." Pew Research Center, 2022. https://www.pewresearch.org/short-reads/2022/07/20/young-adults-in-u-s-are-much-more-likely-than-50-years-ago-to-be-living-in-a-multigenerational-household/.

Fry, Richard, and Dana Braga. "Older Workers Are Growing in Number and Earning Higher Wages." Pew Research Center, December 14, 2023. https://www.pewresearch.org/social-trends/2023/12/14/older-workers-are-growing-in-number-and-earning-higher-wages/.

Frymer, Paul, and Jacob M. Grumbach. "Labor Unions and White Racial Politics." *American Journal of Political Science* 65 (2021): 225–240.

Fulford, Scott, Samyak Jain, Greta Li, Elizabeth Saunders, and Eric Wilson. *Making Ends Meet in 2022: Insights from the CFPB Making Ends Meet Survey*. Consumer Financial Protection Bureau, 2022. https://www.consumerfinance.gov/data-research/research-reports/insights-from-making-ends-meet-survey-2022/.

Fuller, Joseph B., and Manjari Raman. *The Caring Company: How Employers Can Help Employees Manage Their Caregiving Responsibilities—While Reducing Costs and Increasing Productivity*. Harvard Business School Report. January 2019. https://www.hbs.edu/faculty/Pages/download.aspx?name=The_Caring_Company.pdf.

Fung, Brian. "The Luxury of Telling Poor People That iPhones Are a Luxury." *Washington Post*, March 8, 2017. https://www.washingtonpost.com/news/the-switch/wp/2017/03/08/the-luxury-of-telling-poor-people-that-iphones-are-a-luxury/.

Gabler, Neal. "The Secret Shame of Middle-Class Americans." *Atlantic*, May 15, 2016.

Gallagher, Charlie, and Silvio Rendon. "CFI in Focus: Understanding Older Student Loan Borrowers." Federal Reserve Bank Philadelphia, 2022. https://www.philadelphiafed.org/consumer-finance/education-finance/understanding-older-student-loan-borrowers.

Garcia, Emma, and Elaine Weiss. *The Teacher Shortage Is Real, Large, and Growing, and Worse Than We Thought*. Economic Policy Institute, March 26, 2019. https://www.epi.org/publication/the-teacher-shortage-is-real-large-and-growing-and-worse-than-we-thought-the-first-report-in-the-perfect-storm-in-the-teacher-labor-market-series/.

Gershenson, Seth, Michael Hansen, and Constance A. Lindsay. *Teacher Diversity and Student Success: Why Racial Representation Matters in the Classroom*. Harvard Education Press, 2021.

Gershenson, Seth, and Nicholas Papageorge. "Through Peer Learning, the Benefits of Teacher Diversity Extend Beyond Classroom Walls." The Brookings Institution, July 18, 2023. https://www.brookings.edu/articles/through-peer-learning-the-benefits-of-teacher-diversity-extend-beyond-classroom-walls/.

Getter, Darryl E. *Introduction to Financial Services: The Housing Finance System*. Congressional Research Service, 2023. https://www.congress.gov/crs-product/IF11715.

Giancola, Jennifer, and Richard D. Kahlenberg. *True Merit: Ensuring Our Brightest Students Have Access to Our Best Colleges and Universities*. Jack Kent Cooke Foundation, January 2016. https://mrodriguez01.wpenginepowered.com/wp-content/uploads/2018/06/JKCF_True_Merit_FULLReport.pdf.

Gillis, Talia B. "The Input Fallacy." *Minnesota Law Review* 106 (2022): 1175–1263.

Glaser, April, and Olivia Solon. "Accused Hate Groups Receive Pandemic Aid." *NBC News*, December 9, 2020. https://www.nbcnews.com/business/business-news/accused-hate-groups-receive-pandemic-aid-n1250474.

Golden, Daniel, and Kunal Purohit. "The Newest College Admissions Ploy: Paying to Make Your Teen a 'Peer-Reviewed' Author." *ProPublica*, May 18, 2023. https://www.propublica.org/article/college-high-school-research-peer-review-publications.

Goldin, Claudia, and Robert A. Margo. "The Great Compression: The Wage Structure in the United States at Mid-Century." *Quarterly Journal of Economics* 107, no. 1 (February 1992): 1–34.

Gonzalez, Xochitl. "What the Comfort Class Doesn't Get: People with Generational Wealth Control a Society That They Don't Understand." *Atlantic*, April 13, 2025. https://www.theatlantic.com/ideas/archive/2025/04/class-money-finances/682301/.

Gould, Elise, and Heidi Shierholz. "The Compensation Penalty of 'Right-to-Work' Laws." Economic Policy Institute, 2011. https://files.epi.org/page/-/old/briefingpapers/BriefingPaper299.pdf.

Gould, Elise, and Jori Kandra. "Inequality in Annual Earnings Worsens in 2021: Top 1% of Earners Get a Larger Share of the Earnings Pie While the Bottom 90% Lose Ground." Economic Policy Institute, 2022. https://www.epi.org/publication/inequality-2021-ssa-data/.

Granville, Peter. "Parent Plus Borrowers: The Hidden Casualties of the Student Debt Crisis." The Century Foundation, 2022. https://tcf.org/content/report/parent-plus-borrowers-the-hidden-casualties-of-the-student-debt-crisis/.

Gravier, Elizabeth. "More Than Half of Federal Student Loan Borrowers Owe Less Than $20,000—Here's Where Everyone Else Stands." *CNBC*, July 12, 2022. https://www.cnbc.com/select/most-federal-student-loan-borrowers-have-small-balances/.

Green, Erica L., and Stacy Cowley. "Broken Promises and Debt Pile Up as Loan Forgiveness Goes Astray." *New York Times*, November 28, 2019.

Greene, Sarah Sternberg. "The Bootstrap Trap." *Duke Law Journal* 67 (2017): 233–311.

Greenhouse, Steven. *Beaten Down, Worked Up: The Past, Present, and Future of American Labor*. Alfred A. Knopf, 2019.

Griffith, Mike, "Who Pays the Tab for K–12 Education? How States Allocate Their Share of Education Costs." *Progress of Education Reform* 14 (August 2013): 1–2.

Griffiths, Brent D. "Grassley Derides Those Who Spend All Their Money 'on Booze or Women or Movies.'" Politico, December 3, 2017. https://www.politico.com/story/2017/12/03/grassley-tax-booze-women-movies-277764.

Grigsby, Sharon. "How Dallas ISD Plans to Stop the Suburban Cheaters Stealing Admission Slots at Prestigious Booker T." *Dallas Morning News*, June 7, 2019.

Groner, Isaac N., and David M. Helfeld. "Race Discrimination in Housing." *Yale Law Journal* 57, no. 3 (1948): 426–458.

Gross, Jenny. "Bank of America Tests No-Down-Payment Mortgages in Black and Hispanic Neighborhoods." *New York Times*, September 1, 2022.

Gruber, Jonathan. "How Should We Provide Benefits to Gig Workers?" The Brookings Institution, June 13, 2024. https://www.brookings.edu/articles/how-should-we-provide-benefits-to-gig-workers/.

Haberle, Megan, and Philip Tegeler. "Coordinated Action on School and Housing Integration: The Role of State Government." *University of Richmond Law Review* 53 (March 2019): 949–978.

Hacker, Jacob S. *The Great Risk Shift: The New Economic Insecurity and the Decline of the American Dream*. Oxford University Press, 2008.

Hacker, Jacob S., and Paul Pierson. *Winner-Take-All Politics: How Washington Made the Rich Richer—And Turned Its Back on the Middle Class*. Simon & Schuster, 2011.

Hailey, Chantel A. "Racial Preferences for Schools: Evidence from an Experiment with White, Black, Latinx, and Asian Parents and Students." *Sociology of Education* 95, no. 2 (2022): 110–132.

Hankerson, Mechelle. "Decades After Brown Decision, Virginia Is Still Grappling with School Segregation." *Virginia Mercury*, August 26, 2019. https://www.virginiamercury.com/2019/08/26/decades-after-brown-decision-virginia-is-still-grappling-with-school-segregation/.

Hannon, Simona M. "Saving for College and Section 529 Plans." Board of Governors of the Federal Reserve System. *FEDS Notes*, February 3, 2016. http://dx.doi.org/10.17016/2380-7172.1684.

Hanson, Melanie. *Average Cost of College by Year*. Education Data Initiative Report. January 2022. https://educationdata.org/average-cost-of-college-by-year.

Hanson, Melanie. *Average Cost of Community College*. Education Data Initiative Report. December 2021. https://educationdata.org/average-cost-of-community-college.

Hanson, Melanie. "College Enrollment & Student Demographic Statistics." Education Data Initiative, December 2024. https://educationdata.org/college-enrollment-statistics.

Hanson, Melanie. "College Graduation Statistics." Education Data Initiative, March 2024. https://educationdata.org/number-of-college-graduates/.

Hanson, Melanie. "Student Loan Debt by Race." Education Data Initiative, 2023. https://educationdata.org/student-loan-debt-by-race.

Hanson, Melanie. "Student Loan Debt Statistics." Education Data Initiative, July 2024. https://educationdata.org/student-loan-debt-statistics.

Harkin, Thomas. *Opening Statement, The Endangered Middle Class: Is the American Dream Slipping Out of Reach for American Families?, Before the Committee on Health, Education, Labor, and Pensions.* 112th Cong. 1 (May 12, 2011). https://www.congress.gov/112/chrg/CHRG-112shrg81792/CHRG-112shrg81792.pdf.

Harris, Naomi. "How Popular Merit College Scholarships Have Perpetuated Racial Inequalities." *Washington Post*, May 7, 2022.

Hasan, Sharique, and Anuj Kumar. "Digitization and Divergence: Online School Ratings and Segregation in America." SSRN, July 23, 2019. https://ssrn.com/abstract=3265316 or http://dx.doi.org/10.2139/ssrn.3265316.

Hasan, Tashfia, Katherine L. McKay, and Joanna Smith-Ramani. *Disparities in Debt: Why Debt Is a Driver in the Racial Wealth Gap.* Aspen Institute Financial Security Program, 2022.

Hegewisch, Ariane. "As Apprenticeships Expand, Breaking Down Occupational Segregation Is Key to Women's Economic Success." Institute for Women's Policy Research, 2024. https://iwpr.org/as-apprenticeships-expand-breaking-down-occupational-segregation-is-key-to-womens-economic-success/.

Heise, Michael. "The Distribution of In-Person Public K–12 Education in the Time of COVID: An Empirical Perspective." *Journal of Empirical Legal Studies* 20 (2023): 305–338.

Hendricks, Galen and Seth Hanlon. "The TCJA 2 Years Later: Corporations, Not Workers, Are the Big Winners." Center for American Progress, December 19, 2019. https://www.americanprogress.org/issues/economy/news/2019/12/19/478924/tcja-2-years-later-corporations-not-workers-big-winners/.

Herbert, Chris, Jennifer Molinsky, Samara Scheckler, and Kacie Dragan. *Health Spending Among Older Adults Before and After Mortgage Payoff.* Joint Center for Housing Studies, 2021. https://www.jchs.harvard.edu/research-areas/journal-article/health-spending-among-older-adults-and-after-mortgage-payoff.

Herbin-Triant, Elizabeth A. *Threatening Property: Race, Class, and Campaigns to Legislate Jim Crow Neighborhoods.* Columbia University Press, 2019.

Hershbein, Brad. "A College Degree Is Worth Less If You Are Raised Poor." The Brookings Institution, February 19, 2016. https://www.brookings.edu/articles/a-college-degree-is-worth-less-if-you-are-raised-poor/.

Hibbert, Jeffrey, Ivan Beutler, and Todd Martin. "Financial Prudence and Next Generation Financial Strain." *Journal of Financial Counseling and Planning* 15 (2004): 51–59.

Hill, Latoya, Nambi Ndugga, Samantha Artiga, and Anthony Damico. *Health Coverage by Race and Ethnicity, 2010–2023.* KFF, February 13, 2025. https://www.kff.org/racial-equity-and-health-policy/issue-brief/health-coverage-by-race-and-ethnicity/.

Himmelstein, David U., Robert M. Lawless, Deborah Thorne, Pamela Foohey, and Steffie Woolhandler. "Medical Bankruptcy: Still Common Despite the Affordable Care Act." *American Journal of Public Health* 109 (2019): 431–433.

Hoachlander, E. Gareth, Phillip Kaufman, Karen Levesque, and James Houser. *Vocational Education in the United States: 1969–1990*. US Department of Education, National Center for Education Statistics, Compendium of Statistics, 1992. https://nces.ed.gov/pubs92/92669.pdf.

Holland, Megan M., and Stefanie DeLuca. "'Why Wait Years to Become Something?': Low-Income Youth and the Costly Career Search in For-Profit Trade Schools." *Sociology of Education* 89 (2016): 261–278.

Holpuch, Amanda. "Which Colleges Offer Free Tuition? Dozens of Schools Say They Provide Free Tuition to Students Whose Families Earn Under a Certain Income: How Does It Work?" *New York Times*, December 7, 2024.

Holzer, Harry, and Sandy Baum. "Overcoming the Stigma of Voc Ed in Today's CTE." Future Ed. 2017. https://www.future-ed.org/overcoming-the-stigma-of-yesterdays-voc-ed-in-todays-cte.

Homans, Charles. "Is the U.S. Ready for Post-Middle-Class Politics?" *New York Times*, April 27, 2016.

Hora, Matthew T. "Unpaid Internships and Inequality: A Review of the Data and Recommendations for Research, Policy, and Practice." Center for Research on College-Workforce Transitions, University of Wisconsin-Madison, 2022. https://ccwt.wisc.edu/publication/unpaid-internships-and-inequality-a-review-of-the-data-and-recommendations-for-research-policy-and-practice-policy-brief-2/.

Horowitz, Alex, and Tushar Kansal. "Converting Offices to Tiny Apartments Could Add Low-Cost Housing." The Pew Charitable Trusts, February 4, 2024. https://www.pew.org/es/research-and-analysis/articles/2025/02/04/converting-offices-to-tiny-apartments-could-add-low-cost-housing.

Horowitz, Juliana Menasce, and Nikki Graf. "Most U.S. Teens See Anxiety and Depression as a Major Problem Among Their Peers." Pew Research Center, February 20, 2019. https://www.pewresearch.org/social-trends/2019/02/20/most-u-s-teens-see-anxiety-and-depression-as-a-major-problem-among-their-peers/.

Houle, Jason N., and Fenaba R. Addo. "Racial Disparities in Student Debt and the Reproduction of the Fragile Black Middle Class." *Sociology of Race and Ethnicity* 5 (2019): 562–77.

Howell, David R. "From Decent to Lousy Jobs: New Evidence on the Decline in American Job Quality, 1979–2017." Working Paper, Washington Center for Equitable Growth, August 2019. https://equitablegrowth.org/working-papers/from-decent-to-lousy-jobs-new-evidence-on-the-decline-in-american-job-quality-1979-2017/.

Howell, David R., and Arne L. Kalleberg. "Declining Job Quality in the United States: Explanations and Evidence." *RSF: Russell Sage Foundation Journal of the Social Sciences* 5, no. 4 (2019): 1–53. https://www.rsfjournal.org/content/5/4/1.

Howell, Junia. "2022 Appraised Update." eruka, 2023. https://static1.squarespace.com/static/62e84d924d2d8e5dff96ae2f/t/6465321aca101a0b82e45344/1684353568112/Howell+2022+Appraised+Update_05_01_23.pdf.

Howell, Junia, and Elizabeth Korver-Glenn. "Neighborhoods, Race, and the Twenty-First-Century Housing Appraisal Industry." *Sociology of Race and Ethnicity* 4 (2018): 439–596.

HUD Exchange. HOME Investment Partnerships Program. Accessed June 14, 2025. https://www.hudexchange.info/programs/home/.

Huelsman, Mark, Tamara Draut, Tatjana Meschede, Lars Dietrich, Thomas Shapiro, and Laura Sullivan. "Less Debt, More Equity: Lowering Student Debt While Closing the Black-White Wealth Gap." Dēmos, 2015. https://www.demos.org/research/less-debt-more-equity-lowering-student-debt-while-closing-black-white-wealth-gap.

In re: Navy Federal Mortgage Discrimination Litigation, Case No. 1:23-cv-01731-LMB-WEF (E.D. Va. 2024). https://www.wavy.com/wp-content/uploads/sites/3/2024/02/Navy-Federal-lending-lawsuit.pdf.

Institute for Women's Policy Research. "Women at Work: Five Years Since the Start of the COVID-19 Pandemic." March 2025. https://iwpr.org/wp-content/uploads/2025/03/Women-at-Work-2025.pdf.

Irwin, Veronique, Josue De La Rosa, Ke Wang, et al. *Report on the Condition of Education 2022*. National Center for Education Statistics, May 2022. https://nces.ed.gov/pubs2022/2022144.pdf.

Irwin, Veronique, Ke Wang, Julia Jung, et al. *Report on the Condition of Education 2024*. National Center for Education Statistics, May 2024. https://nces.ed.gov/pubs2024/2024144.pdf.

Jackson, Alphonso. "Briefing for the Council of Urban Professionals and the Network Professionals Association." Prepared Remarks, Washington, DC, September 28, 2007. https://archives.hud.gov/remarks/jackson/speeches/2007-09-28.cfm.

Jackson, Victoria, Brittani Williams, and Jalil B. Mustaffa. *Parent PLUS Loans Are a Double-Edged Sword for Black Borrowers*. The Education Trust, June 2023. https://edtrust.org/rti/parent-plus-loans-are-a-double-edged-sword-for-black-borrowers/.

Jacobson, Elizabeth M. Affidavit, *Mayor & City Council of Baltimore v. Wells Fargo*, 631 F. Supp. 2d 702 (D. Md. 2009).

Jaschik, Scott. "Feeling the Heat: The 2013 Survey of College and University Admissions Directors." *Inside Higher Ed*, September 18, 2013. https://www.insidehighered.com/news/survey/feeling-heat-2013-survey-college-and-university-admissions-directors.

Johnson, Rucker. "Long-Run Impacts of School Desegregation & School Quality on Adult Attainments." National Bureau of Economic Research Working Paper No. 16664. January 2011. https://www.nber.org/system/files/working_papers/w16664/w16664.pdf.

Joint Center for Housing Studies. "High-Income Black Homeowners Receive Higher Interest Rates than Low-Income White Homeowners." February 16, 2021. https://www.jchs.harvard.edu/blog/high-income-black-homeowners-receive-higher-interest-rates-low-income-white-homeowners.

Jones, Jeffrey M. "What Percentage of Americans Own Stock?" Gallup, May 24, 2023. https://news.gallup.com/poll/266807/percentage-americans-owns-stock.aspx.

Kaiser-Schatzlein, Robin. "Alabama Takes from the Poor and Gives to the Rich." *New York Times*, July 27, 2022.

Kamin, Debra. "Black Homeowners Face Discrimination in Appraisals." *New York Times*, August 25, 2020.

Kamin, Debra. "She Made an Offer on a Condo: Then the Seller Learned She Was Black." *New York Times*, May 31, 2024.

Kane, Tom, and Sean Reardon. "Parents Don't Understand How Far Behind Their Kids Are in School." *New York Times*, May 11, 2023.

Kasakove, Sophie. "The College Admissions Scandal: Where Some of the Defendants Are Now." *New York Times*, October 9, 2021.

Kasakove, Sophie, and Robert Gebeloff. "The Shrinking of the Middle-Class Neighborhood." *New York Times*, July 6, 2022.

Katz, Lawrence F., and Alan B. Krueger. "The Rise and Nature of Alternative-Work Arrangements in the United States." National Bureau of Economic Research Working Paper Series No. 22667. September 2016. https://www.nber.org/papers/w22667.pdf.

Katznelson, Ira. *When Affirmative Action Was White: An Untold History of Racial Inequality in Twentieth-Century America*. W. W. Norton, 2005.

Kellam, Brandi, and Louis Hansen. "The Last Houses of Shoe Lane: How a Virginia College Expanded by Uprooting a Black Neighborhood." *ProPublica*, September 5, 2023. https://www.propublica.org/article/how-virginia-college-expanded-by-uprooting-black-neighborhood.

Kelly, Emily, and Tara Adam. "Trends in Undergraduate Nonfederal Grant and Scholarship Aid by Demographic and Enrollment Characteristics: Selected Years, 2003–04 to 2015–16." National Center for Education Statistics, August 2019. https://nces.ed.gov/pubs2019/2019486.pdf.

Kelly, Emily, and Laura Holian. "Education, Employment, and Earnings: Expectations of 2009 Ninth-Graders in 2016." Institute of Education Sciences, 2020. https://nces.ed.gov/pubs2021/2021056.pdf.

Kiersz, Andy. "The Percentage of Workers in Government Is at a 54-Year Low." *Business Insider*, January 9, 2015.

Kim, Jinhee, and Swarn Chatterjee. "Childhood Financial Socialization and Young Adults' Financial Management." *Journal of Financial Counseling and Planning* 24 (2013): 61–79.

Kim, Mee Jung, Kyung Min Lee, J. David Brown, and John S. Earle. "Black Entrepreneurs, Job Creation, and Financial Constraints." United States Census Bureau, Working Paper Number CES-21-11. 2021. https://www.census.gov/library/working-papers/2021/adrm/CES-WP-21-11.html.

Kimmelman, Michael. "Downtowns Are Full of Empty Buildings: Universities Are Moving In." *New York Times*, November 17, 2023.

Kirk, Mimi. "The NIMBY Fight That Rocked an Iowa City." *Bloomberg*, September 8, 2016. https://www.bloomberg.com/news/articles/2017-09-08/the-iowa-nimbys-who-fought-affordable-housing-and-lost.

Klein, Aaron. *The Great Student Swap*. Brookings Mountain West, 2021.

Klopp, Harrison. "'Mow to Own' Program Allows Man to Possess Vacant Lot." *WREG News Channel 3*, May 21, 2025. https://wreg.com/news/local/mow-to-own-program-allows-man-to-possess-vacant-lot/.

Kochhar, Rakesh, Ana Gonzalez-Barrera and Daniel Dockterman. "Through Boom and Bust: Minorities, Immigrants and Homeownership." Pew Hispanic Center, May 12, 2009. https://www.pewresearch.org/hispanic/wp-content/uploads/sites/5/2009/05/Pew-Hispanic-Center_Through-Boom-and-Bust-Minorities-Immigrants-Homeownership_2009-05-12.pdf.

Kochhar, Rakesh, and Anthony Cillufo. "How Wealth Inequality Has Changed in the U.S. Since the Great Recession, by Race, Ethnicity and Income." Pew Research Center, November 1, 2017. https://www.pewresearch.org/short-reads/2017/11/01/how-wealth-inequality-has-changed-in-the-u-s-since-the-great-recession-by-race-ethnicity-and-income/.

Kochhar, Rakesh, and Stella Sechopoulos. "COVID-19 Pandemic Pinches Finances of America's Lower-and Middle-Income Families." Pew Research Center, April 20, 2022. https://www.pewresearch.org/social-trends/2022/04/20/covid-19-pandemic-pinches-finances-of-americas-lower-and-middle-income-families/.

Koller, Dionne. *More Than Play: How Law, Policy, and Politics Shape American Youth Sports*. University of California Press, 2025.

Koren, James Rufus. "Former Wells Fargo Workers Say They Targeted Immigrants and Native Americans." *Los Angeles Times*, May 5, 2017.

Kroeger, Teresa, and Graham Wright. "Entrepreneurship and the Racial Wealth Gap: The Impact of Entrepreneurial Success or Failure on the Wealth Mobility of Black and White Families." *Journal of Economic Race Policy* 4 (2021): 183–195.

Kuh, George D., Jillian Kinzie, Jennifer A. Buckley, Brian K. Bridges, and John C. Hayek. *What Matters to Student Success: A Review of the Literature*. National Postsecondary Education Cooperative, 2006. https://nces.ed.gov/npec/pdf/kuh_team_report.pdf.

Kusito, Laura. "As Land Use Rules Rise, Economic Mobility Slows, Research Says." *Wall Street Journal*, October 18, 2016.

Landry, Bart. *The New Black Middle Class*. University of California Press, 1987.

Larson, Ryan, Sarah Shannon, Aaron Sojourner, and Chris Uggen. "Felon History and Change in U.S. Employment Rates." *Social Science Research* 102 (2022): 1–14. https://www.sciencedirect.com/science/article/pii/S0049089X21001265?via%3Dihub.

Laurison, Daniel, and Sam Friedman. *The Class Ceiling: Why It Pays to Be Privileged*. Bristol University Press, Policy Press, 2019.

Lawyers for Civil Rights: Boston. "Federal Civil Rights Complaint Challenges Harvard's Legacy Admissions." Accessed June 14, 2025. http://lawyersforcivilrights.org/our-impact/education/federal-civil-rights-complaint-challenges-harvards-legacy-admissions/.

Lederer, Anneliese, and Sara Oros. "Lending Discrimination Within the Paycheck Protection Program." National Community Reinvestment Coalition, 2020. https://www.ncrc.org/lending-discrimination-within-the-paycheck-protection-program/.

Lee, Amber, Bruce Mitchell, and Anneliese Lederer. *Disinvestment, Discouragement and Inequity in Small Business Lending*. National Community Retirement Coalition, 2019. https://ncrc.org/disinvestment.

Leslie, Chistopher R. "Banking Deserts, Structural Racism, and Merger Law." *Minnesota Law Review* 108(2) (2023): 695–794.

Levey, Noam N. "100 Million People in America Are Saddled with Medical Debt." *Texas Tribune*, June 16, 2022. https://www.texastribune.org/2022/06/16/americans-medical-debt/.

Levine, Ilan, Ama Takyi-Laryea, Phillip Oliff, and Lexi West. "Borrowers with Certain Educational Experiences Appear More Likely to Default." The Pew Charitable Trusts, January 30, 2024. https://www.pew.org/en/research-and-analysis/articles/2024/01/30/borrowers-with-certain-educational-experiences-appear-more-likely-to-default.

Levitin, Adam J. "How to Start Closing the Racial Wealth Gap." *American Prospect*, June 17, 2020. https://prospect.org/economy/how-to-start-closing-the-racial-wealth-gap/.

Lewis, Sue, and Flore-Anne Messy. "Financial Education, Savings and Investments: An Overview." OECD Working Papers on Finance, Insurance and Private Pensions, 2012. https://www.oecd.org/en/publications/financial-education-savings-and-investments_5k94gxrw760v-en.html.

Lieber, Ron. "Another Admissions Advantage for the Affluent: Just Pay Full Price." *New York Times*, March 15, 2019.

Lieber, Ron. "Colleges Know How Much You're Willing to Pay." *New York Times*, May 1, 2025.

Lin, Judy T., Christopher Bumcrot, and Tippy Ulicny. *Financial Capability in the United States*. FINRA Investor Education Foundation, 2016. https://finra

foundation.org/sites/finrafoundation/files/NFCS-Report-Fifth-Edition-July-2022.pdf.

Lippman Laura, Lina Guzman, Julie Dombrowski Keith, Akemi Kinukawa, and Rebecca Shwalb. *Parent Expectations and Planning for College*. National Center for Education Statistics, 2008. https://nces.ed.gov/pubs2008/2008079.pdf.

Liu, Albert Y., Laura Burns, and Lisa Hudson. *Public High School Students' Career and Technical Education Coursetaking: 1992–2013*. Institute of Education Sciences, November 2020. https://nces.ed.gov/pubs2020/2020010.pdf.

LoGerfo, Laura, Elise M. Christopher, and Kristin Denton Flanagan. *The High School Longitudinal Study of 2009: A First Look at Fall 2009 Ninth-Graders*. National Center for Education Statistics, 2011. https://nces.ed.gov/pubs2011/2011327.pdf.

Looney, Adam, and Constantine Yannelis. "Borrowers with Large Balances: Rising Student Debt and Falling Repayment Rates." The Brookings Institution, 2018. https://www.brookings.edu/wp-content/uploads/2018/02/es_20180216_looneylargebalances.pdf.

Looney, Adam, and Constantine Yannelis. "A Crisis in Student Loans? How Changes in the Characteristics of Borrowers and in the Institutions They Attended Contributed to Rising Loan Defaults." *Brookings Papers on Economic Activity* 46 (2015): 1–89. https://www.brookings.edu/bpea-articles/a-crisis-in-student-loans-how-changes-in-the-characteristics-of-borrowers-and-in-the-institutions-they-attended-contributed-to-rising-loan-defaults/.

Lopes, Lunna, Audrey Kearney, Alex Montero, Liz Hamel, and Mollyann Brodie. *Health Care Debt in the U.S.: The Broad Consequences of Medical and Dental Bills*. KFF, 2022. https://www.kff.org/health-costs/report/kff-health-care-debt-survey/.

Lowrey, Annie. "Where Did the Government Jobs Go?" *New York Times Magazine*, April 27, 2016.

Lowry, Robert C. "The Effects of State Higher Education Policies and Institutions on Access by Economically Disadvantaged Students." *Research in Higher Education* 60 (2019): 44–63.

Ma, Jennifer, and Sandy Baum. "Trends in Community Colleges: Enrollment, Prices, Student Debt, and Completion." College Board Research, April 2016. https://research.collegeboard.org/media/pdf/trends-community-colleges-research-brief.pdf.

Ma, Jennifer, Sandy Baum, Matea Pender, and C. J. Libassi. "Trends in College Pricing 2018." College Board Research, 2018. https://research.collegeboard.org/pdf/trends-college-pricing-2018-full-report.pdf.

Ma, Jennifer, Matea Pender and Meredith Welch. *Education Pays 2019: The Benefits of Higher Education for Individuals and Society*. College Board

Research, 2017. https://research.collegeboard.org/media/pdf/education-pays-2019-full-report.pdf.

Macey, Jonathan. "Fair Credit Markets: Using Household Balance Sheets to Promote Consumer Welfare." *Texas Law Review* 100 (2022): 683–745.

Manyika, James, Susan Lund, Jacques Bughin, Kelsey Robinson, Jan Mischke, and Deepa Mahajan. *Independent Work: Choice, Necessity, and the Gig Economy*. McKinsey Global Institute, 2016. https://www.mckinsey.com/featured-insights/employment-and-growth/independent-work-choice-necessity-and-the-gig-economy.

Markovits, Daniel. *The Meritocracy Trap: How America's Foundational Myth Feeds Inequality*. Penguin Press, 2019.

Martinez, Mel. *Statement, Increasing Minority Homeownership, and Expanding Homeownership to All Who Wish to Attain It*. 112th Cong. 15 (2003). https://www.banking.senate.gov/imo/media/doc/martinez.pdf.

Marto, Ricardo. "Who Applies to and Enrolls at Selective Colleges?" *On the Economy Blog*, Federal Reserve Bank of St. Louis, December 12, 2024. https://www.stlouisfed.org/on-the-economy/2024/dec/who-applies-enrolls-selective-colleges.

Mather, Mark, and Beth Jarosz. "The Demography of Inequality in the United States." *Population Bulletin* 69 (2014). https://www.prb.org/wp-content/uploads/2014/11/united-states-inequality.pdf.

McCarthy, Justin. "U.S. Approval of Labor Unions at Highest Point Since 1965." Gallup, August 10, 2022. https://news.gallup.com/poll/398303/approval-labor-unions-highest-point-1965.aspx.

McCarty, Maggie. *Introduction to Public Housing*. Congressional Research Service, 2014. https://fas.org/sgp/crs/misc/R41654.pdf.

McClelland, Robert, Livia Mucciolo and Safia Sayed. "New Evidence on the Effect of the TCJA on the Housing Market." Tax Policy Center, March 2022. https://taxpolicycenter.org/publications/new-evidence-effect-tcja-housing-market.

McGough, Matthew, Emma Wager Twitter, Aubrey Winger, Nirmita Panchal, and Lynne Cotter. "How Has U.S. Spending on Healthcare Changed over Time?" KFF, February 7, 2023. https://www.healthsystemtracker.org/chart-collection/u-s-spending-healthcare-changed-time/.

McKernan, Signe-Mary, Caroline Ratcliffe, Margaret Simms, and Sisi Zhang. "Do Financial Support and Inheritance Contribute to the Racial Wealth Gap?" *The Urban Institute's Opportunity and Ownership Project* 26 (2012). https://www.urban.org/sites/default/files/alfresco/publication-pdfs/412644-Do-Financial-Support-and-Inheritance-Contribute-to-the-Racial-Wealth-Gap-.PDF.

McNamee, Stephen, and Robert Miller Jr. *The Meritocracy Myth*. Rowman & Littlefield, 2004.

Merrill Lynch. *Finances in Retirement: New Challenges, New Solutions.* 2017. https://static1.squarespace.com/static/56f9b1fc746fb96413a0fcbc/t/597b4793e4fcb5787a165daf/1501251482362/ML_Finance-Study-Report_2017.pdf.

Mervosh, Sarah, Claire Cain Miller, and Francesca Paris. "What the Data Says About Pandemic School Closures, Four Years Later." *New York Times,* March 18, 2024.

Meschede, Tatjana, Jamie Morgan, Andrew Aurand, and Dan Threet. *Misdirected Housing Supports: Why the Mortgage Interest Deduction Unjustly Subsidizes High-Income Households and Expands Racial Disparities.* National Low Income Housing Coalition, 2021. https://nlihc.org/sites/default/files/NLIHC-IERE_MID-Report.pdf.

Meschede, Tatjana, Joanna Taylor, Alexis Mann, and Thomas Shapiro. "Family Achievements? How a College Degree Accumulates Wealth for Whites and Not for Blacks." *Federal Reserve Bank of St. Louis Review* (2017). https://heller.brandeis.edu/iere/pdfs/racial-wealth-equity/racial-wealth-gap/family-achievements.pdf.

Meyer, Brent, and Mark E. Schweitzer. "The Impact of the Pandemic on US Businesses: New Results from the Annual Business Survey." Policy Hub 94151. Federal Reserve Bank of Atlanta, 2022. https://www.atlantafed.org/-/media/documents/research/publications/policy-hub/2022/03/22/03--impact-of-pandemic-on-us-businesses--new-results-from-annual-business-survey.pdf.

Mezza, Alvaro, Daniel Ringo, and Kamila Sommer. "Can Student Loan Debt Explain Low Homeownership Rates for Young Adults." *Federal Reserve Board Division of Research and Statistics* 1 (2019): 2–6. https://www.federalreserve.gov/publications/2019-january-consumer-community-context.htm,

Michney, Todd M., and LaDale Winling. "New Perspectives on New Deal Housing Policy: Explicating and Mapping HOLC Loans to African Americans." *Journal of Urban History* 46 (2020): 150–180.

Mills, Claire Kramer, and Jessica Battisto. "Double Jeopardy: COVID-19's Concentrated Health and Wealth Effects in Black Communities." Federal Reserve Bank of New York, 2020. https://www.newyorkfed.org/medialibrary/media/smallbusiness/DoubleJeopardy_COVID19andBlackOwnedBusinesses.

Mirer, Jeanne. "Right-to-Work Laws: History and Fightback." *National Law Guild Review* 70 (2013): 30–40.

Mishel, Lawrence. "The Enormous Impact of Eroded Collective Bargaining on Wages." Economic Policy Institute, 2021. https://www.epi.org/publication/eroded-collective-bargaining/.

Mishel, Lawrence and Jori Kandra. "CEO Pay Has Skyrocketed 1,322% Since 1978." Economic Policy Institute, 2021. https://www.epi.org/publication/ceo-pay-in-2020/.

Mitchell, Keri. "How Suburbanites Cheat Their Way into Booker T. Washington." *Advocate Lakewood/East Dallas,* May 17, 2019. https://lakewood.advocatemag.com/suburbans-cheating-booker-t-washington/.

Mitchell, Michael, Michael Leachman, and Matt Saenz. "State Higher Education Funding Cuts Have Pushed Costs to Students, Worsened Inequality." Center on Budget and Policy Priorities, 2019. https://www.cbpp.org/sites/default/files/atoms/files/10-24-19sfp.pdf.

Monarrez, Tomas E. "School Attendance Boundaries and the Segregation of Public Schools in the United States." *American Economic Journal: Applied Economics* 22 (2023): 210–237.

Mondragon, John, and Johannes Wieland. "Housing Demand and Remote Work." Federal Reserve Bank of San Francisco Working Paper 2022-11. 2022. https://www.frbsf.org/research-and-insights/publications/economic-letter/2022/09/remote-work-and-housing-demand/.

Morrissey, Monique, Siavash Radpour, and Barbara Schuster. "The Older Workers and Retirement Chartbook." Economic Policy Institute, 2022. https://www.epi.org/publication/older-workers-retirement-chartbook/.

Mueller. "Frequently Asked Questions." November 17, 2004. https://www.austintexas.gov/sites/default/files/files/Redevelopment/Redevelopment_Projects/Mueller/faq.pdf.

Munnell, Alicia H., Jean-Pierre Aubry, and Gal Wettstein. "Wills, Wealth, and Race." Wharton Pension Research Council Working Paper No. 2023-16. 2023. https://ssrn.com/abstract=4590303.

Muro, Mark, and Siddharth Kulkarni. "Voter Anger Explained—in One Chart." The Brookings Institution, March 15, 2016. https://www.brookings.edu/articles/voter-anger-explained-in-one-chart/.

Myers, Elizabeth A., and John J. Topoleski. "A Visual Depiction of the Shift from Defined Benefit (DB) to Defined Contribution (DC) Pension Plans in the Private Sector." Congressional Research Service, 2021. https://www.congress.gov/crs-product/IF12007.

Natella, Stefano, Tatjana Meschede, and Laura Sullivan. "Wealth Patterns Among the Top 5% of African-Americans." Credit Suisse and Institute on Assets and Social Policy, 2014. https://heller.brandeis.edu/iere/pdfs/racial-wealth-equity/racial-wealth-gap/top-5-percent.pdf.

Nathenson, Robert A., Andrés Castro Samayoa, and Marybeth Gasman. "Moving Upward and Onward: Income Mobility at Historically Black Colleges and Universities." Rutgers Graduate School of Education, 2019. https://cmsi.gse.rutgers.edu/sites/default/files/EMreport_R4_0.pdf.

National Association of Realtors. "The Impact of Student Loan Debt." September 2021. https://www.nar.realtor/sites/default/files/documents/2021-the-impact-of-student-loan-debt-report-executive-summary-09-14-2021.pdf.

National Center for Education Statistics. "Employment and Unemployment Rates by Educational Attainment." May 2024. https://nces.ed.gov/programs/coe/indicator/cbc/employment-unemployment-rates.

National Center for Education Statistics. "Table 303.25, Total Fall Enrollment in Degree-Granting Postsecondary Institutions, by Control and Level of

Institution: 1970 Through 2018." In *Digest of Education Statistics*. https://nces.ed.gov/programs/digest/d19/tables/dt19_303.25.asp.

National Employment Law Project. "Big Business, Corporate Profits, and the Minimum Wage Data Brief." August 2012. https://s27147.pcdn.co/wp-content/uploads/2015/03/NELP-Big-Business-Corporate-Profits-Minimum-Wage.pdf.

National Employment Law Project. "Unemployment Insurance Provisions in the Coronavirus Aid, Relief, and Economic Security (CARES) Act." March 27, 2020. https://www.nelp.org/publication/unemployment-insurance-provisions-coronavirus-aid-relief-economic-security-cares-act/.

National Fair Housing Alliance. *The Crisis of Housing Segregation: 2007 Fair Housing Trends Report*. National Fair Housing Alliance, 2007. https://nationalfairhousing.org/wp-content/uploads/2017/04/2007_fair_housing_trends_report.pdf.

National Historic Landmarks Program. *World War II & The American Home Front*. Bibliograph, 2007. https://www.nps.gov/articles/000/the-american-home-front-and-world-war-ii.htm.

National Student Clearinghouse Research Center. "Current Term Enrollment Estimates." May 22, 2025. https://nscresearchcenter.org/current-term-enrollment-estimates/.

Neuman, Katherine. *The Missing Class*. Beacon Press, 2007.

Neumann, Zach, and Alastair Fitzpayne. "Building a Lifelong Learning System: A Roadmap for Cities." Aspen Institute Future of Work Initiative, December 1, 2020. https://www.aspeninstitute.org/wp-content/uploads/2025/05/Building-a-Lifelong-Learning-System_December-2020_Aspen-Institute-Future-of-Work-Initiative.pdf.

New York Times. "Excerpts from the Times's Interview with Trump." July 19, 2017.

New York Times. "Transcript of First TV Debate Among Bush, Clinton and Perot." October 12, 1992.

New York Times. "Transcript of Speech by Clinton Accepting Democratic Nomination." July 17, 1992.

New York Times. "The Zoning Law and Its Benefits." June 25, 1922.

Noe-Bustamante, Luis, Sahana Mukherjee, and Jens Manuel Krogstad. "A Majority of Latinas Feel Pressure to Support Their Families or to Succeed at Work." Pew Research Center, May 14, 2024. https://www.pewresearch.org/race-and-ethnicity/2024/05/14/a-majority-of-latinas-feel-pressure-to-support-their-families-or-to-succeed-at-work/.

NPR. "Discrimination in America: Experiences and Views." Robert Wood Johnson Foundation and Harvard T. H. Chan School of Public Health, 2017. https://www.rwjf.org/en/library/research/2017/10/discrimination-in-america--experiences-and-views.html.

NPR. "Personal Experiences of U.S. Racial/Ethnic Minorities in Today's Difficult Times." Robert Wood Johnson Foundation & Harvard T. H. Chan School of Public Health, 2022. https://www.rwjf.org/en/insights/our-research/2022/08/personal-experiences-of-u-s-racial-ethnic-groups-in-todays-difficult-times.html.

O'Brien, Rourke. "Depleting Capital? Race, Wealth and Informal Financial Assistance." *Social Forces* 91 (2012): 375–396.

O'Brien, Sarah. "Secure 2.0 Clears Congress as Part of Omnibus Appropriations Bill, Will Bring More Changes to U.S. Retirement System." *CNBC*, December 23, 2022. https://www.cnbc.com/2022/12/23/secure-2pointo-clears-congress-will-bring-changes-to-retirement-system.html.

Onkst, David H. "'First a Negro . . . Incidentally a Veteran': Black World War Two Veterans and the G. I. Bill of Rights in the Deep South, 1944–1948." *Journal of Social History* 31 (1998): 517–543.

Orfield, Gary. Foreword to *Who Should We Help? The Negative Consequences of Merit Scholarships*. The Civil Rights Project at Harvard University, 2002.

Orozco, Marlene, Inara Sunan Tareque, Paul Oyer, and Jerry I. Porras. "The Ongoing Impact of COVID-19 on Latino-Owned Businesses." Stanford Latino Entrepreneurship Initiative, August 2020. https://www.gsb.stanford.edu/faculty-research/publications/ongoing-impact-covid-19-latino-owned-businesses.

Owens, Ann, Sean F. Reardon, Demetra Kalogrides, Heewon Jang, and Thalia Tom. "Trends in Racial/Ethnic and Economic School Segregation, 1991–2020." Segregation Index Research Brief, 2022. http://socialinnovation.usc.edu/wpcontent/uploads/2022/05/Trends-in-Racial-Ethnic-Segregation_FINAL.pdf.

Palmer, Aneliese. "Strategies for Sustainable Growth in Community Land Trusts." Harvard Joint Center for Housing Studies, 2019. https://www.jchs.harvard.edu/sites/default/files/media/imp/harvard_jchs_palmer_strategies_sustainable_growth_community_land_trusts_2019.pdf.

Park, Julie J., Brian Heseung Kim, Nancy Wong, Jia Zheng, Stephanie Breen, Pearl Lo, Dominique J. Baker, Kelly Ochs Rosinger, Mike Hoa Nguyen, and OiYan Poon. "Inequality Beyond Standardized Tests: Trends in Extracurricular Activity Reporting in College Applications Across Race and Class." *EdWorkingPaper* (2023): 23–743. https://edworkingpapers.com/ai23-749.

Parker, Kim, and Richard Fry. "More Than Half of U.S. Households Have Some Investment in the Stock Market." Pew Research Center, March 25, 2020. https://www.pewresearch.org/fact-tank/2020/03/25/more-than-half-of-u-s-households-have-some-investment-in-the-stock-market/.

Parker, Kim, Rachel Minkin, and Jesse Bennett. "Economic Fallout from Covid-19 Continues to Hit Lower-Income Americans the Hardest." Pew Research Center, 2020. https://www.pewresearch.org/social-trends/2020/09

/24/economic-fallout-from-covid-19-continues-to-hit-lower-income-americans-the-hardest/.

Peetz, Johanna, Jennifer Robson, and Silas Xuereb. "The Role of Income Volatility and Perceived Locus of Control in Financial Planning Decisions." *Frontiers in Psychology* 12 (2021): 1–13.

Pell Institute for the Study of Opportunity in Higher Education. *Indicators of Higher Education Equity in the United States: 2022 Historical Trend Report.* 2022. https://www.pellinstitute.org/pell-institute-indicators-2022/.

Pension Benefit Guaranty Corporation. "Maximum Monthly Guarantee Tables." Accessed June 22, 2025. https://www.pbgc.gov/about/faq/pg/general-faqs-about-pbgc.

Perlmeter, Ryder. "How PPP Loans Eluded Small Businesses of Color." Federal Reserve Bank of Dallas, November 29, 2021. https://www.dallasfed.org/cd/communities/2021/1129.

Perry, Andre M., Hannah Stephens, and Manann Donoghoe. "Black Wealth Is Increasing, but So Is the Racial Wealth Gap." The Brookings Institution, January 9, 2024. https://www.brookings.edu/articles/black-wealth-is-increasing-but-so-is-the-racial-wealth-gap/.

Perry, Andre M., Hannah Stephens, and Manann Donoghoe. "The Supreme Court's Decision to Strike Down Affirmative Action Means That HBCU Investment Is More Important Than Ever." The Brookings Institution, June 29, 2023. https://www.brookings.edu/articles/the-supreme-courts-decision-to-strike-down-affirmative-action-means-that-hbcu-investment-is-more-important-than-ever/.

Perry, Mark. "New US Homes Today Are 1,000 Square Feet Larger Than in 1973 and Living Space per Person Has Nearly Doubled." American Enterprise Institute, June 5, 2016. https://www.aei.org/carpe-diem/new-us-homes-today-are-1000-square-feet-larger-than-in-1973-and-living-space-per-person-has-nearly-doubled/.

Pew Research Center. "Americans More Upbeat on the Economy; Biden's Job Rating Remains Very Low." The Pew Charitable Trusts, January 25, 2024. https://www.pewresearch.org/politics/2024/01/25/views-of-the-nations-economy.

Pew Research Center. "Despite Recovery, Fewer Americans Identify as Middle Class." April 2019. https://www.bankrate.com/pdfs/pr/20190425-summer-vacation-survey.pdf.

Pew Research Center. "Employer-Sponsored Retirement Plan Access, Uptake, and Savings." The Pew Charitable Trusts, 2016. https://www.pewtrusts.org/-/media/assets/2016/09/employersponsoredretirementplanaccessuptakeandsavings.pdf.

Pew Research Center. "How Debt Collectors Are Transforming the Business of State Courts." The Pew Charitable Trusts, 2020. https://www.pewtrusts.org/

-/media/assets/2020/06/debt-collectors-to-consumers.pdf; https://joebiden.com/racial-economic-equity/.

Pew Research Center. "The State of Gig Work in 2021." The Pew Charitable Trusts, December 8, 2021. https://www.pewresearch.org/internet/2021/12/08/the-state-of-gig-work-in-2021/.

Phippen, J. Weston. "How Toyota May Have Started Overcharging Minority Customers." *Atlantic*, February 3, 2016. https://www.theatlantic.com/business/archive/2016/02/toyota-car-loans-restitution/459678/.

Pinsker, Joe. "Why So Many Americans Don't Talk About Money." *Atlantic*, March 2, 2020. https://www.theatlantic.com/family/archive/2020/03/americans-dont-talk-about-money-taboo/607273/.

Planas, Antonio. "After She Concealed Her Race, Black Indianapolis Owner's Home Value More Than Doubled." *NBC News*, May 17, 2021. https://www.nbcnews.com/news/us-news/after-concealing-her-race-black-indianapolis-owner-s-home-value-n1267710.

Powell, Jerome H. "Getting Back to a Strong Labor Market." Board of Governors of the Federal Reserve System, February 10, 2021. https://www.federalreserve.gov/newsevents/speech/powell20210210a.htm.

Powell, Jerome H. *The Semiannual Monetary Policy Report to the Congress, Before the Senate Committee on Banking, Housing, and Urban Affairs.* 116th Cong. (June 16, 2020). https://www.banking.senate.gov/hearings/06/08/2020/the-semiannual-monetary-policy-report-to-the-congress.

Practical Money Skills. "Financial Football." Accessed June 22, 2025. https://www.practicalmoneyskills.com/en/resources/videos/financial-football/visa_unveils_nfl-themed_financial_football_video_game.html.

Putnam, Robert D. *Our Kids: The American Dream in Crisis.* Simon & Schuster, 2015.

Quinn, David M., and Morgan Polikoff. "Summer Learning Loss: What Is It, and What Can We Do About It?" The Brookings Institution, September 14, 2017. https://www.brookings.edu/articles/summer-learning-loss-what-is-it-and-what-can-we-do-about-it/.

Rademacher, Ida, Tim Shaw, and Delaney Crampton. "Rise and Shine: Improving Retirement and Enhancing Savings." Aspen Institute, 2022. https://www.aspeninstitute.org/blog-posts/rise-and-shine-improving-retirement-and-enhancing-savings/.

Ravikumar, B., and Lin Shao. "Labor Compensation and Labor Productivity: Recent Recoveries and the Long-Term Trend." *Economic Synopses*, no. 16 (2016). https://research.stlouisfed.org/publications/economic-synopses/2016/08/12/labor-compensation-and-labor-productivity-recent-recoveries-and-the-long-term-trend/.

Ray, Rayshawn, Andre M. Perry, David Harshbarger, Samantha Elizondo, and Alexandra Gibbons. "Homeownership, Racial Segregation, and Policy

Solutions to Racial Wealth Equity." The Brookings Institution, September 2021. https://www.brookings.edu/articles/homeownership-racial-segregation-and-policies-for-racial-wealth-equity/.

Reeves, Richard V. "The Dangerous Separation of the American Upper Middle Class." The Brookings Institution, September 3, 2015. https://www.brookings.edu/articles/the-dangerous-separation-of-the-american-upper-middle-class/.

Reeves, Richard V. *Dream Hoarders: How the American Upper Middle Class Is Leaving Everyone Else in the Dust, Why That Is a Problem, and What to Do About It.* The Brookings Institution Press, 2017.

Reeves, Richard V., Katherine Guyot, and Eleanor Krause. "Defining the Middle Class: Cash, Credentials, or Culture?" The Brookings Institution, May 7, 2018. https://www.brookings.edu/articles/defining-the-middle-class-cash-credentials-or-culture/.

Reidy, Patrick E., C.S.C. "Churching NIMBYs: Creating Affordable Housing on Church Property." *Yale Law Journal* 133, no. 4 (2024): 1039–1400.

Reutschlin, Catherine, and Dedrick Asante-Muhammad. "The Challenge of Credit Card Debt for the African American Middle Class." Dēmos and NAACP, 2013. https://naacp.org/wp-content/uploads/2016/04/CreditCardDebt-Demos_NAACP.pdf.

Rhee, Nari. "Race and Retirement Insecurity in the United States." National Institute on Retirement Security, 2013. https://www.nirsonline.org/reports/race-and-retirement-insecurity-in-the-united-states/.

Roche, Tara. "The Time Has Come to Help America's Forgotten Homebuyers." The Pew Charitable Trusts, September 23, 2024. https://www.pew.org/en/about/news-room/opinion/2024/09/23/the-time-has-come-to-help-americas-forgotten-homebuyers.

Rojas, Rick. "Louisiana Will Get a New City After a Yearslong Court Battle." *New York Times*, April 28, 2024.

Roksa, Josipa, and Peter Kinsley. "The Role of Family Support in Facilitating Academic Success of Low-Income Students." *Research in Higher Education* 60 (2019): 415–436.

Roper Center for Public Opinion Research. "The Meaning of Middle Class." May 2015. https://ropercenter.cornell.edu/blog/meaning-middle-class.

Rosalsky, Greg. "Affirmative Action for Rich Kids: It's More Than Just Legacy Admissions." *NPR*, July 24, 2023. https://www.npr.org/sections/money/2023/07/24/1189443223.

Rosen, Sam. "Atlanta's Controversial 'Cityhood' Movement." *Atlantic*, April 26, 2017. https://www.theatlantic.com/business/archive/2017/04/the-border-battles-of-atlanta/523884/.

Rosenfeld, Jake. *You're Paid What You're Worth: And Other Myths of the Modern Economy.* Harvard University Press, 2021.

Rosenfeld, Jake, Patrick Denice, and Jennifer Laird. "Union Decline Lowers Wages of Nonunion Workers: The Overlooked Reason Why Wages Are Stuck and Inequality Is Growing." Economic Policy Institute, 2016. https://www.epi.org/publication/union-decline-lowers-wages-of-nonunion-workers-the-overlooked-reason-why-wages-are-stuck-and-inequality-is-growing/.

Rosenfeld, Jake, and Meredith Kleykamp. "Organized Labor and Racial Wage Inequality in the United States." *American Journal of Sociology* 117 (2012): 1460–1502.

Ross, Abbi. "A Snapshot of Pandemic Life for Adjunct Faculty Members." *Chronicle of Higher Education*, February 24, 2022.

Rothwell, Jonathan. "Black Students at Top Colleges: Exceptions, Not the Rule." The Brookings Institution, February 3, 2015. https://www.brookings.edu/articles/black-students-at-top-colleges-exceptions-not-the-rule.

Rothwell, Jonathan, Tracy Hadden Loh, and Andre Perry. "The Devaluation of Assets in Black Neighborhoods: The Case of Commercial Property." Brookings Metro, 2022. https://www.brookings.edu/articles/the-devaluation-of-assets-in-black-neighborhoods-the-case-of-commercial-property/.

Ruckelshaus, Catherine, and Sarah Leberstein. "Manufacturing Low Pay: Declining Wages in the Jobs That Built America's Middle Class." National Employment Law Project, November 2014. https://www.nelp.org/insights-research/manufacturing-low-pay-declining-wages-in-the-jobs-that-built-americas-middle-class/.

Rusk, David. "The 'Segregation Tax': The Cost of Racial Segregation to Black Homeowners." The Brookings Institution, 2001. https://www.brookings.edu/wp-content/uploads/2016/06/rusk.pdf.

Saad, Linda, and Jeffery M. Jones. "What Percentage of Americans Own Stock?" Gallup, May 12, 2022. https://news.gallup.com/poll/266807.

Saez, Emmanuel, and Gabriel Zucman, "Wealth Inequality in the United States Since 1913: Evidence from Capitalized Income Tax Data." *Quarterly Journal of Economics* 131 (2016): 563–578.

Sallie Mae. *How America Pays for College*. Ipsos Public Affairs, 2019. https://www.ipsos.com/en-us/news-polls/how-america-pays-for-college-2019.

Sanghi, Siddhartha, Maggie Isaacson, Barton H. Hamilton, Andrés Hincapié, and Prasanthi Ramakrishnan. "What Can be Done to Promote Black Entrepreneurship?" Federal Reserve Bank of St. Louis, 2022. https://www.stlouisfed.org/publications/regional-economist/2022/jan/what-can-be-done-promote-black-entrepreneurship.

Saul, Stephanie. "College Enrollment Drops, Even as the Pandemic's Effects Ebb." *New York Times*, May 26, 2022.

Schindler, Sarah, and Kellen Zale. "The Harms of Liminal Housing Tenure: Installment Land Contracts and Tenancies in Common." *Journal of Affordable Housing* 29 (2021): 523–534.

Schmitt, John, and Ben Zipperer. "The Decline in African-American Representation in Unions and Manufacturing, 1979–2007." Center for Economic and Policy Research, 2008. http://cepr.net/documents/publications/unions_aa_2008_02.pdf.

Schneider, Daniel, Orestes P. Hastings, and Joe LaBriola. "Income Inequality and Class Divides in Parental Investments." *American Sociological Review* 83 (2018): 475–507.

Schuetz, Jenny. "Under US Housing Policies, Homeowners Mostly Win, While Renters Mostly Lose." The Brookings Institution, 2018. https://www.brookings.edu/research/under-us-housing-policies-homeowners-mostly-win-while-renters-mostly-lose/.

Schumann, Richard E. "Compensation from World War II Through the Great Society." Bureau of Labor Statistics, January 30, 2003. https://www.bls.gov/opub/mlr/cwc/compensation-from-world-war-ii-through-the-great-society.pdf.

Schwartz, Heather. *Housing Policy Is School Policy: Economically Integrative Housing Promotes Academic Success in Montgomery County, Maryland.* The Century Foundation, 2010. https://tcf.org/content/report/housing-policy-school-policy-economically-integrative-housing-promotes-academic-success-montgomery-county-maryland/.

Scott-Clayton, Judith. *The Looming Student Loan Default Crisis Is Worse Than We Thought.* The Brookings Institution, 2018. https://www.brookings.edu/wp-content/uploads/2018/01/scott-clayton-report.pdf.

Shaver, Katherine. "Single-Family Zoning Preserves Century-Old Segregation, Planners Say: A Proposal to Add Density Is Dividing Neighborhoods." *Washington Post*, November 20, 2021.

Shierholz, Heidi. "Strengthening Labor Standards and Institutions to Promote Wage Growth." The Hamilton Project, The Brookings Institution, 2018. https://www.brookings.edu/research/strengthening-labor-standards-and-institutions-to-promote-wage-growth/.

Shu, Suzanne, and John W. Payne. "Social Security Claiming Intentions: Psychological Ownership, Loss Aversion, and Information Displays." National Bureau of Economic Research Working Paper No. 31499. July 2023. https://www.nber.org/papers/w31499.

Shupe, Cortnie, Greta Li, and Scott Fulford. "Consumer Use of Buy Now, Pay Later: Insights from the CFPB Making Ends Meet Survey." Consumer Financial Protection Bureau, March 2023. https://www.consumerfinance.gov/reports/consumer-use-of-buy-now-pay-later/.

Siegel, Tara. "Workers Tap Retirement Savings as a Last Resort." *New York Times*, December 17, 2020.

Silver-Greenberg, Jessica, Stacy Cowley, and Natalie Kitroeff. "When Unpaid Student Loan Bills Mean You Can No Longer Work." *New York Times*, November 18, 2017.

Silvestrini, Elaine. "Borrowers over 50 with Student Loan Debt." Kiplinger, September 15, 2022. https://www.kiplinger.com/personal-finance/credit-debt/loans/student-loans/605222/borrowers-over-50-with-student-loan-debt.

Singletary, Michelle. "Many Americans Are Car Poor from Their Auto Loans: Here's Why," *Washington Post*, October 16, 2024.

Sinnock, Bonnie. "HUD Approves Pact Resolving Appraisal Bias Charges at JPMorgan Chase." *National Mortgage News*, March 9, 2021.

Sjoquist, David L., and John V. Winters. "The Effects of State Merit Aid Programs on Attendance at Elite Colleges." *Southern Economic Journal* 83 (2016): 529–530.

Smith, Christian M., Amber D. Villalobos, Laura T. Hamilton, and Charlie Eaton. "Promising or Predatory? Online Education in Non-Profit and For-Profit Universities." *Social Forces* 102 (2024): 952–977.

Smith, Denise A. "Achieving Financial Equity and Justice for HBCUs." The Century Foundation, September 14, 2021. https://tcf.org/content/report/achieving-financial-equity-justice-hbcus/.

Smith, Hedrick. *Who Stole the American Dream?* Random House, 2013.

Smythe, Andria. "Child-to-Parent Intergenerational Transfers, Social Security, and Child Wealth Building." *AEA Papers and Proceedings* 112 (2022): 53–57.

Smythe, Andria. "The Impact of Social Security Eligibility on Transfers to Elderly Parents and Wealth-Building Among Adult Children." Center for Financial Security, 2019. https://cfsrdrc.wisc.edu/publications/working-paper/jsit19-05.

Social Security Administration. "Historical Background and Development of Social Security." Accessed June 13, 2025. https://www.ssa.gov/history/briefhistory3.html.

Social Security Administration. *A Summary of the 2024 Annual Social Security and Medicare Trust Fund Reports*. 2024. Accessed June 19, 2025. https://www.ssa.gov/oact/trsum/. https://www.ssa.gov/oact/trsum/.

Sommer, Kamila, and Paul Sullivan. "Implications of US Tax Policy for House Prices, Rents, and Homeownership." *American Economic Review* 108 (2018): 241–274.

Stavins, Joanna. "Credit Card Debt and Consumer Payment Choice: What Can We Learn from Credit Bureau Data?" Federal Reserve Bank of Boston Working Paper No. 18-7. October 2018. https://papers.ssrn.com/sol3/papers.cfm?abstract_id=3281512.

Stiglitz, Joseph E. *The Price of Inequality: How Today's Divided Society Endangers Our Future*. W. W. Norton, 2013.

Strohl, Jeff, Zachary Mabel, and Kathryn Peltier Campbell. *The Great Misalignment: Addressing the Mismatch Between the Supply of Certificates and Associate's Degrees and the Future Demand for Workers in 565 US Labor Markets*. Georgetown University Center on Education and the Workforce, 2024. https://cew.georgetown.edu/GreatMisalignment.

Student Borrower Protection Center. "Educational Redlining." 2020. https://protectborrowers.org/wp-content/uploads/2020/02/Education-Redlining-Report.pdf.

Suddath, Claire. "The Middle Class." *Time Magazine*, February 27, 2009.

Sullivan, Laura, Tatjana Meschede, Thomas Shapiro, and Fernanda Escobar. "Stalling Dreams: How Student Debt Is Disrupting Life Chances and Widening the Racial Wealth Gap." Institute on Assets and Social Policy, September 2019. https://heller.brandeis.edu/iere/pdfs/racial-wealth-equity/racial-wealth-gap/stallingdreams-how-student-debt-is-disrupting-lifechances.pdf.

Susaneck, Adam Paul. "Mr. Biden, Tear Down This Highway." *New York Times*, September 8, 2022.

Tamborini, Christopher R., and Chang Hwan Kim. "Education and Contributory Pensions at Work: Disadvantages of the Less Educated." *Social Forces* 95 (2017): 1577–1606.

Tavernise, Sabrina. "The U.S. Birthrate Has Dropped Again: The Pandemic May Be Accelerating the Decline." *New York Times*, May 5, 2021.

Taylor, Barrett J., Brendan Cantwell, Kimberly Watts, and Olivia Wood. "Partisanship, White Racial Resentment, and State Support for Higher Education." *Journal of Higher Education* 91 (2020): 858–887.

Taylor, Keeanga-Yamahtta. *Race for Profit: How Banks and the Real Estate Industry Undermined Black Homeownership*. University of North Carolina Press, 2019.

Taylor, Paul, Rakesh Kochhar, Richard Fry, Gabriel Velasco, and Seth Motel. "Wealth Gaps Rise to Record Highs Between Whites, Blacks, and Hispanics." Pew Research Center, 2011. https://www.pewresearch.org/wp-content/uploads/sites/3/2011/07/SDT-Wealth-Report_7-26-11_FINAL.pdf.

Taylor, Paul, Rich Morin, D'Vera Cohn, Richard Fry, Rakesh Kochhar, and April Clark. "Inside the Middle Class: Bad Times Hit the Good Life." Pew Research Center, April 9, 2008. https://www.pewresearch.org/social-trends/2008/04/09.

Tedeneke, Alem. "What Are 'Pandemic Pods,' and Why Are They a Problem for Diversity?" World Economic Forum, November 10, 2020. https://www.weforum.org/agenda/2020/11/pandemic-pods-inequality/.

Telesford, Imani, Shameek Rakshit, Matthew McGough, Emma Wager, and Krutika Amin. "How Has U.S. Spending on Healthcare Changed over Time?" *Peterson-KFF Health System Tracker*, February 7, 2023. Accessed

June 19, 2025. https://www.healthsystemtracker.org/chart-collection/u-s-spending-healthcare-changed-time/.

Tennessee College of Applied Technology Northwest. "TCAT Northwest and UT Martin Articulation Agreement." *TCAT Northwest News*, June 5, 2024. https://tcatnorthwest.edu/news/tcat-northwest-and-ut-martin-articulation-agreement-2024-10.

Treisman, Rachel. "University of Texas, MIT and Others Announce Free Tuition for Some Undergraduates." *NPR*, November 22, 2024. https://www.npr.org/2024/11/22/nx-s1-5202754.

Truesdale, Beth C. "Better Jobs, Longer Working Lives: Proposals to Improve the Low-Wage Labor Market for Older Workers." Brookings Economic Studies, 2020. https://www.brookings.edu/articles/better-jobs-longer-working-lives-proposals-to-improve-the-low-wage-labor-market-for-older-workers/.

Trump, Donald J., and Ben Carson. "We'll Protect America's Suburbs: We Reject the Ultraliberal View That the Federal Bureaucracy Should Dictate Where and How People Live." *Wall Street Journal*, August 16, 2020.

Tseng, Phuong, Heather Bromfield, Samir Gambhir, and Stephen Menendian. *Opportunity, Race, and Low Income Housing Tax Credit Projects*. Haas Institute, 2017. https://www.novoco.com/sites/default/files/atoms/files/hass_institute_lihtc_analysis_031617.pdf.

Tucker, John C. *Trial and Error: The Education of a Courtroom Lawyer*. Carroll & Graf Publishers, 2003.

Turner, Margery Austin, and Solomon Green, "Causes and Consequences of Separate and Unequal Neighborhoods." Urban Institute. Accessed June 13, 2025. https://www.urban.org/racial-equity-analytics-lab/structural-racism-explainer-collection/causes-and-consequences-separate-and-unequal-neighborhoods.

Turner, Sarah, and John Bound. "Closing the Gap or Widening the Divide: The Effects of the G.I. Bill and World War II on the Educational Outcomes of Black Americans." *Journal of Economic History* 63 (2003): 145-177.

Turnham, Jennifer. "Attitudes to Savings and Financial Education Among Low-Income Populations: Findings from the Financial Literacy Focus Groups." University of Wisconsin-Madison Center for Financial Security Working Paper No. 10-7. October 2010. https://centerforfinancialsecurity.files.wordpress.com/2010/10/turnham2010_attitudesbrief.pdf.

UNCF. "The Impact of HBCUs on Diversity in STEM Fields." Accessed June 13, 2025. https://uncf.org/the-latest/the-impact-of-hbcus-on-diversity-in-stem-fields.

United States Senate. *Nomination of Alan Greenspan: Hearing Before the Committee on Banking, Housing, and Urban Affairs*. 106th Cong. (January 26, 2000). https://fraser.stlouisfed.org/title/nomination-alan-greenspan-277

US Bureau of Economic Analysis. *Personal Saving Rate (PSAVERT)*. Federal Reserve Bank of St. Louis FRED. Accessed June 25, 2025. https://fred.stlouisfed.org/series/PSAVERT.

US Census Bureau. "Historical Households Tables, Table HH-4, HH-6." November 2024. https://www.census.gov/data/tables/time-series/demo/families/households.html.

US Census Bureau. *Quarterly Residential Vacancies and Homeownership, Second Quarter 2020*. https://www.census.gov/housing/hvs/files/currenthvspress.pdf.

US Commission on Civil Rights. "Targeted Fines and Fees Against Communities of Color." 2017. https://www.usccr.gov/files/pubs/2017/Statutory_Enforcement_Report2017.pdf.

US Department of Commerce. *Middle Class in America*. Economics and Statistics Administration, 2010. https://www.commerce.gov/sites/default/files/migrated/reports/middleclassreport.pdf.

US Department of Education. "Education Department Releases Proposed Regulations to Protect Veterans and Service Members, Increase College Oversight, and Increase College Access for Incarcerated Individuals." Press release, July 26, 2022. https://www.ed.gov/news/press-releases/education-department-releases-proposed-regulations-protect-veterans-and-service-members-increase-college-oversight-and-increase-college-access-incarcerated-individuals.

US Department of Education. *National Assessment of Career and Technical Education: Final Report to Congress*. 2014. https://s3.amazonaws.com/PCRN/uploads/NACTE_FinalReport2014.pdf.

US Department of Education. "U.S. Department of Education Releases *COVID-19 Handbook*, Volume 2, *Roadmap to Reopening Safely and Meeting All Students' Needs*." Press release, April 9, 2021. https://www.ed.gov/news/press-releases/us-department-education-releases-covid-19-handbook-volume-2-roadmap-reopening-safely-and-meeting-all-students-needs.

US Department of Education, National Center for Education Statistics. "Integrated Postsecondary Education Data System (IPEDS), Table 32472, Average Undergraduate Tuition and Required Fees, by Control and Level of Institution, Academic Year." 2025. https://nces.ed.gov/ipeds/search/viewtable?tableId=32472.

US Department of Housing and Urban Development. "Unequal Burden: Income and Racial Disparities in Subprime Lending in America." 2000. https://www.huduser.gov/publications/pdf/unequal_full.pdf.

US Department of Justice, Civil Rights Division. *Investigation of the Ferguson Police Department*. 2015. https://www.justice.gov/sites/default/files/opa/press-releases/attachments/2015/03/04/ferguson_police_department_report.pdf.

US Department of Labor. "Past Secretaries of Labor." Accessed June 13, 2025. https://www.dol.gov/general/aboutdol/history/sec-chrono.

US Department of Labor. "Trade Adjustment Assistance Community College and Career Training." https://www.dol.gov/agencies/eta/skills-training-grants/community-colleges.

US Department of Labor, Bureau of Labor Statistics. "Education Pays: Unemployment Rates and Earnings by Educational Attainment." 2024. https://www.bls.gov/emp/chart-unemployment-earnings-education.htm.

US Department of Labor, Bureau of Labor Statistics. "Employment Projections: Earnings and Unemployment Rates by Educational Attainment, 2024." https://www.bls.gov/emp/chart-unemployment-earnings-education.htm.

US Department of Labor, Bureau of Labor Statistics. *Occupational Outlook Handbook*. Last modified April 18, 2025. https://www.bls.gov/ooh/most-new-jobs.htm.

US Department of Labor, Wage and Hour Division. "Fact Sheet #71: Internship Programs Under the Fair Labor Standards Act." April 2010. https://www.dol.gov/agencies/whd/fact-sheets/71-flsa-internships.

US Department of the Treasury. "Labor Unions and the Middle Class." 2023. https://home.treasury.gov/system/files/136/Labor-Unions-And-The-Middle-Class.pdf

US Department of the Treasury. "The State of Labor Market Competition." 2022. https://home.treasury.gov/system/files/136/State-of-Labor-Market-Competition-2022.pdf

US Government Accountability Office. "Income and Wealth Disparities Continue Through Old Age." 2019. https://www.gao.gov/products/gao-19-587.

US Government Accountability Office. "Low Defined Contribution Savings May Pose Challenges." May 2016. https://www.gao.gov/assets/gao-16-408.pdf.

US Government Accountability Office. "Most Households Approaching Retirement Have Low Savings." GAO-19-442R. 2019. https://www.gao.gov/products/gao-19-442r.

US Government Accountability Office. "The Nation's Retirement System." February 2019. https://www.gao.gov/products/gao-19-342t.

US Government Accountability Office. "Retirement Security: Debt Increased for Older Americans over Time, but the Implications Vary by Debt Type." May 2021. https://www.gao.gov/products/gao-21-170.

US Government Accountability Office. "Shorter Life Expectancy Reduces Projected Lifetime Benefits for Lower Earners." 2016. https://www.gao.gov/assets/680/676086.pdf.

US Government Accountability Office. "A Small Percentage of Families Save in 529 Plans." 2012. https://www.gao.gov/assets/gao-13-64.pdf.

US Government Accountability Office. *Student Population Has Significantly Diversified, But Many Schools Remain Divided Along Racial, Ethnic, and Economic Lines*. 2022. https://www.gao.gov/products/gao-22-104737.

US Government Accountability Office. "Which Workers Are the Most Affected by Automation and What Could Help Them Get New Jobs?" *WatchBlog*, August 23, 2022. https://www.gao.gov/blog/which-workers-are-most-affected-automation-and-what-could-help-them-get-new-jobs.

US President. "Executive Order: Ending Illegal Discrimination and Restoring Merit-Based Opportunity." January 21, 2025. https://www.whitehouse.gov/presidential-actions/2025/01/ending-illegal-discrimination-and-restoring-merit-based-opportunity/.

University of Michigan. "Health and Retirement Study, 1992–2018." Ann Arbor, MI.

University of Northern Iowa. "Materials Science and Engineering." Department of Applied Engineering and Technical Management. Accessed June 10, 2025. https://chas.uni.edu/aetm/materials-science-and-engineering.

Van Dam, Andrew. "Sending Your Kids to College Increases Chances You'll Lose Your House." *Washington Post*, August 6, 2018.

Van Green, Ted. "Majorities of Adults See Decline of Union Membership as Bad for the U.S. and Working People." Pew Research Center, April 19, 2023. https://www.pewresearch.org/short-reads/2023/04/19/majorities-of-adults-see-decline-of-union-membership-as-bad-for-the-u-s-and-working-people/.

Wakabayashi, Daisuke. "Google's Shadow Work Force: Temps Who Outnumber Full-Time Employees." *New York Times*, May 28, 2019.

Wang, Ruoniu, Claire Cahen, Arthur Acolin, and Rebecca J. Walter. "Tracking Growth and Evaluating Performance of Shared Equity Homeownership Programs During Housing Market Fluctuations." Lincoln Institute of Land Policy, 2019. https://www.lincolninst.edu/publications/working-papers/tracking-growth-evaluating-performance-shared-equity-homeownership/.

Warren, Elizabeth. *This Fight Is Our Fight: The Battle to Save America's Middle Class.* Macmillan, 2017.

Warren, Elizabeth, and Amelia Warren Tyagi. *The Two-Income Trap: Why Middle-Class Mothers and Fathers Are Going Broke.* Basic Books, 2003.

Weber, Lauren. "Some of the World's Largest Employers No Longer Sell Things, They Rent Workers." *Wall Street Journal*, December 28, 2017.

Weil, David. *The Fissured Workplace.* Harvard University Press, 2014.

Weller, Christopher, and David Madland. "Union Membership Narrows the Racial Wealth Gap for Families of Color." Center for American Progress, September 2018. https://www.americanprogress.org/issues/economy/reports/2018/09/04/454781/union-membership-narrows-racial-wealth-gap-families-color/.

The White House. "The American Jobs Plan." March 31, 2021. https://www.whitehouse.gov/briefing-room/statements-releases/2021/03/31/fact-sheet-the-american-jobs-plan/.

The White House. "Biden-Harris Administration Announces New Actions to Build Black Wealth and Narrow the Racial Wealth Gap." June 1, 2021. https://www.whitehouse.gov/briefing-room/statements-releases/2021/06/01/fact-sheet-biden-harris-administration-announces-new-actions-to-build-black-wealth-and-narrow-the-racial-wealth-gap/.

The White House. "Fact Sheet: President Biden Announces Student Loan Relief for Borrowers Who Need It Most." August 24, 2022. https://www.whitehouse.gov/briefing-room/statements-releases/2022/08/24/fact-sheet-president-biden-announces-student-loan-relief-for-borrowers-who-need-it-most/.

The White House. "President Clinton and Vice President Gore, Bringing Homeownership Rates to Historic Levels." Accessed June 13, 2025. https://clintonwhitehouse5.archives.gov/WH/Accomplishments/housing_accomps.html.

The White House. "President George W. Bush, a Home of Your Own: Expanding Opportunities for All Americans." Accessed June 13, 2025. http://georgewbush-whitehouse.archives.gov/infocus/homeownership/toc.html.

The White House. "President George W. Bush, Expanding Homeownership." December 16, 2003. https://georgewbush-whitehouse.archives.gov/infocus/achievement/chap7.html.

The White House. "The State of Our Unions." September 5, 2022. https://www.whitehouse.gov/cea/written-materials/2022/09/05/the-state-of-our-unions.

Wilson, Erika K. "White Cities, White Schools." *Columbia Law Review* 123 (2023): 1221–1270.

Wolfe, Alan. *One Nation, After All.* Penguin Books, 1998.

Wolff, Edward N. "The Asset Price Meltdown and the Wealth of the Middle Class." National Bureau of Economic Research Working Paper No. 18559. November 2012. https://www.nber.org/papers/w18559.

Wolff, Sarah, and Deven Carlson. "Who Chooses Donors? Submission and Funding Patterns on the Nation's Largest Education Crowdfunding Platform." *Educational Researcher* 50 (2021): 355–367.

Woo, Jennie H., Alexander H. Bentz, Stephen Lew, Erin Dunlop Velez, and Nichole Smith. "Repayment of Student Loans as of 2015 Among 19g95–96 and 2003–04 First-Time Beginning Students: First Look." National Center for Education Statistics, 2017. https://nces.ed.gov/pubs2018/2018410.pdf.

Woo, Jennie H., and Susan P. Choy. "Merit Aid for Undergraduates: Trends from 1995–96 to 2007–08." National Center for Education Statistics, 2011. https://nces.ed.gov/pubs2012/2012160.pdf.

York, Erica. "Tax Treatment of Worker Training." Tax Foundation, March 21, 2019. https://taxfoundation.org/research/all/federal/tax-treatment-of-worker-training.

Youngman, Joan. *A Good Tax: Legal and Policy Issues for the Property Tax in the United States.* Lincoln Institute of Land Policy, 2016.

Zessoules, Daniella, and Olugbenga Ajilore. "Wage Gaps and Outcomes in Apprenticeship Programs." Center for American Progress, December 11, 2018. https://www.americanprogress.org/article/wage-gaps-outcomes-apprenticeship-programs/.

Zipperer, Ben, Celine McNicholas, Margaret Poydock, Daniel Schneider, and Kristen Harknett. "National Survey of Gig Workers Paints a Picture of Poor Working Conditions, Low Pay." Economic Policy Institute, 2022. https://www.epi.org/publication/gig-worker-survey/.

Index